BUSINESS
TAXATION
Policy & Practice

The VNR Series in Accounting and Finance

Consulting Editor
John Perrin, Emeritus Professor of the University of Warwick
and Price Waterhouse Fellow in Public Sector Accounting
at the University of Exeter

J.M. Cope
Business Taxation: Policy and Practice

J.C. Drury
Management and Cost Accounting

J.C. Drury
Management and Cost Accounting:
Students' Manual

J.C. Drury
Management and Cost Accounting:
Teachers' Manual

C.R. Emmanuel and D.T. Otley
Accounting for Management Control

D. Henley *et al.*
Public Sector Accounting and
Financial Control (2nd edn)

G.A. Lee
Modern Financial Accounting (4th edn)

G.A. Lee
Student Manual for Modern Financial Accounting (4th edn)

T.A. Lee
Income and Value Measurement (3rd edn)

T.A. Lee
Company Financial Reporting (2nd edn)

T.A. Lee
Cash Flow Accounting

S.P. Lumby
Investment Appraisal (2nd edn)

S.P. Lumby
Investment Appraisal (2nd edn)

S.P. Lumby
Investment Appraisal:
A Student Workbook

J.M. Samuels and F.M. Wilkes
Management of Company Finance (4th edn)

F.M. Wilkes and R.E. Brayshaw
Company Finance and its Management
principles, practice problems and solutions

BUSINESS
TAXATION
Policy & Practice

TAX YEAR 1987/88 EDITION

J. M. COPE

**Department of Accounting and Finance
University of Lancaster**

Van Nostrand Reinhold (UK) Co. Ltd

First published in 1987 by
Van Nostrand Reinhold (UK) Co. Ltd
Molly Millars Lane, Wokingham, Berkshire, England

Typeset in 10 on 11pt Sabon by Witwell Ltd, Liverpool

Printed and bound by
T.J. Press (Padstow) Ltd
Padstow, Cornwall

British Library Cataloguing in Publication Data

Cope, J.M.
Business taxation: policy and practice.
—— (The VNR series in accounting and finance).
1. Tax accounting —— Great Britain
I. Title
657'.46'0941   HF5681.T3

ISBN 0-278-00006-1

Contents

Preface

This book is designed to show how the system of taxation works in the United Kingdom. The main features of the significant taxes are explained and these features are then put into a comparative and analytical context. I hope that by interlacing the descriptive and the analytical the latter will become more meaningful. I hope too that the discussion of possible alternatives will induce a deeper understanding of the important policy issues. Studying taxation involves a variety of academic disciplines: economics, law, accounting, psychology, politics, history and so on. The interaction between them can be an important determinant of tax policy and reference is made to them where this seems to be the case.

The book is intended for use on university and college courses in accounting and business studies at undergraduate, diploma and postgraduate levels. Many students on such courses will go on to seek professional qualifications and it is with this in mind that I have included at the end of most chapters Exercises which are taken from the examinations of the professional bodies. However, it should be noted that the book does not pretend to cover the professional syllabuses in full as those include many points of detail which are not appropriate to the purpose of the book as described above. I have assumed that readers will already possess an elementary knowledge of the principles of economics and accountancy.

In using the book students should work through the Examples placed near the end of many chapters as and when reference is made to them in the text. Detailed References are also placed at the end of each chapter and these, as well as providing justification for the statements made in the text, point the way to a more detailed investigation of the topics concerned. They include many references to the statute and case law which is the foundation of tax practice in the UK. A decision about tax liability on any particular set of facts depends on the exact wording of the statute law and on any judgements of the courts which have been based on similar facts. The full titles of the case report series are given in the list of abbreviations which follows immediately: there are several such series and reference has, in general, been given for two of them, usually the Reports of Tax Cases and the All England Reports, for each case quoted.

Although the general principles of the UK system change very little from year to year the detail of the calculations changes frequently, partly because of indexation provisions adopted to deal with rising price levels. The problem that this creates for the textbook writer has been dealt with here by inserting an Appendix shortly before publication. This shows the main current and recent rates of tax and allowances etc. (which will be needed in attempting may of the Exercises) and records any recent changes in tax law which may affect topics discussed in the main text.

Taxes are imposed directly and indirectly on people, young and old, male and female. Unfortunately there is no word in the language which conveniently describes individuals irrespective of their sex. This book has adopted the conventional approach of using 'he' to include 'she' unless the context makes it clear that only males are intended. In general tax legislation applies equally to male and female except in so far as there is discriminatory treatment of married couples (a topic which is discussed in Chapter 4).

I am grateful to Her Majesty's Stationery Office for permission to reproduce the figures in Tables 1.1, 1.2, 1.3, 1.5, 11.1 and 11.2 and to the various professional bodies for permission to use their past examination questions. I am grateful also to my publishers, especially John Perrin, Stephen Wellings and anonymous referees, for the help and guidance which have made this a much better book than it would have been otherwise. Finally I must thank my past and present students for reacting constructively as I developed in my teaching some of the ideas which now appear in the book. Any faults and errors which remain are entirely my own responsibility.

JOHN COPE
Lancaster
November 1986

Abbreviations used

AC	Appeal Cases (law reports)
ACT	Advance corporation tax
All ER	All England Reports (law reports)
AP	Accounting period
BES	Business Expansion Scheme
BIR	Board of Inland Revenue
CBI	Confederation of British Industry
CCE	Commissioners of Customs and Excise
CGT	Capital gains tax
CIT	Comprehensive income tax
CTT	Capital transfer tax
CT	Corporation tax
DHSS	Department of Health & Social Security
DIY	Do-it-yourself
EC	European Communities
FII	Franked investment income
FY	Financial year
GNP	Gross national product
ICAEW	The Institute of Chartered Accountants in England & Wales
ICSA	Institute of Chartered Secretaries and Administrators
IFS	Institute for Fiscal Studies
IHT	Inheritance tax
IoT	Institute of Taxation
IRC	Commissioners of Inland Revenue (used in tax case titles)
IT	Income tax
IHT Act	Inheritance Tax Act
MCT	Mainstream corporation tax
MIRAS	Mortgage interest relief at source
NEDO	National Economic Development Office
NI	National insurance
NICS	National insurance contributions
NPV	Net present value
NSC's	National Savings Certificates
OECD	Organization for Economic Co-operation and Development

PAYE	Pay-as-you-earn
PEP	Personal equity plan
PET	Potentially exempt transfer
PRT	Petroleum revenue tax
PSBR	Public Sector Borrowing Requirement
SAYE	Save-as-you-earn
SET	Selective employment tax
Taxes Act	Income and Corporation Taxes Act
TC	Tax Cases (law reports)
USM	Unlisted securities market
VAT	Value added tax
WDA	Writing down allowance

1   Introduction

Taxation is a compulsory levy by the state and exists in countries of all political and social complexions. Few people like to pay taxes but, if pressed, most of them will agree that they accept that some of the purposes for which taxes are levied are both necessary and desirable. They will still be able to cite other purposes of which they disapprove.

However, taxation should not be thought of solely in terms of a financial levy used to finance specified expenditures. The way in which it is imposed can have important effects on the nation's economic well-being and its design may require modification as economic and social changes occur. Tax policies which are suitable for one country may be quite unsuitable for another, an obvious example of this being the quite different circumstances in developed and underdeveloped countries.

In this book we shall look in some detail at the main features of one tax system, that of the UK, but we will put it into a world-wide context so that its characteristics can be judged in a broader perspective. Alternatives will be taken from other countries and from proposals which have not yet been adopted anywhere. In this chapter we shall consider first why taxes exist at all, and then go on to look at the range of taxes levied in the UK and elsewhere.

WHY ARE TAXES IMPOSED?

There are several different problems which lead to the existence of taxes and the brief analysis which follows outlines both the problems and the role that taxes may play in solving them.[1] It is because both the problems and the solutions may differ that the level and pattern of taxation varies between countries and through time.

The first problem is the existence of public goods. This is the technical term used by economists to describe those goods and services which do not lend themselves to allocation via a market price because the buyer cannot confine enjoyment of them to himself or herself. If I erect a light outside my house at my own expense I cannot prevent others from enjoying the benefit of it as they pass by.

The solution to this problem will often take the form of a publicly financed provision paid for by taxation. Of course the extent of the provision may be varied (bright or dull lights, fewer lamp posts) and the amount of tax needed to pay for it will vary accordingly. Nor need the provision be made by the public authority directly. It could be provided by private contractors who are employed by the public body but the latter still has the ultimate responsibility for collecting the taxes and providing the service.

Another kind of problem arises with so-called merit goods. Unlike public goods the direct benefit of these can be confined to one buyer, but the government in its wisdom may decide that there would be additional benefits to the community if more people acquired them than would have done so under normal free market conditions.

The leading example is education. It is perfectly easy for education to be made available only to those who can afford it and who wish to buy it for themselves or for their children. They may decide to buy it because they think it will increase their, or their children's, future earning power or because they think it will improve the quality of their lives. The additional argument which turns education into a merit good is that if all (or nearly all) of a nation's population become more literate and numerate the level of social, economic and technical organization in society can be raised. The expected result of this is that everyone, including the wealthy, will be better off.

Taxes may be involved too in attempts to counter the effects of externalities. An externality is a cost of production which does not fall on the producer. Economic analysis suggests that if this is not corrected it will result in greater production (at a lower selling price) than if the producer had borne the full cost. In other words the economic balance is distorted so that it is no longer optimum. The usual example of this is pollution. If people living near a factory suffer damage, dirt and inconvenience as a result of pollution created by it they are bearing part of the true cost of production.

The tax system may then be involved in two ways. A tax may be imposed on the offending product so as to increase the cost of it, and hence the selling price. The tax yield may or may not be used to recompense those who suffer from the pollution. Alternatively, regulations may be made to impose additional requirements (and costs) on the producer so that the pollution is reduced and this may involve the tax system in financing the regulatory arrangements.

Some economic activities constitute natural monopolies. The distribution of electricity to houses and factories does not lend itself to competitive activity (except for some limited competition between different forms of energy) because of the high cost of duplicating or triplicating the distribution network. The trouble is that an uncontrolled monopoly may exploit its power and charge very high prices.

One solution that has been adopted is to supply such products under public ownership, and this need involve no taxation at all in so far as capital costs are met by borrowing and current outlays are covered by the charges made to consumers. The alternative approach, which has been used with British Telecom, involves public regulation of a private sector monopoly and this may require some tax revenue to finance the regulatory arrangements. That tax may come from the general body of taxpayers or from the industry.

Finally, taxation is used on a massive scale in the UK (and elsewhere) to finance support for pensioners, the unemployed, the sick and other welfare beneficiaries. This reflects a positive decision that the working population shall support those who are in need. Taxes may also be used in an attempt to reduce inequalities of income between income earners.

Clearly such a use of taxation is the result of a political response to the problem of need and it may not be appropriate in all kinds of society. In some societies support of the elderly and infirm is provided by the younger and fitter members of an extended family. A country which is economically backward may not be in a position to consider the provision of state financed welfare and the prevention of death from starvation and disease may then depend on outside agencies and international charities. The fact that many advanced economies have decided that the tax system shall be used to redistribute income between different groups of people has important effects on people's behaviour and expectations.

THE TAX STRUCTURE IN BRITAIN

Taxes may be collected at any level of public administration so the design of the total tax system depends on the political structure of the country. In a federation, such as Australia and the USA, significant taxes are levied by both the federal government and by the states. Taxes may be levied by municipalities as well.

In the UK taxes are levied by central government and, to a much lesser extent, by municipalities. The pattern is made more complicated by two features.

1. There can be three layers of municipal government – county, town and parish – but only one of these, the town, acts as a tax collector. It acts as an agent for the others and passes over to them the tax revenue to which they are entitled.
2. Taxes levied by the municipalities produce less than half the revenue they require to finance the services they provide. The main reason is that they are responsible for the high cost of education. As they receive more than half their revenue from central government the line of responsibility is blurred. This has important political consequences as in the last resort the main paymaster will be able to call the tune.

Decisions about the size and nature of the central government taxes are the responsibility of the Chancellor of the Exchequer advised by the Treasury, of which he is the political head. His decisions depend in turn on government policies laid down on a much wider front. It is these which will determine the outlays to be incurred and the economic and monetary policies to be followed.[2]

Once his decisions have been made, and approved by Parliament, the administration and collection of the taxes to be levied becomes the responsibility of three civil service bodies. The Board of Inland Revenue (BIR) is responsible for the collection of taxes imposed directly on people and companies. The Commissioners of Customs and Excise (CCE) are concerned with the taxes on goods and services. The Department of Health and Social Security (DHSS) is responsible for collecting National Insurance Contributions (NICS) based on employment and other income on a weekly or monthly basis.

The main central government taxes (other than NICS) are shown in Table 1.1, which is taken from Table 6.B.3 in the *Red Book*.[3] This information is published annually at the time of the Chancellor's budget speech, usually in March or April. Unlike many other countries which use the calendar year the UK's financial year starts on 1 April. We will now look briefly at the various taxes shown in the table with further reference to the chapters in which they are discussed in greater detail.

The list of taxes starts with those administered by the BIR and the first of these is income tax (IT). Not only does this produce the largest yield of any tax, it is also the most visible in the sense that people are very conscious of it. For most people it is

Table 1.1 Consolidated Fund revenue

	£ million		
	1985–86		1986–87
	Budget forecast	Latest estimate	Forecast
Inland Revenue			
Income tax[1]	35 200	35 100	38 500
Corporation tax[2,3]	10 100	10 700	11 700
Petroleum revenue tax[4]	8 200	6 400	2 400
Capital gains tax	790	930	1 050
Development land tax	55	60	35
Capital transfer tax (inheritance tax)[5]	760	890	910
Stamp duties	1 100	1 230	1 430
Total Inland Revenue	**56 200**	**55 300**	**56 000**
Customs and Excise			
Value added tax	18 300	19 300	20 700
Petrol, derv etc. duties	6 500	6 500	7 300
Cigarettes and other tobacco	4 300	4 300	4 700
Spirits, beer, wine, cider and perry	4 200	4 200	4 400
Betting and gaming	700	730	800
Car tax	760	880	980
Other excise duties	20	20	20
EC own resources[6]			
Customs duties, etc.	1 400	1 200	1 300
Agricultural levies	100	160	160
Total Customs and Excise	**36 300**	**37 300**	**40 400**
Vehicle excise duties[7]	2 500	2 400	2 500
National Insurance surcharge	30	30	—
Gas levy	520	520	500
Broadcasting receiving licences	790	990	1 000
Interest and dividends	870	910	840
Other[8]	9 200	8 400	7 400
Total Consolidated Fund revenue	**106 500**	**105 800**	**108 600**

[1] See paragraph 6.B.1.
[2] Includes advance corporation tax

(net of repayments)	3 600	3 800	4 100
[3] North Sea corporation tax	2 800	3 000	2 700
of which satisfied by setting off ACT	1 200	1 200	1 200

Liability to corporation tax arising in respect of North Sea production may be satisfied by setting off ACT arising on dividends paid in previous periods in respect of both onshore and offshore activities. Dividends and ACT associated with North Sea activities alone cannot be identified.
[4] Includes advance payments of petroleum revenue tax.
[5] Includes estate duty.
[6] Customs duties and agricultural levies are accountable to the European Communities as

'own resources'; actual payments to the Communities are recorded in Table 6.B.2.

[7] Includes driving licence receipts.

[8] Includes the 10 per cent of 'own resources' refunded by the European Communities to meet the costs of collection, other receipts from the European Communities, privatisation proceeds and oil royalties (see Table 1.2).

Source: H.M. Treasury Financial Statement and Budget Report 1986/7. Reproduced by permission of the Controller, Her Majesty's Stationery Office © Crown copyright.

deducted from their salary or wage and is actually paid on their behalf by their employer. Because it affects millions of people quite small changes can have a significant effect on total tax revenue and this fact goes a long way to explain the obstacles in the way of reforming its present structure. (See Chapters 2, 3 and 4.)

Corporation tax (CT) is very similar to IT except that it is levied on companies' incomes and on their capital gains (see below). It has been a separate tax since 1965. (See Chapter 7.) Petroleum revenue tax (PRT) is a special and complicated tax which is levied on the profits earned from the extraction of oil and gas from the North and Irish seas. It is levied in addition to CT, largely because the profit potential from such operations is considerable.

Capital gains tax (CGT) is levied on transactions which produce a profit, but not in the form of 'income'. A typical example would be the gain made by an investor on the sale of shares which he bought and sold through a stock exchange. (See Chapter 5.) Capital transfer tax (CTT) is now called inheritance tax (IHT) and is levied on the transfer of wealth on death and on certain other occasions. (See Chapter 6.) Stamp duties are taxes on new capital issued by companies and on the legal transfers of title to real property, shares and other assets.

The figures for the taxes administered by the CCE also show that one is dominant. This is value added tax (VAT) which is levied (at 15%) on the net selling prices of a wide range of goods and services. It is intended to be borne by the consumer, not by the trader. The taxes on petrol, cigarettes, spirits, etc., are sometimes referred to as the excise taxes. They are imposed as special taxes on the defined commodities because it has been decided that the rate of tax should exceed substantially the normal rate of VAT. The car tax, imposed on the sale of new cars, comes into a similar category. Again these takes are assumed to be borne by the consumer. (See Chapters 10 and 11.)

The betting and gaming taxes reflect an attempt to tax various aspects of these leisure activities. Customs duties are imposed on imported goods. At one time they were a very important feature of the tax system but have now become comparatively unimportant, as the figures show. For the most part they reflect the agreed rates of tax applied by all members of the European Community (EC) to imports from outside the member states. states.

Turning now to the miscellaneous group at the end of the table, the vehicle excise duty is the annual licence fee and should not be confused with the car tax referred to above. (See Chapter 11.) The revenue from broadcast receiving licences is intended to finance the BBC and in so far as it is payable whether or not you watch BBC television, and irrespective of how long if you do, it has some of the characteristics of a tax. Of course you pay for ITV by buying the advertised products but that is not compulsory.

Before leaving Table 11.1 a final comment is prompted by the entry 'Gas levy'. A nationalized industry may be used as a form of hidden taxation where it is able to raise its prices beyond the cost of production and is instructed to do so. In effect the consumer

Table 1.2 Public sector transactions by sub-sector and economic category

£ billion[1]

1985–86 Latest estimate

General government

	Line[2]	Central government	Local authorities	Total	Public corporations	Public sector
Current and capital receipts						
Taxes on income, and oil royalties	1	54.0	—	54.0	−0.3	53.8
Taxes on expenditure	2	42.9	13.7	56.6	—	56.6
Taxes on capital	3	2.5	—	2.5	—	2.5
National insurance and other contributions	4	24.3	—	24.3	—	24.3
Gross trading surplus	5	−0.3	0.3	−0.1	7.5	7.4
Rent and miscellaneous current transfers	6	0.3	2.9	3.2	0.5	3.7
Interest and dividends from private sector and abroad	7	2.9	0.6	3.5	1.1	4.7
Interest and dividends within public sector	8	5.5	−2.6	2.9	−2.9	—
Imputed charge for non-trading capital consumption	9	0.9	1.4	2.3	—	2.3
Capital transfers from private sector	10	—	—	—	0.2	0.2
Total	11	133.0	16.3	149.2	6.2	155.5
Current and capital expenditure						
Current expenditure on goods and services	12	−46.4	−28.2	−74.6	—	−74.6
Subsidies	13	−5.6	−1.2	−6.8	—	−6.8
Current grants to personal sector	14	−43.2	−4.1	−47.2	—	−47.2
Current grants paid abroad	15	−2.6	—	−2.6	—	−2.6
Current grants within public sector	16	−20.2	20.2	—	—	—
Debt interest	17	−16.1	−1.5	−17.7	−0.6	−18.2
Gross domestic fixed capital formation	18	−3.1	−3.5	−6.6	−6.0	−12.6
Increase in stocks	19	−0.5	—	−0.5	−0.1	−0.6
Capital grants to private sector	20	−2.1	−0.7	−2.9	−0.1	−3.0
Capital grants within public sector	21	−1.2	0.7	−0.6	0.6	—
Total	22	−141.1	−18.4	−159.4	−6.2	−165.7
Unallocated Reserve	23	—	—	—	—	—
Financial surplus/deficit	24	−8.1	−2.1	−10.2	—	−10.2
Financial transactions						
Net lending to private sector and abroad	25	−0.1	0.2	0.1	−0.2	—

£ billion[1]

1986–87 Forecasts

General government

Line[2]	Central govern- ment	Local authori- ties	Total	Public corpora- tions	Public sector	
						Current and capital receipts
1	52.9	—	52.9	−0.2	52.8	Taxes on income and oil royalties
2	46.3	15.6	61.9	—	61.9	Taxes on expenditure
3	2.8	—	2.8	—	2.8	Taxes on capital
4	26.2	—	26.2	—	26.2	National insurance and other contributions
5	−0.6	0.3	−0.3	7.7	7.4	Gross trading surplus
6	0.3	2.9	3.3	0.5	3.8	Rent and miscellaneous current transfers
7	3.2	0.6	3.8	1.0	4.8	Interest and dividends from private sector and abroad
8	5.7	−3.1	2.6	−2.6	—	Interest and dividends within public sector
9	1.0	1.4	2.4	—	2.4	Imputed charge for non-trading capital consumption
10	—	—	—	0.2	0.2	Capital transfers from private sector
11	**137.8**	**17.8**	**155.6**	**6.7**	**162.2**	**Total**
						Current and capital expenditure
12	−49.1	−28.5	−77.6	—	−77.6	Current expenditure on goods and services
13	−5.8	−0.9	−6.7	—	−6.7	Subsidies
14	−44.9	−4.2	−49.1	—	−49.1	Current grants to personal sector
15	−2.5	—	−2.5	—	−2.5	Current grants paid abroad
16	−21.1	21.1	—	—	—	Current grants within public sector
17	−17.0	−1.2	−18.2	−0.6	−18.7	Debt interest
18	−3.3	−3.4	−6.7	−5.6	−12.2	Gross domestic fixed capital formation
19	−0.2	—	−0.2	—	−0.2	Increase in stocks
20	−2.1	−0.6	−2.7	−0.1	−2.8	Capital grants to private sector
21	−1.4	0.7	−0.6	0.6	—	Capital grants within public sector
22	**−147.3**	**−17.0**	**−164.3**	**−5.6**	**−169.9**	**Total**
23					−4.5	Unallocated Reserve
24					**−12.2**	**Financial surplus/deficit**
						Financial transactions
25	−0.2	0.3	—	−0.1	—	Net lending to private sector and abroad

Table 1.2   continued

Cash expenditure on company securities (net) (including privatisation proceeds)	26	2.7	—	2.7	—	2.7
Transactions concerning certain public sector pension schemes	27	0.4	—	0.4	—	0.4
Accruals adjustments	28	-0.4	0.1	-0.3	0.4	0.1
Miscellaneous financial transactions	29	0.5	-0.3	0.3	-0.1	0.2
Borrowing requirement	30	**4.9**	**2.1**	**7.0**	**-0.2**	**6.8**

[1]Sign convention: receipts positive, payments negative.
[2]Relationship between lines: (24) = (11) + (22) + (23) = – (25) to (30)

is paying an additional tax based on his consumption of the particular product. This fact may not be apparent from the taxation statistics, although in this case it is.

Turning now to Table 1.2 (Table 6.5 in the *Red Book*) we find a complete summary of all taxes, central and local, and how they have been spent. It may be observed that in the 1986/87 forecast expenditure was due to exceed receipts by £billion 7.1. This is the Public Sector Borrowing Requirement (PSBR).

Two taxes were not shown in Table 1.1. National Insurance Contributions (NICS) are second only to IT in total yield and the greater part of this consists of employers' contributions. The remainder will appear as a deduction from employees' wages. Despite its name this is a true tax as it is used to pay current benefits. Unlike a private pension scheme the contributions are not invested in a special fund. (See Chapter 2.)

Local rates are the municipal tax and appear as 'Taxes on expenditure' in the column headed 'Local authorities'. They are levied on the basis of the 'annual value' of property located in the municipal area. They are a tax on the occupation, not ownership, of the property but they may be paid by a landlord and recovered from the occupier by means of an appropriate increase in the rent charged. (See Chapter 10.) Examination of the 'Local authorities' column in the 1986–87 forecasts reveals that the yield of rates at £billion 15.6 fall well short of grants received amounting to £billion 21.1

Public expenditure is further analysed in Table 1.3 (Table 5.1 in the *Red Book*). This shows the heavy burden of social security and the substantial sums being spent on defence, health and education and, at the bottom of the list, interest on the National Debt. The figure for Scotland, Wales and Northern Ireland relates to spending under the control of the respective secretaries of state and does not represent the total spending in those parts of the kingdom.

TAX CATEGORIZATION AND COMPARISON

Before international and other comparisons can be made we need to try to put these taxes into categories so that similar taxes can be compared despite differences of detail. It has been argued by Kay and others that all taxes fall ultimately to be borne by people.[4] Institutions are only intermediary in this process. Nevertheless we can still categorize taxes by the way in which they are imposed.

					Cash expenditure on company securities (net) (including
26	4.8	—	4.8	—	4.8	privatisation proceeds)
					Transactions concerning certain public sector
27	0.6	—	0.6	—	0.6	pension schemes
28	−0.1	—	−0.1	—	−0.1	Accruals adjustments
29	0.2	−0.4	−0.2	−0.1	−0.3	Miscellaneous financial transactions
30					7.1	**Borrowing requirement**

Source: H.M. Treasury Financial Statement and Budget Report 1986/7. Reproduced by permission of the Controller, Her Majesty's Stationery Office © Crown copyright.

A commonly used division is that between direct and indirect taxes. Income tax, it is argued, is a direct tax because it is imposed directly on those who are intended to bear it. This is a plausible contention in the case of people, but not quite so clear in the case of

Table 1.3 Public expenditure

	£ billion				
	1984–85 Outturn	1985–86 Estimate	1986–87 Provision	1987–88 Plans	1988–89 Plans
Department					
DHSS – Social security	38.1	41.3	42.9	44.4	45.9
Defence	17.2	18.0	18.5	18.8	19.0
DHSS – Health and personal social services	15.8	16.7	17.7	18.4	19.1
Scotland, Wales and Northern Ireland	13.7	14.5	15.0	15.0	15.2
Education and science	14.0	14.3	14.3	14.4	14.5
Other	33.0	31.7	31.2	31.2	31.6
Privatisation proceeds	−2.1	−2.6	−4.7	−4.7	−4.7
Reserve			4.5	6.3	8.0
Adjustments			−0.4[1]		
Public expenditure planning total	129.6	133.9	139.1	143.9	148.7
General government gross debt interest[2]	16.1	17.7	18.2	19	19
Other adjustments[2]	4.3	6.2	6.1	7	7
General government[2] expenditure	150.0	157.7	163.4	170	175
Planning total in real terms (base year 1984–85)	129.6	126.3	126.6	126.2	126.0
General government expenditure as percentage of GDP	46	44	42½	41½	40½

[1]External finance of – £400 million for nationalised industries to be privatised in 1986–87.
[2]1987–88 and 1988–89 figures rounded to nearest £ billion.

Source: H.M. Treasury Financial Statement and Budget Report 1986/7.

companies where it may be argued that the tax is intended to be borne by the shareholders. Direct taxes may be subdivided between taxes such as income tax which are imposed on an annual flow, and taxes levied on a stock of capital or wealth at some instant in time.

The indirect taxes are imposed on goods and services with the intention that they will be borne by the final consumer through a price increase sufficient to recoup the tax actually paid by the suppliers. It does not follow that the consumer will know how much tax he has borne when he buys and consumes, say, a bottle of wine. The wine may have borne customs duty when imported, excise duty when released from bond, and a value added or sales tax at various stages in its progress from the vineyard to the dining table.

One sub-division of indirect taxes can be important for budgetary policy. This is the distinction between specific and *ad valorem* taxes. The former are imposed according to some physical attribute such as the weight of the product. The latter are imposed as a percentage of the selling price. When prices are rising the implications are clear, one is buoyant in its revenue, the other is not.

NICS, known in most countries as social security taxes, do not fit comfortably into these categories. The employee's contributions can be likened to an income tax but the employers' contributions are more like an indirect tax imposed on industrial costs using payroll as the basis. Thus we find that this tax is sub-divided into the two components in Table 1.4 below.

It should be borne in mind that the distinction between direct and indirect taxes is not quite so clear as the preceding discussion may suggest. The question whether direct taxes are really borne in full by the apparent taxpayer and whether indirect taxes are really passed on in full to the final consumer/taxpayer has been subjected to considerable investigation the results of which are inconclusive. It is a question to which we shall return.

The categories we have just discussed are set out in Table 1.4.

Table 1.4 Categorization of taxes

	Taxes imposed on	
	People	Institutions
Direct taxes — flow	Income taxes	Corporation tax
— static measure	Capital taxes	Capital taxes
Indirect (expenditure) taxes		
— specific	Rates	Tobacco tax
— *ad valorem*	—	VAT
Social security	NICS	NICS

We can now consider some international comparisons, taking first the UK and the other developed countries which are members of OECD. The figures in Table 1.5 enable us to compare total taxes and then to look at the components thereof.

It will be seen that in terms of total taxes the UK is somewhere near the middle of the group. The countries with the lowest taxes are Japan, Switzerland and the USA and it may be that this is because those countries have the least developed public welfare

Table 1.5 International comparison of taxation

Figures are for 1980 and are % of GNP.

	Total tax	Income taxes People	Income taxes Corporations	Expenditure taxes	Social security Total	Social security Employer
UK	42	13	4	19	7	4
Australia	35	16	4	15	–	–
Austria	49	13	2	19	15	–
Belgium	48	17	3	13	14	10
Canada	36	13	5	14	4	2
Finland	39	15	2	17	6	–
France	48	7	3	18	21	14
W. Germany	44	12	2	14	16	8
Greece	–	5	1	15	10	–
Irish Repub.	–	–	–	20	7	–
Italy	38	10	2	12	14	10
Japan	28	7	5	8	8	4
Netherlands	52	14	3	14	20	10
Norway	59	–	–	–	14	–
Spain	–	4	2	7	13	–
Sweden	55	23	1	15	16	15
Switzerland	31	12	2	7	9	3
USA	33	13	3	9	8	5

Source: *Economic Trends*, December 1982. Reproduced by permission of the Controller, Her Majesty's Stationery Office. © Crown copyright.

programmes. Welfare provision may, of course, be provided in other ways. There is plenty of scope for arguing about the reasons. Are these three countries wealthy because of their low taxes, or is the fact that they are wealthy responsible for the low taxes? Is their GNP so large that taxes appear to be low in proportion to it?

Looking at the individual taxes leads us to some interesting insights into government policies. France has a high level of social security taxes, both for employer and employee, but has kept income taxes low, so offsetting the social security burden on the employee. Australia takes the opposite approach with a high level of income taxes and no social security taxes at all. For a country with an average level of taxation (in this context) the UK has a very high level of expenditure taxes.

The figures suggest that tax policy, even within a group of developed nations, may vary with the level of government expenditure, with the nature of that expenditure (e.g. whether a social security tax is needed) and with the country's traditions and social attitudes. Thus a country which may look attractive to a potential immigrant because of low rates of direct taxes may be less attractive when it is realized that other taxes are proportionately heavier even if less obvious.

Moving to a comparison with other types of country produces even greater differences. Poorer countries are unlikely to be able to afford welfare provision and the design of the system may be limited by widespread illiteracy and by the fact that much of the economic activity is production for own consumption (subsistence farming) where few market transactions take place.

It is difficult to obtain up-to-date statistics in sufficient detail but a study made in 1982 shows the pattern in developing countries.[5] As can be seen in Table 1.6 direct taxes

Table 1.6 Direct taxes as % of total tax revenue

	Group of poorest countries	Group of developed countries
Personal income taxes	9.0	25.9
Taxes on corporate income	10.3	11.1
Other taxes	6.8	12.2
Total	26.1	49.2

for 1966–68 represented only 26.1% of total taxes in the poorest countries (GNP less than $250 per capita), but 49.2% in 1970 for a group of developed countries. At that time the UK percentage was 57.7. Of the direct taxes in the poorest group only about one-third of the yield came from personal income tax, which was lower than the yield from taxes on corporate income. In the developed group personal income taxes were nearly 26% of total taxes compared with just over 11% for taxes on corporate incomes.

The comparative deficiency in the poorest countries' income tax yield is made up by indirect taxes. Taking a similar group of the poorest countries export taxes provided 10.6% of tax revenue and import taxes 28.2%. Such taxes are of little importance in the developed countries but the figures for the two groups are much closer in the case of excise and sales taxes. In looking at these comparisons it should be remembered that in the poorer countries total taxes tend to be a lower proportion of a low GNP.

Finally two special features of some tax systems are worth a comment. In oil producing countries royalties may be a very high proportion of government revenue. In Kuwait the proportion in 1977 was 96.6%. In countries with centrally planned (socialist) economies state enterprise surpluses may be significant. In 1977 they amounted to 45% of government revenue in Syria, and in some other countries the offical figures may be misleading because they account for taxes on the profits of such enterprises in different ways.

NOTES AND REFERENCES

1. For a fuller treatment see Chapter 2 of Brown, C.V. and Jackson, P.M., *Public Sector Economics*, Martin Robertson, Oxford (1982).
2. See Robinson, A. and Sandford, C. *Tax Policy-Making in the United Kingdom*, Heinmann Educational Books, London (1983), for an interesting account of the many influences at work.
3. H.M. Treasury, *Financial Statement and Budget Report, 1986–87*, HMSO, London (1986).
4. See, for example, Chapters 12 and 14 of Kay, J.A. and King, M.A., *The British Tax System*, Oxford University Press, Oxford (1983).
5. The figures in the remainder of this chapter are taken from Askari, H., Cummings, J.T. and Glover, M., *Taxation and Tax Policies in the Middle East*, Butterworths, London (1982).

EXERCISES AND DISCUSSION TOPICS

1. Discuss for any country (not just the UK) whether and for what reasons the following activities necessitate the use of a tax system.

   (a) Judicial proceedings in a court of law.

(b) University education.
(c) Household refuse disposal.
(d) Providing post-retirement income.

2. Governments justify high taxes on cigarettes and tobacco on the grounds that they help to discourage a habit which 'can damage your health'. These excise taxes produce substantial revenue (see Table 1.1). Supposing that this policy of discouragement succeeded brilliantly and that consumption of tobacco virtually ceased, what results, apart from the immediate loss of tax revenue, would you expect to see? Consider direct, indirect, long- and short-term effects including those on government spending. Would the government have to find other sources of revenue?

3. A friend of yours is considering the offer of a job in another country where the tax rate on income is normally 10%, which is much lower than in the UK. The salary level is higher but she is particularly excited about the prospect of paying so little tax. Should you try to calm her down? If so, why? (Concentrate on the possible financial offsets rather than on social and other non-financial problems.)

2   Income taxes in the UK

In this chapter we shall look at the way in which the income of individuals is taxed in the UK. Apart from the question of what is classified as income and how it may be taxed we must consider the question of whose incomes can be taxed under the UK tax laws. The special problems that may arise in taxing families will be left for fuller discussion in Chapter 4. Illustrative examples will be found at the end of the chapter and are all cross-referenced from the text.

WHO AND WHAT IS SUBJECT TO UK INCOME TAX

It is clear that a Brazilian peasant who earns his only income from farming in his home village will not be taxable on that income in the UK. But where should the tax frontier be drawn in this modern world when millions of people cross over national boundaries every year?

The main concept for this purpose is called *residence*. If I am resident in the UK I am, potentially at least, liable to UK tax on my income arising anywhere in the world. Even if I am not resident in the UK I may be liable on income arising in the UK. This would apply, for instance, to income arising on investments situated in the UK.

It should be apparent that if other countries levy taxes on the same basis (and many do so) some income will be taxable in two countries. Such a result could be damaging to the international allocation of investment funds so most countries provide relief either by giving credit for foreign tax suffered by their own residents or by exempting income already taxed elsewhere. This is a rather specialized topic which will not be pursued in this book.

Returning, however, to the question of residence there can be a serious problem in determining a person's status because individual circumstances vary in so many ways. The main guidelines used in the UK are that a person entering the country is resident if:

1. he is actually present in the country for more than one half of a tax year, or
2. he visits the country on a regular basis for 3 months or more per tax year over a series of years.

A person who is already resident remains so unless absent for a complete tax year. The tax year in the UK starts on 6 April each year.

It may be noted here that not all countries use the same definitions and guidelines as the UK. In the USA, for example, citizenship is the vital factor. Thus it is possible for the same person to be resident in two or more countries at the same time.[1]

Two related concepts must now be defined as they will be encountered later in this chapter. *Ordinary residence* implies something more than mere residence: it refers to the country in which a person usually resides. This can mean that for a particular year a person may be ordinarily resident but not resident in a country if he is actually out of the country for the whole year. *Domicile* means, roughly, one's home country. It can be changed from the domicile acquired at birth but only as a result of a very clear course of action going beyond a mere change of nationality as that, by itself, may be insufficient.

To sum up, a German citizen could emigrate to the UK while remaining domiciled in West Germany, take a temporary job in Spain so as to be resident there for one year, and remain ordinarily resident in the UK. All or any of these features could be relevant to his UK tax liability.

Having decided that someone is going to be liable to UK tax on all or part of his income the next requirement is to define and quantify that income. There are some well-known general definitions of income. As Goude puts it 'There is an extensive and tedious literature on the subject, enlivened by a few notable contributions.'[2] The trouble is that whether we go to Adam Smith or J. R. Hicks, or any of the other authors, we look in vain for a definition that is operational for the purposes of tax administration. This problem of definition is not a trivial one because the theoretical deficiencies of the practical solutions lead to potential loopholes in the system and hence to complex legislation designed to close those loopholes.

The practical solution adopted in the UK is to describe income in the legislation source by source, and then to calculate an annual liability based on the total income from all those sources. This scheme has the added advantage that each source can have its own appropriate rules for making the necessary income calculations.

Using an old legal form based on the original 1842 legislation the sources are listed as Schedules, some of which are sub-divided into Cases. Before we look at them in turn we should note that this is not a 'schedular' system of taxation as used in some other countries (e.g. Italy and Hong Kong). There the word implies that there is a separate tax on each source, possibly using different tax rates, and there need be no aggregation of sources to produce a total income figure.

Schedule A covers rent and other receipts from land (and buildings thereon) situated in the UK. It does not include the profits of businesses merely because they use land, nor does it apply to income from property which is let fully furnished.

Deductions are allowed in a fairly predictable way for the cost of maintenance, repairs, insurance and management, although repairs may be subjected to some of the restrictions that apply for the calculation of business profits (see Chapter 9). Rent paid to a superior lessor is also deductible. A claim can be made for a depreciation allowance on eligible assets such as plant and machinery, again following the scheme applicable to business assets. Relief is available for losses suffered.[3]

Schedule B applies to income from woodlands and this poses a special problem because of the length of time it takes growing timber to reach maturity. The tax is charged on one-third of the 'annual value' of the land, but the occupier of the land may elect to be taxed under Schedule D on a trading basis.[4]

Schedule C applies to most of the interest paid on government securities and requires that tax at the 'basic rate' (which is specified annually) shall be deducted from the payment. When the correct tax actually due from the recipient has been determined a refund or further payment of tax may be necessary. The main exclusion from the generality of Schedule C is interest on government securities held on the Post Office or Trustee Savings Bank registers.[5] These are taxed under Schedule D.

Schedule D is sub-divided into 6 Cases, each of which is important in its own right.

Cases I and II together cover the profits of trades, professions and vocations. The calculation rules are dealt with in detail in Chapter 9.

Case III levies tax on interest, annuities, annual payments, discounts and some other items. It charges tax on the full amount receivable with no deductions for any expenses incurred. There are some important questions of definition, some of which will be discussed in Chapter 5.[6]

Cases IV and V cover income arising outside the UK, such as interest and dividends on foreign investments and the profits of trades carried on abroad. We shall not delve deeper into this category in this book.[7]

Case VI is a residual category but it cannot be used to tax items which are different in nature from those listed elsewhere in the Schedules. Thus it catches activity of a minor nature which is similar to a trade but on a lesser scale. An example would be the receipt of insurance commissions on an occasional basis which falls far short of being a trade in the proper sense.[8]

Schedule E covers the emoluments of 'offices and employments' together with pensions from them. It also covers some of the state welfare benefits. Some of the difficulties of defining emoluments will be considered in Chapter 5. Two other points can be made here about this schedule.

1. There are three Cases but, unlike those under Schedule D, they do not deal with different kinds of income as such, as the following summary will show.[9]
    (a) *Case I.* Any emoluments for duties in the UK or elsewhere if the recipient is both resident and ordinarily resident in the UK.
    (b) *Case II.* Any emoluments, but only for duties in the UK, if the recipient is not resident, or if resident not ordinarily resident.
    (c) *Case III.* Any emoluments actually received in the UK if the recipient is resident but not domiciled in the UK and the employer is not resident in the UK.
    Thus Cases II and III restrict the UK tax liability on those employments where the connection with the UK is impermanent or tenuous.
2. The deduction allowed for expenses incurred is notoriously narrow and restrictive – although rather curiously it still preserves the possibility of a claim for the cost of travelling on horseback! The case law derived from the appeals procedure makes it clear, for instance, that dual purpose expenditure is wholly disallowed (e.g. the cost of a meal which was more expensive than usual because of circumstances arising from the employment) as is any cost incurred while not actually performing the duties (e.g. getting to work, evening classes to improve skills).[10]

Schedule F governs the income received in the form of dividends paid on the shares of UK companies. The topic will be covered in detail in Chapter 7. As with Schedule C the recipient is credited with tax at the basic rate and a further payment or refund may then be found to be needed.

Various receipts may make us better off without being classified as income under Schedules A – F. Few would expect gifts and inherited wealth to be so treated but in other circumstances the point may not be so clear. Such cases can be divided into three broad categories.

1. Accountants are well aware of the hazy borderline between capital and income matters. Capital receipts, such as those which arise from the sale of investments, are not income, although in the UK they may be taxed as capital gains (Chapter 5).

2. Some receipts may arise as windfalls or escape the income tax net in some other way, even though they are received as a consequence of some income earning activity. Thus compensation paid to an employee for a loss suffered when he moved house as a result of a new posting within the same company was held not to be income.[11] Nor is compensation paid to a professional firm on an *ex gratia* basis following the loss of a regular engagement through no fault of its own.[12] Such cases do, however, tend to be exceptional. More frequently encountered are prizes and betting winnings which fall right outside the tax net because they are unrelated to any income earning activity, but note that bookmakers do carry on such an activity and receive taxable income.[13]

3. The third category covers a miscellaneous group of receipts which are clearly income but are excluded from the statutory definition by government decision. The reasons vary. Some social welfare benefits, being means tested, may just as well be left free of tax, but this exclusion does not apply to state retirement pensions and unemployment benefits. Another example is the exemption of certain forms of national savings such as National Savings Certificates. The low rate of interest offered reflects their tax-free nature. Unfortunately the investor who is not liable to tax, a child without other income for instance, suffers the low rate of interest but can claim no tax refund. Finally, the income on some British government securities is tax exempt if the investor is not ordinarily resident in the UK.

ASSESSMENT

The listing and definition of income is only a first step in the process of actually collecting the tax that is due. From the point of view of the Treasury it is important that tax revenue shall flow on a regular and predictable basis. Without this, and especially with such an important tax as IT the government's financial planning would be hopelessly prejudiced and there could be serious economic consequences. The government might find itself with a sudden need to borrow large sums on the money markets and this could result in widely fluctuating interest rates. In this section we shall see how this sort of problem is overcome in the UK.

Income tax and many other taxes are assessed and collected on an annual basis. The one-year period had an agricultural origin (one harvest per year in the UK) and is widely used as the base period for many financial measures. In fact the IT year in the UK is not the usual financial year starting on 1 April but the period from 6 April in one year to 5 April twelve months later. Thus a year described as 1986/87 means the year starting on 6 April 1986. This idiosyncratic choice derives first from the traditional quarter days, one of which was Lady Day on 25 March, and secondly from the change of 10 days in the Gregorian calendar in 1582 when the old calendar had moved out of phase with the seasons.[14]

However odd these dates may seem they could not be changed easily and the scheme that has developed is that every individual liable in the UK can be required annually to report his income for the year ended 5 April. For most people the official forms are received in April and are intended to provide the tax office with information about the income for the year just ended. Chapter 14 deals with these administrative arrangements in more detail.

Unfortunately the UK tax system has a further complication in store for us. For Schedules A, B, C, E and F the income to be reported is that arising in the tax year itself. For most of the Schedule D sources the income to be reported is that of the previous tax year.[15] Thus interest due to be received in 1986/87 and payable gross is taxed as if it were part of the total income of the tax year 1987/88 (6 April 1987 to 5 April 1988). The main virtue of this arrangement, the so-called 'preceding year basis', is that the taxable income is known at the beginning of the tax year and so the tax due can be collected promptly and accurately within the year itself. Thus the interest actually received in 1986/87 gives rise to tax liability for 1987/88 which is collectable on 1 January 1988. This arrangement creates two problems.

Problem 1

What is to happen when interest first arises and when it ceases? The answer lies in special rules for the opening and closing years. For the opening years they are as follows:

1st tax year	Actual interest (for year or part year).
2nd tax year	Actual interest for the year.
3rd tax year	Preceding year's interest.
4th tax year	Preceding year's interest.

It will be seen that the second year's interest is taxed twice. The taxpayer has an option to have the third tax year assessed on actual interest which means that it is then the third year's interest which is taxed twice.

The *quid pro quo* for this double taxation comes when the source ceases. The rules then are as follows:

Final tax year	Actual interest.
Year before that	Preceding year's interest.
Year before that	Preceding year's interest.

On this basis the interest of the penultimate year is not taxed at all. Again there is an option, but this time it is only available to the Inland Revenue. The option is to tax the penultimate tax year on actual interest, thus moving the 'gap' to the ante-penultimate year.

The present trend is to tax more interest at source, as under Schedule C, in which case these rules do not apply and the interest becomes income of the tax year in which it is receivable.

Problem 2

What about trading profit? The rules for the opening and closing years of the trade are a bit more complicated than those for interest. The reason for this is that while business accounts are usually prepared for one year at a time they are seldom prepared to cover the tax year. Thus the preliminary question is what is meant by 'income arising in the preceding year'? The answer is that an accounting year ending in a tax year is treated as if it were coterminous with that tax year. Thus profit calculated for the calendar year 1986 is treated as income arising in tax year 1986/87 and becomes the taxable income for 1987/88.

Again there are special rules for the opening and closing years, their effect being to tax one year's profits twice (or more) in the opening years and to leave a gap in the closing years. These can best be explained by means of a simple example.

Suppose that a business started to trade on 1 January 1980 and existed for 8 years, ending on 31 December 1987. Accounts were drawn up for the 8 calendar years and showed the following taxable profits:

	£		£
1980	4 000	1984	5 600
1981	5 000	1985	4 800
1982	3 600	1985	3 200
1983	6 000	1986	2 000

The income for IT purposes will be calculated as follows, under the statutory rules.

		£
1979/80	Actual profits, apportioned 4 000 × 3/12	1 000
1980/81	First 12 months (1980 calendar year)	4 000
1981/82	Preceding year's profit (normal basis)	4 000
1982/83	do.	5 000
1983/84	do.	3 600
1984/85	do.	6 000
1985/86	do.	5 600
1986/87	do.	4 800
1987/88	Final tax year, actual profit, apportioned 2 000 × 9/12	1 500

Note how in practice the odd 5 days in April are ignored and the apportionment calculations done in complete months. Simple arithmetic reveals that this business made a total profit of £34 000 over its whole life whereas the tax assessments total £35 500. This seems to be rather unsatisfactory but the legislation does allow two modifications to be made.

1. The second and third tax years can be modified jointly at the taxpayer's option to the actual apportioned profits, viz.

1980/81	4 000 × 9/12	3 000	
	5 000 × 3/12	1 250	4 250

1981/82	5 000 × 9/12	3 750	
	3 600 × 3/12	900	4 650

It is clear that this would not be a favourable option on these figures.

2. The Inland Revenue has a similar option in respect of the 2 years immediately preceding the final tax year, viz.

1985/86	4 800 × 9/12	3 600	
	3 200 × 3/12	800	4 400
1986/87	3 200 × 9/12	2 400	
	2 000 × 3/12	500	2 900

Again it is all too clear that the option will not be exercised. Thus we are still left with the unsatisfactory position that taxable income exceeds actual income by £1 500.

Because these rules are rather artificial it can be shown that tax liability may be affected substantially by the choice of a starting date (especially around 5/6 April) and by the choice of accounting year.

To sum up this section we can conclude that a person's total income for a tax year may be an aggregate of items taken from different periods and that it may, over several years, differ from the total income that he perceives himself as having actually received. Example 2.1 illustrates the point and should be studied carefully.

COLLECTION

Let us now turn to the actual collection of tax revenue. The Treasury seeks to achieve a smooth flow of revenue by collecting tax during the tax year itself and at a time when the taxpayer can afford to pay. This means that tax should be collected soon after, but not before, the income is received.

In fact tax on a wide range of incomes is collected under arrangements whereby it is withheld at source. The best known example of this is the Pay As You Earn scheme (PAYE) under which employers are required to withhold from wages and salaries the estimated tax due from the employee week by week or month by month. This is achieved by issuing to the employer a code number for each employee. This is then applied to the gross wage using standard tables which are supplied as well. Because the calculations are done on a cumulative basis through the tax year periodic variations in emoluments can be absorbed into the calculation and for most employees the result at the end of the tax year is very accurate.

The other main arrangement for withholding tax at source applies to payments of interest and other annual payments. In these cases all the tax is withheld at the specified 'basic rate' so the end result may be inaccurate and there may have to be further payments or refunds.

The recipients of all such income, including wages, are entitled to full credit for the tax deducted whether or not that tax has been accounted for and paid by the person who made the deduction.[16] This is a desirable corollary of the recipient's obligation to allow the tax to be withheld from his income.

Deduction of tax at source does not apply to all interest payments. It applies if it is paid by a company, but not if paid by an individual unless the recipient is not resident in the UK. In the case of interest paid or credited by banks and building societies to individuals, but not companies etc., there are special arrangements. The bank etc. pays tax on the interest at a 'composite rate' (which is lower than the basic rate) and recipients are then treated as if they had paid tax at the basic rate. The snag is that none of this composite rate tax can be refunded, so an investor whose income is below the tax threshold suffers tax whereas none would have been due if the investment had been made in, say, government securities on the Post Office register where interest is paid gross.

If tax is not withheld at source under any of these arrangements payment has to be made direct to a collector of taxes. The timing of these payments is laid down in the legislation and in the case of Schedules A and B and Schedule D, Case III, is required on 1 January of the relevant tax year.[17] In the case of Schedule A this is done on a provisional basis as the exact income for the whole year is not yet known.[18]

Cases I and II of Schedule D are dealt with slightly differently. The tax is payable in two equal instalments, the first on 1 January in the relevant tax year, the second six months later.[19] Sometimes it is assumed that this rule, combined with the preceding year basis discussed above, means that the trader does not have to pay tax on his profits until many months, even years, after those profits were made. Referring to Example 2.1 it may be concluded that no tax is payable on the 1985 trading profit, which provides the basis for the taxable income of 1986/87, until 1 January 1987.

There is a fallacy in this conclusion, however, because tax would have been paid twice or more on the profits of the first year of trading (see the example on p. 19 above) and so some tax is due and payable in every tax year from the start of the business. All that is being deferred is the extra tax that results from any increase in current profits over 'preceding year' profits.

THE STRUCTURE OF INCOME TAXES

The main virtue claimed for a tax on income is that it attempts to tax people by reference to their ability to pay, or 'taxable capacity'. A poll tax imposed equally on everyone is disliked because it bears lightly on the rich and may be an almost impossible burden on the poor. Such a tax is called a regressive tax.

It may seem reasonable to suggest that a tax on income should be levied in proportion to that income, and indeed it would be very convenient in many ways, not least in that the rate of tax to be deducted at source would be known precisely. However, it was recognized from the early beginnings of the tax in the UK that such a tax imposes an unfair burden on those with very low incomes and would be comparatively expensive to collect at that level. So it is that in most systems the first slice of income is exempted and those taxpayers whose income is above the exempt slice pay tax only on the excess.

One effect of this scheme is to cause the average rate of tax to rise as income rises above the threshold. The point can be shown with some simple figures.

	£	£	£
Income	1 000	2 000	4 000
Threshold	1 000	1 000	1 000
Income taxed at 30%	Nil	1 000	3 000
Total tax	Nil	300	900
Average rate of tax (%)	Nil	15	22½

Income taxes of this type are called 'progressive' and the marginal rate of tax will always exceed the average rate (except below the threshold where both are zero).

It may now be asked what factors determine the level at which the threshold shall be set? Three such factors will be considered.

1. The first is the influence of family circumstances. The UK system provides for an enhanced threshold for a married man who is living with his wife (although, as Chapter 4 will show, this concept is being challenged). In 1986/87 this enhancement, compared with the threshold for a single man or woman, amounted to 56.33%. Other responsibilities may also be taken into account. For many years an extra amount was given for each child, but since 1979 this has been replaced by a cash payment on the grounds that the actual cash benefit of tax relief may be minimal or even zero for those who are so poor that they pay little or no tax. It is interesting too to observe that some countries enhance the threshold in respect of dependant children, but only for a few as they are trying to discourage large families and thereby reduce the birthrate.[20] The UK system still enhances the threshold to recognize other commitments such as the extra costs resulting from blindness and, in special circumstances, the cost of a housekeeper or of the services of a son or daughter. A special threshold is given to the elderly, those over 65 years. In 1986/87 this increased the normal level by 22%. The purpose of this seems to be that it exempts a state pensioner who has little other income from liability to IT. Details of this arrangement are shown in Example 2.2.

2. The second factor is the response of the threshold to general price inflation. We have just seen that as income rises above the threshold the average rate of tax rises. This means that if a person's salary is raised by 10% to meet rising prices the average tax rate, and the real burden of tax, will rise. Putting it another way, the tax due will rise by more than 10%. If the tax yield is not to rise by stealth (a process referred to as 'fiscal drag') it is necessary for the threshold to rise by 10% as well. In the UK system this problem has been dealt with by legislation which requires the threshold to be raised each year in proportion to the Retail Prices Index unless Parliament makes a specific decision to alter it by some greater or lesser amount.[21] It may decide to do so if economic or social policy seem to justify it.

3. We have left until last the most fundamental issue of all, how should the basic threshold be quantified? It could be argued that it should aim to exclude from tax liability all those whose income provides no more than a bare existence. In fact the present level in the UK is below the lowest wage paid to anyone in full-time employment.[22] What has happened is that through the twentieth century IT has ceased to be a tax payable by a small minority and is now payable by virtually the

whole of the working population.[23] We may conclude therefore that there is no general principle underlying the quantification of the threshold and that it depends as much as anything on fiscal need. Nevertheless, as we shall see in Chapter 3, the present low level creates some intractable problems.

The simple model of a progressive income tax system which has been outlined can be modified to include more than one rate of tax. This can cause the rate of progression to steepen as the increasing marginal rate influences the average rate. If in the previous example (p. 22) income is charged to tax at 30% for the first £2,000 above the threshold and at 40% thereafter, the average rate of tax on an income of £4 000 would be 25% instead of 22½%, £100 being added to the tax bill. The UK system in 1986/87 provided a broad band at the basic rate of tax (29%) followed by a series of steps as the rate rose to 60% (see Example 2.3). Thus the average rate of tax on an income of £100 000 is seen to be 50.7%.

Like the threshold the tax rate bands may be eroded by rising prices. If prices rise by 10% and incomes rise similarly then the average rate of tax will rise unless the rate bands are widened by 10% as well. Note that it is the spread of the band, not the rate of tax, which is important. Again the UK legislation makes the necessary arrangements.[24]

For many decades until 1984 the UK system had a variant on the higher rates which is not found elsewhere. This was a special rate, or surcharge, on investment income. In later years this consisted of an addition of 15% to the rate of tax (i.e. 60% became 75%) on all investment above a separate annual threshold. The arguments for this surcharge go back to the early years of the century and are based on the idea that investment income is more secure and therefore capable of being taxed at a higher rate.

RELIEFS AGAINST PARTICULAR SOURCES OF INCOME

Under the rules found in the Schedules most kinds of income are calculated net of the outlays incurred in the process of earning or acquiring them. Thus we find deductions for the expenses incurred in the processes of property letting, trading and earning the emoluments of an employment. Certain other deductions are allowed by UK legislation, but they also relate to particular kinds of income. In this section we will deal with pension provision and with losses. Other more general deductions will be covered on pp. 26-8.

The first of the particular deductions, then, is that for pension contributions. The idea that people should be encouraged to provide funds for their retirement is one that has found favour with governments in the UK and elsewhere and it has led to some very favourable tax reliefs. These reliefs apply to pension arrangements over and above the state's own retirement pension scheme which is discussed on p. 29.

Pension schemes are a complex and specialized field of study but their broad outline is easily described. Most schemes are company-based and provide for regular contributions by the employer and the employee (occasionally by the employer alone). The funds subscribed are held by trustees who invest them directly or under the terms of an arrangement with an insurance company. In due course the individual employee retires and is entitled to a regular predetermined pension until he dies. The scheme will have rules covering entitlements on withdrawal from the scheme, on death before retirement and on support for a dependant after the death of a pensioner.

What then are the tax benefits? The first is that the contributions are deductible in arriving at the amount of the employee's taxable wage or salary and in arriving at the employer's taxable profit.[25] The second is that the income earned by the invested fund is completely free of tax.[26] The value of this exemption is substantial. If funds are invested for 20 years at an annual rate of return of 5% they will yield an overall gain of 165% if free of tax, but only 109% if liable to tax at, say, 25% (the annual rate of return being reduced to 3.75%).[27]

When the pension is paid the tax on it is payable normally, but often at a much lower rate (because of a lower income after retirement) than that which would bave been paid on the salary and profits out of which the contributions were made. Furthermore, it is also possible under the tax rules to receive one-quarter of the value of the pension rights in the form of a lump sum paid free of tax. If this lump sum is then used to purchase a life annuity from an insurance company the so-called 'capital element' in each annuity payment will continue to be tax exempt.[28]

These very favourable tax rules have resulted in some important economic and social consequences. There has been a steady expansion of the pension fund 'industry', enormous sums of money are invested each year and contributions account for the great bulk of personal savings in the UK economy.[29] No doubt there is a useful addition to social welfare when people feel a sense of security about their financial provision for old age and infirmity.

Nevertheless several objections have been made to the present state of affairs. The main ones are as follows.

1. It places a small number of large financial institutions in a dominant position in the financial markets with little outside control over their investment policies.
2. The small saver who would like to make his own arrangements is at a disadvantage both because of the absence of tax relief and because the investment markets are dominated by these large institutions.
3. In so far as the large institutions take the safe line (and the pension fund trust deeds may require them to do so) and invest only in other large organizations the flow of investment funds is being distorted to the possible disadvantage of the economy.
4. The employee who changes jobs frequently is disadvantaged because pensions are not generally 'portable' and this can lead to an undesirable degree of immobility in the labour market. It should be noted, however, that it is possible to earn a full pension in 20 years of service and stay within the rules governing tax relief.

It seems unlikely that significant changes will be made to the present arrangements, so all-pervading have they become. The tendency has been to extend them further. Thus it was argued successfully that people who owned their own businesses or were in non-pensionable jobs should be allowed to enter into formal pension schemes with similar benefits. Such schemes, which are offered by those insurance companies who do pension business, are now common. The legislation allows relief for an annual premium which may fluctuate as income varies provided only that it does not exceed 17½% of the 'net relevant earnings'.[30]

One of the general policy issues that arises from these reliefs is the development of portable pensions, namely the ability of employees to transfer their pension rights with them when they change jobs. At present such employees may be entitled only to a deferred pension payable at retirement age on the basis of their earnings while with the former employer. In some cases they may be able to claim a refund of their own contributions (less a tax charge of 10%), the employer's contributions remaining in the fund for the benefit of others. In effect the employee who leaves may be abandoning a potential future benefit to which the employer had already contributed. However, the problems lie more in the economics and technicalities of pension funds than in the relevant tax laws.

Turning now to the relief for losses, this is not applicable to income such as interest, wages and salaries. Either there is such income or there is not. On the other hand, property letting and trading may well produce a deficit when the income calculation has been completed. The question then is how should this deficit, or loss, be relieved, if at all? The reliefs are the subject of legislative rules and we illustrate them by looking at Schedule A and at Schedule D, Cases I and II.

The Schedule A rules appear quite complex but their underlying rationale is reasonably clear.[31] They aim to exclude all losses which arise because property is being let at an artificially low rent (e.g. to another member of the family.) These apart, relief can be claimed in two ways.

1. A loss on one property can be deducted from a profit on another in the same tax year (subject to a restriction where one of the properties is let to a tenant who is responsible for all repairs, the so-called 'full repairing lease').
2. A loss on a property can be carried forward and deducted from profits arising on the same property in a future tax year provided it is let at a full rent continuously or is unused between lettings.

Most people who own several properties will choose the first relief where possible because it takes effect earlier.

The reliefs under Schedule D follow a similar pattern.

1. There is an automatic right to carry forward losses of a trade against future profits of the same trade. The loss must be used as soon as possible and this means that it may reduce income which is already below the threshold, thereby wasting part of the relief. The relief is only available if the trade is the same one, so a change of activity designed to improve profitability may eliminate the right to relief. If I make losses while running a bookshop I will not be able to use them against my future profits when I turn my business into a newsagency.[32]
2. The other relief requires a specific claim but enables the trader to set off the loss against all other income of the same tax year.[33] This has the effect, rather oddly it may seem, that the loss may be used to reduce the trading profit of the previous year, but a simple example will show how this works. If a trader makes a profit of £10 000 in the calendar year 1985 this would be the income for tax purposes of 1986/87 on the preceding year basis. In the following year, 1986, there is a loss of £4 000. This loss means that there is no trading income for 1987/88, but the loss itself is treated as a loss suffered in 1986/87. Thus it can be set off against the profits assessed for that year or it can be carried forward to be used, if there are profits, in 1988/89. Example 2.4 illustrates some of the problems that may arise.

In addition to the reliefs described above there are additional loss reliefs for the trader and these reflect the special circumstances of the opening and closing years of a business when losses may be more likely.

GENERAL RELIEFS

The remaining reliefs are available to reduce total income and are not confined to particular kinds of income. They are called 'charges' and consist of payments made under a legal obligation. The idea that payments which become income of the recipient should be treated as a reduction in the income of the payer is one that goes far back into the nineteenth century. To qualify, the payment must be wholly income of the recipient (a payment to the greengrocer for cabbages does not qualify) and there must be a legal obligation to make it.[34] The relief is now much restricted because of the scope it gave for tax avoidance.

Another preliminary point to note is that in the normal case the payer is responsible for the tax due thereon at the basic rate. Thus with a basic rate of 29% the payer pays only 71% of the sum actually due and accounts for 29% to the tax collector. Thus there may be no visible reduction in the tax bill of the payer but he receives the relief in the form of the reduced payment.

This normal rule applies to payments such as annuities, royalties and maintenance payments. A common example is a payment made under a deed of covenant (a legal obligation entered into voluntarily) which qualifies if it is capable of lasting for more than 6 years in the case of an individual recipient, or for more than 3 years if the recipient is a charity. The deed must not be for the benefit of a minor child of the covenantor.

Example 2.5 shows how this works when a father signs a deed in favour of his daughter who is at university. The father is assumed to want to pay £1 000 per year for the period of study. This can be achieved by making the deed one for 7 years 'or for the period of full-time education if shorter'. Earlier death of either party will also cancel it. With a basic rate of tax of 29% he pays £710 each year and accounts for £290 to the tax collector, directly or indirectly. His daughter can claim a refund of £290 from the Inland Revenue as she is not liable to tax on the figures used in the example. The net result is that she benefits by £1 000 at a cost to her father of £710.

This system may well be thought to be unwieldy, and indeed it is. Because of this it has been modified for those cases where a court orders regular payments to be made for the support of a spouse, ex-spouse or children following the breakdown of a marriage. If the payments are 'small' (as defined) they can be made without deduction of basic rate tax and the tax bill of the payer is reduced accordingly. The chances are that the recipients will be below the tax threshold but if they are not any tax due is collected from them directly.

Payments of interest may also be treated as 'charges' but they raise some special problems, not least in defining what is 'interest'. For present purposes we will assume the normal meaning, a regular and agreed payment for the use of money. To qualify the interest must be annual, which excludes interest on short-term loans such as a bank overdraft. It may qualify simultaneously as an expense deductible in the calculation of profit as in the operation of any trading or professional activity which needs loan finance. Where there is a dual qualification only one form of relief is allowed.

Relief for interest as a 'charge' has been restricted quite severely. Interest paid on money borrowed to finance the purchase of a private car, for instance, no longer qualifies. Relief is restricted to a list of qualifying purposes, and this may result in people borrowing up to the hilt for a qualifying purpose and using their own money for the non-qualifying purposes! The qualifying purposes are, in outline, as follows.[35]

1. Acquisition of an interest in a closely controlled company (see Chapter 7), a partnership, a co-operative or an employee-controlled company.
2. Purchase of plant and machinery.
3. Payment of inheritance tax (see Chapter 6).
4. Purchase of a life annuity – but with limiting conditions.
5. Purchase of or improvement to land or buildings occupied as only or main residence of self, former spouse or dependant relative, relief being limited to interest paid on loans of £30 000 maximum.

Interest is different from other charges in the way the relief is given. Deduction at source does not apply unless the payment is made by a company or to a person not resident in the UK. In other cases the payer gets direct relief for the payment in his tax calculation and the recipient is accountable for the tax due under Schedule D, Case III.

However, in order to simplify administration the interest paid on loans acquired to buy a house is dealt with quite differently again. Most such borrowing is from large institutions such as building societies. It has therefore been arranged that when the monthly payments are made by borrowers the society will calculate the interest element so that it is a net amount which takes into account the tax relief due at the basic rate. The society in turn will then be able to claim from the Inland Revenue a sum equal to the tax relief it has, in effect, given to the borrowers. The system is known as MIRAS (Mortgage Interest Relief At Source).[36]

Nevertheless, the scheme is not perfect. Many mortgages are taken out on a gradual repayment basis whereby, if interest rates are unchanged, a fixed sum is paid each month and is calculated to pay off over the agreed period the capital plus the interest due on the outstanding balances (i.e. the annuity formula). The practical problem is that the interest component of the payment varies, and matters are made even more difficult when interest rates change in mid-year. Under MIRAS there is a small imbalance between borrower and lender in so far as the former pays, in effect, a lower interest rate spread over the entire period of the loan, whereas the latter receives the tax relief on the basis of a yearly calculation.

MIRAS cannot deal with the relief that is due on IT rates above the basic rate. In those cases a separate refund of tax has to be calculated for the borrower, this refund being based on the difference between the higher and basic rate on that top slice of income which is covered by the gross equivalent of the interest paid. The point is illustrated in Example 2.6.

Although not a 'charge' one other relief deserves passing mention. For many years the UK legislation gave tax relief for premiums on life assurance policies provided they were secured on the life of the payer or of the payer's spouse. This encouraged provision for the dependant family in case of unexpectedly early death. It also applied to endowment policies which provide a lump sum at the end of a stated period or death if earlier. These policies are a form of regular saving and can be used as a tax shelter for those who pay high rates of IT as tax is charged on the sums invested to cover the policy at a modest rate. Policies could be used in more sophisticated ways to reduce tax liability.

In the circumstances the relief was withdrawn from new policies as from March 1984.[37] Old policies continue to get the relief until they mature but this has no effect on the calculation of the policyholder's tax liability as a system like MIRAS operates. The relief is 15% of the premium and is given by a reduction in the premium actually payable, the insurance company being reimbursed directly by the Inland Revenue.

NATIONAL INSURANCE

We have seen already in Chapter 1 that a high proportion of the UK government's budget (and indeed those of other European countries) is accounted for by the social security system. This system can also have important effects on the IT system, as we shall see in Chapter 3. For present purposes we shall confine discussion to the main features of the contributions and benefits. This broad outline will be sufficient for our purposes but there exists a mass of detail most of which is of interest only to those individuals who are directly affected by it.

The rates of contribution vary with personal circumstances. In the case of employees both they and their employer contribute if weekly earnings exceed a lower threshold (which stands at a level only found in part-time work). Above the threshold contributions are paid at various rising percentages of earnings by both employer and employee, but for the latter further contributions cease above an upper limit. (See Examples 2.7(a) and (b) and the Appendix.)

Two features of this scheme may now be apparent.

1. The contributions, if borne as intended, represent a tax on employment so far as the employer is concerned and an additional tax on earnings for the employees.
2. The upper limit falls short of the point at which higher rates of IT become payable and this gives the odd result that the combined marginal rate of tax for employees (IT plus NICS) actually falls at this upper limit. This effect may be obscured for many people by the fact that IT is calculated on an annual basis whereas NICS are based on monthly or weekly pay.

We saw on p. 24 that tax benefits accrue to a company pension scheme. Such schemes can also be approved so as to be 'contracted out' of part of the state pension. In these cases both employer and employee pay a lower rate of NICS. Of course they will be subscribing to the company scheme as well so that the total cost, despite the tax relief, may be greater (see Example 2.7(c)).

This raises an interesting semantic point in passing. If NICS are a tax how do we define the (compulsory) payment to a private funded scheme which replaces part of the NICS? The point is that some of the things that are financed by taxation in one context may have to be met by payments in the private sector in another. The same sort of issue can arise in the payment for medical treatment in different countries, a state scheme versus virtually unavoidable private medical insurance. It all makes international tax comparisons difficult to achieve.

NICS are not confined to employees. People who are, in the jargon, self-employed are entitled to some of the benefits and in return make weekly flat rate payments under Class 2, unless their earnings are very small, plus a percentage of profits between lower and upper thresholds under Class 4, the upper limit being equal to the upper earnings limit for employees (see Example 2.7 (d)). As with employees, contributions are not due from those who are above pensionable age, 65 for men and 60 for women.

On the other side of the picture there are many kinds of social security benefit, some paid in cash, others taking the form of a reduction in outgoings. The main division for present purposes is between the taxable and non-taxable benefits. Four of them have been chosen for discussion.

The retirement pension is taxable and its amount will vary with marital status and with the earnings and contribution record. It is often argued that it should not be taxed at all. As we have seen a normal pension by itself falls below the IT threshold as enhanced for those of pensionable age. Nevertheless, there is a feeling that it is a reward for long years at work and that it is unfair to consider taxing such a reward.

The counter argument is that not all retired people are poor and that the pension is undoubtedly income under any general definition. If IT is to be collected equitably, with the well-to-do paying at progressively higher rates, there seems to be no strong reason why their state pension should be omitted.

Unemployment benefit is taxable as well. This may seem odd at first sight as it is a benefit which, with supplementary benefit, is intended to provide a bare living for those who are out of work. However, there is a counter argument. IT is collected on an annual basis and there seems to be no reason to exempt money received during a short period of unemployment in what is otherwise a prosperous and well-paid year. More technically the effect of exempting it from tax can be very haphazard. A period of unemployment spanning two tax years can have a quite different effect from one which falls wholly within one tax year. Example 2.9 should make this point quite clear.

Child benefit is not taxable. We have noted already the argument which leads to a cash payment rather than tax relief. It has been argued too that there is a social reason for paying cash to the mother rather than paying cash or giving tax relief to the father in so far as the mother may be more likely to use the cash for the child's benefit directly.

Whether or not this is true, the question of who should benefit and to what extent remains an open one. The arguments may be summarized as follows.

1. Tax relief for children by increasing the IT threshold:
   — does not help the very poor at all;
   — maximizes the benefit for the rich (because the relief is effective at their higher rates of tax).
2. Tax relief as a lump sum reduction of the tax bill:
   — is still of no benefit to the poor;
   — but removes the relative advantage to the rich.
3. Cash payment (untaxed):
   — benefits the poor;
   — compared with (1) leaves the rich at a relative disadvantage.

If, then, it is accepted that a cash payment is the better solution and that the cost of paying it out for every child is not prohibitive there remains the question whether it should be taxed. The argument for doing so is that this would reduce the benefit to the rich, who it may be argued do not need it anyway. On the other hand it would complicate the IT system so far as it applied to the overwhelming majority of the population who fall into the basic rate band. The amounts involved for individuals may be thought not to justify such increased complication.

Supplementary benefits are not taxable unless they are related to unemployment. They are the ultimate safety net of the social security system. They seem to exist mainly for those who are in a state of more or less permanent poverty, unlike the unemployed whose poverty may be temporary. They are paid out only after an investigation of personal circumstances. The argument for not taxing them is that these are not the sort of cases where the annual income, including the benefit, is likely to rise above the tax threshold. Making them taxable, except where they are linked to unemployment, would increase the cost of administration, make unreasonable demands on the very poor and yield little or no additional tax revenue.

EXAMPLES

In these examples actual rates of tax for 1985/86 and 1986/87 have been used. Later rates of tax are shown in the Appendix as are any subsequent changes which may affect the validity of the point being demonstrated.

Example 2.1   Income for the tax year

N. Traill has traded as a butcher since 1978 and draws up his accounts for the calendar year. Recent profits have been as follows:

1985	£10 400
1986	£11 200

Other income has been received as well:

Tax year	1985/6	1986/7
	£	£
Property letting	2 000	2 300
Interest on £4 000 nominal of		
5% Treasury stock	140	142
Premium bond prize	—	250
Dividends from UK company	70	105

The income for the tax year 1986/87 is calculated as follows:

	£	
Schedule D, Case I (trade)	10 400	(preceding year)
Schedule A (property letting)	2 300	(actual)
Interest on Treasury stock	200	(tax at 29% added back)
Schedule F (dividend)	148	(do.)
Total	£13 050	

Notes:

1. The premium bond winnings are not income for tax purposes.
2. If the business had ceased on 31 December 1986 the trading income for 1986/87 would have

been £11 200 × 9/12 = £8 400 and the figures for 1985/86 and 1984/85 would have been open to adjustment at the Inland Revenue's option.

3. The basic rate of IT for 1986/87 was 29%. Thus gross interest of £200 is reduced to £142 by deduction of tax under Schedule C. The net company dividend is deemed to have been taxed similarly. Tax deducted at source will be taken into account in calculating the tax actually payable by Traill. The preceding year basis under Schedule D, Case III, is not applicable as tax has been deducted at source.

Example 2.2 Tax calculation with age relief

The extra relief only applies in full if the income is below £9 400. Above that figure the relief is reduced by two-thirds of the excess. Thus:

	£	£
Income		9 700
Age relief (single person *less* ⅔ of	2850	
9 700–9 400)	200	2 650
Taxable income		£7 050
Tax thereon at 29%		£2 044.50

Notes:

1. The abatement must not be used to reduce the relief below £2 335 (which is the relief for everyone else).
2. In this example the normal figure of £2 335 applies when the income reaches £10 173. Because of the abatement formula the marginal rate of tax between £9 400 and £10 173 is 48.3% instead of 29%.

Example 2.3 Calculation of IT at higher rates

		£
Income		100 000
Personal relief (threshold)		2 335
Taxable income		£97 665
Tax at 29% on	£17 200	4 988
40% on	£3 000	1 200
45% on	£5 200	2 340
50% on	£7 900	3 950
55% on	£7,900	4 345
60% on	£56 465	33 879
Total tax due		£50 702
Average rate of tax		50.7%

Example 2.4 Trading losses

Use the same facts given in Example 2.1 (N. Traill) but add a profit for 1984 of £7 400 and assume a loss of £9 000 for 1985 instead of the profit shown. This loss is deemed to be a loss of the tax year 1985/86.

(a) *Loss carry-forward*. The loss could be used to reduce the income assessable for 1987/88 as follows:

	£
Trading profit	11 200(the 1986 profit)
less Loss	(9 000)
	2 200
Other income (assumed)	2 500
Total income	4 700
Personal relief	2 335
Taxable at 29%	£2 365
Tax due	£685.85*

*It has been assumed that rates of tax and relief are the same as for 1986/87, but see Appendix for the correct rates.

The income for 1986/87 will consist of the other income of £2 650 as shown in Example 2.1 and the tax liability will be:

$$(£2 650 - £2 335) \text{ at } 29\% = £91.35$$

(b) *Loss set-off*. The loss of £9 000 could be used to reduce all other income assessed for 1985/86, viz.

	£
Trading income (the 1984 profit)	7 400
Property letting	2 000
Treasury stock interest (tax added back)*	200
UK dividends (gross amount)*	100
Total income	9 700
less Loss as above	9 000
	700
less Personal relief (threshold)	2 205

*Tax rates etc. for 1985/86 – see Appendix.

No tax is due and that suffered on the dividends and interest will be refunded.

1986/87	£
Trading profit (1983 loss)	Nil
Other income	2 650
Tax as in (a) above	£91.35

1987/88

Trading profit	11 200
Other income (as in (a))	2 500
Total income	13 700
Personal relief	2 335
Taxable at 29%	11 365*
Tax thereon	£3 295.85.

*Rates of tax etc. as for 1986/87 – but
see Appendix for correct rates.

Thus in 1985/86 some of the loss is wasted as it eliminates income which is already covered by the personal relief, but on the other hand keeping the loss relief to use in 1987/88 means a long wait.

Example 2.5 Deeds of covenant

Assume that a father's income is £18 000 for 1986/87, that his personal relief is for a single person (he is divorced or a widower), that the child is over 18 and that the covenant is for £1 000 per annum gross.

	With covenant	Without covenant
	£	£
Father's income	18 000	18 000
Personal relief	2 335	2 335
Taxable income	£15 665	£15 665
Tax at 29%	4 542.85	4 542.85
Student's income:		
Grant	Exempt	Exempt
Covenanted payment	£0	710
Tax refund	0	290
	£0	£1 000

Thus the father pays the same tax bill but if we assume that the daughter would need support of £1 000 anyway we get:

	£	£	£	£
Father's gross income		18 000		18 000
less: Payment made	1 000		710	
Tax paid	4 543	5 543	4 543	5 253
Income after tax		£12 457		£12 747
Net benefit				£290

Example 2.6 Mortgage interest relief

Assume that a taxpayer has borrowed £25 000 at 12% from a building society on mortgage and that interest relief is due for 1986/87.

	£
Interest payable	3 000
less Tax relief at 29%	870
Interest actually paid	£2 130

The tax relief is refunded directly to the building society which therefore receives £3 000. Turning now to the taxpayer we get:

	£
Taxpayer's income, say	25 000
Personal relief	2 335
Taxable	£22 665
Tax at 29% (on £17 200)	4 988
Tax at 40% (on £3 000)	1 200
Tax at 45% (on £2 465)	1 109.25
	7 297.25

less: Higher rate relief on interest paid under MIRAS		
	£	
£2 465 at (45% – 29%)	394.40	
£535 at (40% – 29%)	58.85	453.25
Tax due		£6 844.00

Example 2.7 National Insurance Contributions (NICS)

(a) Cain, a single man, receives a wage of £90 per week. His company has no pension scheme and he relies on the state pension alone.

	£
NICS per week at 7%	6.30
(7% applies to the whole wage if it lies between £60 and £94.99.)	
NICS per year (52 weeks)	327.60
(The employer's contribution would be the same.)	
Income tax:	
Income (annual)	4 680
Personal relief	2 335

Taxable	£2345
Tax at 29%	680.05
Total deductions (21.53% of income)	£1007.65

(b) Charles, also a single man, receives a wage of £300 per week, and again there is no company pension scheme.

	£
NICS per week	
(Maximum as wage exceeds £284.99.)	25.65
NICS per year (52 weeks)	1333.80
(The employer's contribution would be 10.45% of the wage.)	

Income tax:	
Income	15600
Personal relief	2335
Taxable	£13265
Tax at 29%	3846.85
Total deductions (33.85% of income)	£5280.65

(c) Colin differs from Charles only in working for a company which has a pension scheme into which he pays 5% of his gross wage.

	£
NICS per week (maximum)	20.34
NICS per year (52 weeks)	1057.68
(The employer would pay £19.65 per week plus 10.45% of the excess of the weekly wage over £285.)	

Income tax:	£	
Income	15600	
less Pension contributions	780	14820
Personal relief		2335
Taxable		£12485
Tax at 29%		3620.65
Total deductions (34.99% of income)		£5458.33

Colin appears to be worse off than Charles but his eventual pension is likely to be higher.

(d) Christopher is also a single man, self-employed and pays NICS under Classes 2 and 4. His trading profit for 1986/87 is £15600 (i.e. the same income as Charles and Colin).

	£
NICS – Class 2 (52 × £3.75)	195.00
– Class 4 (maximum)	653.31

Income tax:		15 600
Income	£	
less 50% of Class 4	327	
Personal relief	2 335	2 662
		£12 938
Tax at 29%		3 752.02
Total deductions (29.49% of income)		£4 600.33

Christopher appears to be better off than Charles but he is entitled to fewer benefits under National Insurance. He could make tax deductible contributions to a retirement annuity scheme in order to produce a better retirement pension and this would make him more comparable with Colin.

Example 2.8 The effects of unemployment

This example ignores NICS as they have no effect on the point that is being made.

(a) Tom does unskilled work at a wage of £80 per week. He is employed for the whole year.

	£
Total income	4 160
Personal relief	2 335
	1 825
Tax at 29%	529.25

(b) Dick has a better job, his wage being £100 per week, but he is unemployed for 12 weeks of the year.

Total income:	
Wage	4 000
Social security (say)	400
	4 400

If the social security benefit *is* taxable, tax due is:

£2 065 at 29%	£598.85

If the social security benefit *is not* taxable, tax due is:

£1 665 at 29%	£482.85

Thus if the benefit is not taxable Dick pays less tax than Tom who has a lower income.

(c)   Harry also earns £100 per week but is unemployed for 40 weeks.

Case 1. If the period of unemployment is divided between 2 tax years (and assuming both have the tax rates of 1986/87) the tax due is as follows according to whether the benefit is taxable or not.

		£
Benefit taxable:		
Income each year: 32 × 100		3 200
20 × 35 (say)		700
		£3 900
Tax for 2 years (£1 565 at 29% × 2)		£907.70
Benefit not taxable (£3 200 taxable each year):		
Tax for 2 years (£865 at 29% × 2)		£501.70

Case 2. If the period of unemployment falls wholly into one year we get:

		£
Benefit taxable:		
Taxable income, year fully employed		5 200
Tax (2 865 at 29%)		830.85

Taxable income, 40 weeks unemployed:		£
40 × £35	1 400	
12 × £100	1 200	2 600
Tax (265 at 29%)		76 .85

NOTES AND REFERENCES

1. The legislation is ss. 49–51, Taxes Act 1970. See also the Inland Revenue booklet *IR 20* and *Tax Digest No. 11*, ICAEW, London (1982).
2. Goude, R., 'The Economic Definition of Income', in Pechman J. A. (ed.), *Comprehensive Income Taxation*, Brookings, Washington DC (1977).
3. Ss. 67–79, Taxes Act 1970.
4. Ss. 91–92, Taxes Act 1970.
5. Ss. 93–107, Taxes Act 1970.
6. Ss. 108–109, Taxes Act 1970.
7. But the legislation can be found in s. 109 and ss. 122–124, Taxes Act 1970.
8. Ss. 109 and 125, Taxes Act 1970.
9. Ss. 181–184, Taxes Act 1970.
10. S. 189, Taxes Act 1970.
11. *Hochstrasser v. Mayes* (1959) 38 TC 673.
12. *Walker* v. *Carnaby, Harrower, Barham and Pykett* (1969) 46 TC 561; and *Simpson* v. *John Reynolds Co. (Insurances) Ltd.* (1975) 49 TC 693.
13. *Graham* v. *Green* (1925) 9 TC 309; and *Southern* v. *AB* (1933) 18 TC 59.
14. Jeffrey-Cook, J., 'A Year Beginning on April 6', at pages 68–69 of *The British Tax Review*, Sweet & Maxwell, London (1977).

15. Ss. 115–124 and s. 4, Taxes Act 1970.
16. S. 52 (1) (d), Taxes Act 1970.
17. S. 4, Taxes Act 1970.
18. S. 69, Taxes Act 1970.
19. S. 4, Taxes Act 1970.
20. Nigeria (4 children), Singapore (3 children).
21. S. 24 (5), Finance Act 1980.
22. At the time of writing it represents about £1.25 per hour for a full-time worker.
23. See the discussion in Chapter 2 of Kay J. A. and King M. A., *The British Tax System*, Oxford University Press, Oxford (1983).
24. S. 24 (1)–(4), Finance Act 1980.
25. S. 21, Finance Act 1970.
26. *Ibid.*
27. £1 invested at 5% compound for 20 years produces $(1.05)^{20}$ = £2.65.
    £1 invested at 5 $(1 - 0.25)$% compound for 20 years produces $(1.0375)^{20}$ = £2.09. Because of compounding a tax rate of 25% reduces the increase in the fund by 34%, viz. 1.09/1.65 = 0.66.
28. S. 230, Taxes Act 1970.
29. See Chapter 3 of Hills, John, 'Savings and Fiscal Privilege', *IFS Report Series No. 9*, IFS, London (1984).
30. Ss. 226–229, Taxes Act 1970.
31. Ss. 71–73 and 2nd Schedule, Taxes Act 1970.
32. S. 171, Taxes Act 1970.
33. Ss. 168–170, Taxes Act 1970.
34. Ss. 52–56, Taxes Act 1970.
35. S. 19 and 1st Schedule, Finance Act 1974 (as amended).
36. S. 26 and 7th Schedule, Finance Act 1982.
37. Ss. 19–21, Taxes Act 1970, and Ss. 72–76, Finance Act 1984.

EXERCISES AND DISCUSSION TOPICS

1. (a) From the following details calculate the total income of Mary Evans, a single woman, for the tax year 1986/87. Show for each item the Schedule (and Case) under which it is taxable.

   (i) Income as author and critic:

Year ended	31.12.84	£10 500
do.	31.12.85	£11 750
do.	31.12.86	£9 420

   (She has been an author etc. since 1972.

   (ii) Rent (less expenses) from letting Red Deeps House:

1984/85	£2 000
1985/86	£2 100
1986/87	£1 900

   (She makes a provisional tax payment in respect of this source on 1 January each year, calculated as basic rate tax on the previous year's net income.)

(iii) Prize in The Times Portfolio competition received on 20 November 1986: £4 000.

(iv) Dividends (cash amounts) received from British Telecom:

1985 September	£19.50
1986 February	£15.00
September	£22.50
1987 February	£15.00

(v)   Interest on £5 000 of 9% Treasury stock 1994.

(vi) Gain on 400 TSB Group shares (partly paid), cost £200, sold for 81p per share free of commission on 1 October 1986.

(vii) Mary took out a retirement annuity policy in 1980 and she pays a premium of £1 200 each year. (The statutory limit for relief is 17½% of net relevant earnings.)

(b) Using the tax rates given in the Appendix calculate how much income tax is due on Mary's total income and how much has still to be paid as at the end of the tax year.

(c) When you show Mary the calculation you have made under (b) above she suddenly remembers that she made a payment on 1 December 1986 under a deed of covenant in favour of Oxfam. The deed provided for 4 annual payments of £100 less tax and this was the first payment.

(i)   How much did she pay to Oxfam?

(ii) What difference does the payment make to the income tax calculated under (b)?

(iii) What is the total benefit to Oxfam and what form does it take?

2. Tom Trollope commenced in business as a toy retailer on 1 July 1979. His accountant suggested that he draw up his accounts to 30 June each year although Tom would have preferred 31 December as this was his slack period and he could take stock on New Year's day. The business continued until 31 December 1987 when Tom had to give up because of ill health.

Now suppose that the taxable profits would have been as follows depending on which accounting date had been chosen. (The total profits are, of course, the same in both cases, viz. £65 600.)

	£		£
Year to 30.6.80	10 000	Period to 31.12.79	7 000
do. 30.6.81	6 000	Year to 31.12.80	7 000
do. 30.6.82	7 200	do. 31.12.81	6 200
do. 30.6.83	8 000	do. 31.12.82	8 000
do. 30.6.84	12 800	do. 31.12.83	10 500
do. 30.6.85	6 600	do. 31.12.84	8 300
do. 30.6.86	10 500	do. 31.12.85	7 700
Period to 31.12.86	4 500	do. 31.12.86	10 900

Required:

(a) Calculate separately the profits assessable for the years from 1979/80 to 1986/87 inclusive on the two sets of accounts.

(b) Examine and comment upon the effect of the choice of accounting date.
3. Bill Thackeray, a single man, has been in business for many years and his recent results, as adjusted for income tax purposes, have been as follows:

Year ended 30 June 1984	Profit £10 000
do. 30 June 1985	Loss £12 000

He is also a company director (part-time) and receives a fee of £1 500 per year and his dividend income has been as follows (including the tax credits):

1985/86	£800
1986/87	£860

The loss is expected to be only temporary and Thackeray thinks he has made a profit of at least £10 000 in the year to 30 June 1986. No substantial change is expected in his other income for 1987/88.

Required:
(a) Show how effect can be given to relief for the loss of £12 000.
(b) Should he decide not to claim relief for the loss against the income of 1985/86? If not, why not?

4. Charlie Dickens works for the Pickwick Paper Co. Ltd. where his gross salary for 1986/87 amounted to £9 650. In addition he received a Christmas bonus of £750. He is a member of the company pension scheme to which he pays 2½% of his salary and bonus. The company scheme is *not* contracted out of the state graduated scheme. Dickens travels daily to his office in London by train and the fares for the year amounted to £540. He would prefer to live near the office but no suitable housing could be found nearby when he was transferred to his present post. Previously he worked for the same company in Lancaster where his travelling expenses were trivial. When he had completed the move to London in April 1986 the company paid him £1 250 reimbursement of removal costs (including estate agents' and legal fees) and made a grant of £2 600 to cover part of the loss suffered on the sale of his house in Lancaster.

Required:
(a) What is the amount of his income taxable under Schedule E?
(b) What is the amount of National Insurance Contributions payable by Pickwick Paper and by Dickens for the year?

5. Describe three ways in which a government may decide to give financial support to parents and guardians of young dependant children and discuss the merits and demerits of each.

(*Note*: Some of the questions at the end of Chapter 4 cover points dealt with in this chapter in addition to the issues arising out of the taxation of families.)

3   Some effects of income taxes

THE ARGUMENTS ABOUT VERTICAL EQUITY

When governments impose a tax they realize that they are doing something which is unlikely to be popular. In such a climate they need to bear in mind the psychology of taxation.[1] It appears that taxation is more acceptable to people if it is seen to be 'fair'. Indeed the government of a western democracy which imposes taxes that are perceived to be unfair is very likely to lose votes at the next election.

This question of fairness, or equity, contains two elements, usually described as vertical and horizontal. The latter concerns the equal treatment of equals and will be discussed in Chapter 5. Vertical equity is about the unequal treatment of those who are, in the economic sense, unequal.

The reason why issues of vertical equity are so important in the context of an income tax is that it is a tax which, above all others, lends itself to making distinctions between different people. It is imposed directly on an identifiable individual. While it is true that indirect taxes are borne by people eventually their precise impact will differ because of differences in personal consumption patterns which may be unrelated to income. The tobacco tax illustrates the point very well. Fewer than half the population of the UK smoke and those who do so come from all walks of life.

While there is wide acceptance of the view that the tax bill should increase as incomes rise it does not follow that value judgements about the rate of increase are unaltering or unalterable. However, it does seem that values change slowly in these matters and there is some evidence that people are inclined to accept the existing pattern as fair perhaps because they are used to it. Let us therefore examine the basis of present policies.

We will start with the proposition that people should be taxed in proportion to their incomes and will assume that income is a satisfactory basis for differentiating between people. The idea of proportionality was found acceptable by Adam Smith[2] but there is one obvious reservation about the very poor. If their income is insufficient or barely sufficient to maintain them at a basic standard of food and shelter then the tax would bite into the lowest levels in the hierarchy of human need.[3] There is strong case for excluding these people from the tax net.

There is one possible doubt about this assertion. People may be poor for a variety of reasons, low intelligence, low levels of skill, ill health, age and infirmity and so on. They may also be poor by choice, which implies that they prefer leisure in poverty to making the effort to earn income. Should this last group be relieved of their tax burden when the imposition of a tax which ignored their poverty might provoke them into using their skills and ability? At first sight this argument may have some appeal, although it reduces the social welfare of the group affected in so far as it distorts their preferred way of life. One problem is that the same argument can be employed at other levels. The factory accountant who has both the skill and opportunity to become finance director, but not the desire, is in a comparable position. Should he be taxed as if he were the finance director? It is apparent that even if the theoretical argument has merit it is not one that can be operationalized.

Thus we reach a point where a proportional tax on income appears to be the fairest provided the very poor are excluded. However, the argument cannot be left at that point. We must consider now whether the tax on incomes should rise at a more than proportional rate. This would imply that rates of tax will rise in one or more steps as incomes rise, as indeed they do in the UK and elsewhere.

The first argument which favours this approach is that those with higher incomes can afford to pay proportionately more tax without suffering extra hardship. A tax which deprives the poorer man of adequate warmth and sufficient calories for good health is seen to be in a different category from one which causes a wealthier man to holiday in Benidorm rather than the Bahamas. This argument can be expressed in terms of a diminishing marginal utility of income. The loss of £1 to a poor man is a greater burden than the loss of £1 to a richer man.[4]

The second argument which favours the levying of taxes more than proportionately is that this contributes to a reduction in inequalities of income. The support given to this argument depends on what kind of inequality people have in mind. Where poverty is due to age, sickness or unemployment there may be a much greater acceptance of the idea of income redistribution than there is when inequality results from other economic forces such as the values placed on different skills. Nevertheless some people take the view that the inequalities resulting from uncontrolled economic forces are too great for social harmony to be maintained and on those grounds (as well as on grounds of general morality) they should be mitigated by taxation.[5]

The final argument about vertical equity is that those with more wealth (and higher incomes?) receive greater benefits from public services such as defence and law and order than do those who are not so well off. They have more to lose and may take more advantage of the legal system and of other publicly financed facilities. But how can the value of such benefits be determined?

This problem of valuation leads us to another fundamental issue in vertical equity. How progressive should the system be? As we shall see in Chapter 5, income may not be a sufficient measure by itself but even if it is there seems to be no way of converting these general arguments of principle into monetary amounts. Should the tax structure be mildly progressive, with a maximum marginal rate of, say, 50%, or should it be confiscatory above a certain level, or somewhere between the two? If there are to be higher rate bands how wide should they be? At what point should taxation start?

All of these questions have been answered differently in the UK over recent decades. The top marginal rate has fallen from 98% in 1978 (virtual confiscation) to 60% today. At the other end of the scale the tax threshold for a single man has fallen from about 80% of the average industrial wage in 1938 to about 25% today.[6]

When progressivity in other countries is compared even wider differences appear. Some of them occur because of the impracticality of operating a wide ranging effective income tax in many underdeveloped countries, but they exist too in the developed western economies. Thus in France in 1981 the yield of income tax at 7.9% of GNP was little more than half that in the UK at 14.4%.[7]

Thus we cannot lay down any clear guidelines to reflect the arguments that we have discussed in this section. Furthermore, there are other arguments which conflict with the ones we have considered so far. They relate primarily to economic efficiency.

ECONOMIC EFFICIENCY ARGUMENTS AFFECTING LABOUR SUPPLY AND SAVINGS

We saw in Chapter 1 that the need for taxation arises out of market imperfections. That discussion carried the implication that in major areas of economic activity the market was the best instrument for allocating economic resources. If this is so it follows that any external influences which distort the existing market equilibrium are likely to result in a loss of economic welfare.

Seen from this viewpoint it is unfortunate that taxation can itself act as an agent of distortion. This disadvantage is characteristic of all types of tax but its impact depends on their design and on their relationship with each other. In this section we shall be looking at the effects on labour supply and on personal savings.

It seems reasonable to assume that people will offer their services in order to secure an income which is adequate for their needs and that, at the margin, they will cease to offer them when the additional reward is insufficient to compensate for the loss of leisure. The words 'loss of leisure' do not imply any moral opprobrium, people may just feel weary as a result of extra work.

A common argument about income taxes is that they reduce the monetary reward for extra work while having no effect on the value of leisure. Thus the amount of work offered (labour supplied) is reduced compared with what would have happened without an income tax. This is known as the 'substitution effect' as it causes leisure to be substituted for work. Clearly this, if correct, is a distortion imposed on the normal market for labour by an external influence.

This result is not clear cut, however. There is another possibility which sees the imposition of a tax on income causing people to try to increase their pre-tax incomes in order to maintain their previous spending power. This is known as the 'income effect' and acts in the opposite direction. This conflict is set out diagrammatically in Technical Note 3.1 at the end of the chapter.

The net effect of these two effects has been the subject of lengthy and wide-ranging discussion and investigation.[8] It has been pointed out that the substitution effect depends on the marginal rate of tax and the income effect on the average rate. Thus the balance between the two effects is likely to depend on the particular rate structure of the tax. It also seems likely that the substitution effect will dominate in the case of higher incomes at high and increasing marginal rates. As we shall see later in this chapter this effect may be quite pronounced for the very poor.

The fact that firm conclusions to the many investigations have proved to be elusive is attributable in part to the variations in circumstances encompassed by the phrase 'distortions in the supply of labour'. We can list a few of these circumstances by way of illustration of the point (it will be convenient to phrase all of them initially in terms which imply that the substitution effect dominates):

1. Unwillingness to work longer hours – which may be reflected day by day under a flexible hours arrangement or may be very long term as normal hours of work change over decades.
2. Unwillingness to take on more responsibility or more difficult work.
3. Unwillingness to take on unpleasant, dangerous or otherwise undesirable jobs.
4. Unwillingness to move house in order to take a better job elsewhere. This affects labour mobility as well.
5. Willingness to move to a job in another country where tax rates are lower.
6. Temptation to do a second, undisclosed job (moonlighting) or to spend time on home maintenance (DIY) instead of working taxed overtime.
7. Deciding to retire early because tax reduces the relative loss of income.
8. Married women unwilling to cross the 'going to work' threshold (discussed in Chapter 4).
9. A preference for those jobs which can offer non-cash rewards provided their value is not fully taxable.

It is clear that in many of these examples the income effect could operate as well. Apart from (1) it could apply to (2), (3), (4), (6) and (7). Furthermore choices are influenced by non-financial factors. Senior executives may relish the power and status that goes with their responsibilities, feeling that they are guiding the fortunes of a large organization. People who might work at a lower level may be bored by a job which is below their capacity. Married women may enjoy social contacts at work which are not easily available at home. The decision to retire may depend only partly, if at all, on the financial consequences.

The conclusion must be that income taxes have ample scope to distort the supply of labour but whether they do, and to what extent, are questions to which the answers will continue to be elusive.

Turning now to the possible effects of income taxes on personal savings, these fall under two headings. The first is whether the total supply of personal savings is affected. The formal analysis again produces the two contrasting effects, income and substitution. The latter depends on the belief that the supply of savings will be reduced if the reward for savings is reduced by the marginal tax rate. Tax reduces the opportunity cost of the alternative of immediate consumption.

The income effect depends on a belief that people save for a purpose so that taxing the income from savings will lead them to try to save more so as to achieve the same net of tax target. Again the arguments cannot be resolved on any general basis especially as the incentive to save is not confined to the expected reward. There is evidence that the level of personal savings rises when people expect a rise in the rate of inflation. They perceive a need for increased precautionary (rainy day) savings and for increased working balances in which the tax system is irrelevant.[9]

The second heading concerns the distortion that may occur in the actual investment of the savings. Not all savings result in rewards that are taxable as income. Investment in ordinary shares may produce both regular dividends (taxable income) and gains in the value of the shares. Investment in antiques will produce no cash income but will give aesthetic pleasure (presumably) and result in a financial gain if the antiques are sold. If only some of these rewards are taxed as income then it is clear that the relative attractions are distorted by the tax on it.

One possibility for changing the tax system to overcome this kind of distortion will be considered in Chapter 5. Meanwhile we will consider a consequential effect which is called 'tax capitalization'.

TAX CAPITALIZATION

We have now seen how the imposton of income taxes can distort the equilibrium which market forces would have imposed without them. In this section we shall look at the ways in which market forces may react to the interference of the tax system. Let us look first at a simple example.

Suppose that in the absence of taxation an investment choice consists of only two possibilities:

1. Investment in loan stock redeemable in two years at £100 and paying interest annually at 10%.
2. Investment in ordinary shares whose price is expected to rise 12% in the next two years and whose expected annual dividend yield is 5% of the price being paid today.

In each case we assume a buying price of £100 (in other words the market has decided they are equal opportunities), the greater financial return on (2) being accounted for by the difference in timing of the cash flows and by the risk factor.

If we now assume an income tax imposed at 50% the effect on the rewards is as follows.

		(1) £	(2) £	Ratio (1)/(2)
No tax:	Interest/dividends	20	10	
	Gain	—	12	
	Total	£20	£22	0.91
With tax:	Interest/dividends	10	5	
	Gains	—	12	
	Total	£10	£17	0.59

It should be clear from the marked change in the ratio that once tax is imposed the buying prices can no longer be equal and that the price of (2) must rise relative to (1). In other words the tax effect will be capitalized in the new market prices.

Tax capitalization has an important effect on existing investors. If we had invested in (2) just before the tax was (unexpectedly) imposed we shall be better off as a result of a windfall gain. If we had invested in (1) the opposite would be true.

The effect of tax capitalization can be seen in the daily quotation of prices for British government (gilt edged) securities in *The Financial Times*. The pre-tax yields to maturity of securities with similar lives vary significantly, and this variation can be seen to relate to the split between the income flows and the (untaxed) capital gain that would be enjoyed by investors. The timing differences in the cash flows are reflected already in the yield calculations and the risk factor will be the same.

The effect of tax capitalization can be seen as well in reactions to the distortions imposed on the labour market. If we assume that people are aware of their personal tax burdens (an assumption which is not always justified) it follows that they will be motivated by their earnings net of tax. If they have been deterred by the tax system from full use of their skills it may be that they have been offered a higher 'price' (gross salary) to overcome their reluctance.

If this is the case it implies that the wage and salary structure will have changed, and that those with scarce skills have had to be offered relatively higher salaries to persuade them to move to the jobs where they are needed. Thus more skilled labour is made available and people are persuaded to move their jobs, but only at the cost of higher outlays for employers. It looks as if the higher salaries will tend to rise relative to lower ones as the taxation effect is capitalized. The idea may be expressed in a different way as the employee shifting part of his tax burden on to his employer (and hence on to his employer's customers?). If he succeeds then the aim of progression in the tax structure will have been frustrated.

Another example of tax capitalization lies in the market for private housing. We saw in Chapter 2 that the UK tax system allows an owner/occupier to deduct interest on loans of up to £30 000 in calculating income for IT purposes. It has been argued that this relief is inappropriate and unfair relative to the treatment of tenant occupiers. However, even if this argument was accepted, instant withdrawal of the relief would pose serious problems because of its effect on house prices. Some owners would be forced to sell their houses as they could no longer afford to pay the loan charges without the benefit of tax relief. Others would decide for similar reasons not to move to a larger house. Yet others, not already home owners, would decide not to buy at all.

The result would be a fall in house prices by varying proportions for different categories of house. Any necessary adjustment in the supply of houses would take a long time to achieve as annual construction and demolition forms only a tiny percentage of the total housing stock. Thus the effect of tax capitalization in the housing market is seen in the windfall losses, and probable hardship, suffered by home owners if the existing tax relief was suddenly withdrawn. The capitalization effect lies in the higher prices currently existing, an effect which offsets all or part of the benefit of the tax relief. A gradual withdrawal of the relief by holding the ceiling constant at £30 000 in money terms while prices are rising could still be achievable.

TAX ON LOWER INCOMES

One of the problems of the UK labour market arises as much from the social security arrangements as from the tax on income, but as the issues are similar to those which have just been discussed above and there is an interaction between them it is appropriate to consider it here. The problem is known as 'the poverty trap'.

We have seen already that the threshold for IT in the UK has declined in recent decades and that it now affects people whose wages can be fairly described as 'very low'. These people are also within the range of eligibility for social welfare benefits such as family income supplement, rent and rates rebates, free school meals and so on. It is a feature of these benefits that they are withdrawn step by step as income rises, not all on the same basis or at the same rate.[10] In general the calculations are made on a weekly or monthly basis as a year would be too long a period for people with no cash reserves and whose circumstances may change unexpectedly.

Unfortunately there has been little co-ordination between the welfare benefits and the tax system with the result that the combined effects of tax liability and loss of benefits can result in a man being actually worse off when he increases his gross earnings. A similar effect may occur as a result of a decision to start work.[11]

Clearly if the effective marginal rate of this 'tax' (tax imposed plus benefits withdrawn) is greater than 100% the income effect is reversed and the substitution effect is reinforced. Both then work in the same direction. It is not suggested that there are many such cases but there are many cases where the effective marginal rate suffered is greater than the top rate of 60% found in the direct tax system alone.

It is believed quite generally that this situation is not acceptable but the proposed solutions to it tend to be very expensive in terms of loss of tax yield or of increased welfare expenditure or both. The subject is a complex one. We will therefore confine discussion to three possibilites which impinge on the tax system.

Part of the problem lies in the very low tax thresholds, and it has been suggested that these should be increased so as to remove from direct taxation those people who are likely to be receiving significant welfare benefits. The trouble with this solution is that the increased thresholds would apply to all taxpayers and that the fall in the tax yield would be considerable. A rise of £1 000 in the threshold for 1986/87 would have meant £290 less tax being paid by most taxpayers and £600 less by the higher income group.

This loss of revenue could, of course, be recouped by reducing the size of the tax rate bands (especially the basic rate) or increasing marginal rates, or both. The changes might attempt to leave those who are above the poverty trap with the same tax bill as before. Unfortunately an increase in marginal rates for all, or for a significant proportion, could not be avoided and that would tend to increase the distortions that have been discussed in the earlier parts of this chapter.

Thus the decision seems to lie in the trade-off between the advantages of reducing the poverty trap effect and the possibly injurious effects on the economy at large of the higher marginal rates imposed on most members of the workforce, and on investors. Confining the increases to the highest paid alone would not recover the previous tax yield because of the smaller numbers of people involved.

A second possibility is to start with a lower rate of tax initially. The threshold would not be changed but a first slice of income would be taxed at a lower rate than the basic rate while still leaving most of that rate band in operation.

At first sight this looks like an attractive compromise, less costly in tax yield but giving some relief to those at the lower end of the income scale. It is true as well that the UK has had a reduced rate band in the recent past. There would be some small increase in complication but this might be acceptable if the effects were otherwise beneficial.

Unfortunately it can be shown that it would have no beneficial effects because of the present level of thresholds and the feasible spread of the new lower rate band. There are two reasons for this.

1. The lower rate of tax would affect mostly part-time and casual workers and would hardly touch those who suffer most from the poverty trap.
2. Compared with a rise in the threshold at an equal public revenue cost it would make the poor relatively poorer and benefit those with higher incomes. These points are explained in Technical Note 3.2 at the end of this chapter.

Finally there is the idea of a negative income tax or social dividend scheme which has been widely discussed, especially in the American literature.[12] One version, the so-called Tax Credit Scheme, was the subject of a Green Paper in the UK in 1972.[13] The concept that lies behind all variants is that there should be a smooth transition from income taxation to the welfare system.

To take a simplified example, if the tax threshold was £2000 then tax at, say, 25% would be collected above the threshold, and cash benefits paid out below it at a rate of 25% of the difference between actual income and the threshold. This would imply a maximum cash benefit of £500 (25% of £2000 if income is zero), and this figure immediately raises the question of adequacy of the support being given. The dilemma is the familiar one of adequacy of support for the poor against the effects of high marginal rates of tax and/or withdrawal of support as income rises.

What looks like a very neat solution turns out to be very costly. Furthermore, at this simple level it fails to deal with special and individual problems such as variations in the cost of housing in different parts of the country.

It looks as if the immediate answer lies in some streamlining of the present UK welfare system to eliminate the very high marginal rates which result from differently administered benefits, while still trying to deal with poverty on an individual basis. It may be hoped that this will lead gradually to a more integrated system which approches closer to the negative income tax ideal.

ADMINISTRATION AND COMPLIANCE COSTS

The earlier part of this chapter has been concerned with the effects of an income tax on the economy and, as part of that topic, its effect on the way people behave as economic beings. It must always be emphasized that these effects, difficult though they are to trace and measure, have a significant impact on the economy's health. We will now look at an effect which may be less important economically but which is quantified more easily. It will be convenient to look separately at the cost of administration (the civil service costs) and the costs of compliance (the taxpayers' costs).

The civil service departments responsible for taxation have several functions to perform. They have to obtain and check information that is relevant to tax liability, ensure that the liability is calculated accurately, and ensure that the tax revenue is received and accounted for properly. In doing this they will have to take steps to force some taxpayers to comply with their legal obligations and may be involved in court proceedings to settle matters that are disputed. These functions are discussed in detail in Chapter 14.

Income and other direct taxes are the responsibility of the Board of Inland Revenue (BIR). In its report for 1985 the BIR stated that its costs in 1984/85 amounted to 1.66% of the tax collected. This figure included the cost of employing about 70000 people.[14] The main tax it administers is IT and this produces about 70% of the tax revenue for which jt is responsible. Costs related to IT are divided into two categories, employment income where they were 1.6% of the yield, and other income where they were 5.2%

The costs of administration depend more heavily on the nature of the tax and on its particular structure than on the internal efficiency of the administering body. Thus the taxes on North Sea and Irish Sea oil and gas are collected in large amounts from few sources and the costs amount to only 0.01% of their yield.

Taxes on employment are collected under PAYE which has been outlined already. Many people in the UK have income which is confined to this category, or nearly so, and their tax position is ascertained quite easily. Although there are about 26 million taxpayers[15] most of the work is simple and routine and quite a lot of it is done by the employer, so civil service costs are low.

Tax on other kinds of income is more varied and involves careful examination of each taxpayer's circumstances. As we have seen in Chapter 2 the computation of taxable income and reliefs can be complicated. Thus the higher percentage cost arises out of the nature of the tax liability. A recent attempt to reduce this cost, otherwise than by improved internal efficiency of the tax administration, can be seen in the change which took place in 1985 in the way interest on bank deposits is taxed.[16] In effect the tax is collected from the banks (of which there are few) rather than from the depositors (of whom there are very many). Only those depositors who are liable to tax at rates above the basic rate need involve the civil servants in further work. The same system has been applied to interest received from building societies for several decades.

The financial and economic cost of tax administration does not stop at the doors of the civil service departments. Taxpayers have compliance costs and these fall into three main categories.[17]

1. *Costs imposed on the taxpayer himself.* These may amount to no more than the time and energy consumed in responding to the legitimate requirements of the tax administration. They may involve the use of professional advice and assistance, or in some cases the use of highly skilled and well rewarded experts in tax planning. It is argued that the use of professional brains in this way is a double loss to the economy.

2. *Costs imposed on employers.* The detailed administration of the PAYE system is the responsibility of the employer. In the case of medium to large firms this may involve little more than a standard computer programme, but the costs of entering amended personal details and acting as initial respondent to tax queries raised by employees should not be underestimated. Smaller employers may be especially conscious of the extra work involved and may, indeed, pay their accountant or other agency to do the work for them.

3. *Other compliance costs.* These consist largely of costs imposed on those bodies, other than employers as such, who are under an obligation to provide information about the income of others. One of the effects of the changed procedure for bank interest was to reduce the burden placed upon the banks under this obligation. It also reduced the civil service cost of processing it. Perhaps the latter had more effect on the decision to change than did the former!

The existence of these costs leads to demands for simplification of the tax system. Not only would this reduce costs, it would also enable the taxpayer and others to achieve a better understanding of the system and thereby enable the whole procedure to be conducted more effectively.

Simplification may relate either to the tax itself or to the way it is administered. The latter covers such questions as ensuring that the only complexity is that which is unavoidable because of the nature of the tax itself. For instance, it is possible to seek information in a straightforward, simply expressed way on a well designed form instead of using a bad design and convoluted sentences on it.

Simplification of the tax itself is likely to be more difficult even if the will to do it exists. There tends to be a conflict between simplicity and equity because a simple system does not allow for the hard cases. The change in the treatment of bank deposit interest to which reference has just been made can be taken as an example of this point. There can be little doubt that the new system is simpler.

Unfortunately the new system is also less equitable as depositors who are not liable to IT cannot claim a tax refund despite receiving interest which is, in effect, net of tax. Furthermore, economic inefficiency may creep in as the choice of investment medium is influenced by these tax consequences, especially as there may be consequential benefits to those investors who do pay tax and who find that investment in bank deposits has become more desirable than, say, national savings opportunities. The bank interest is, of course, taxed at a composite rate and this is lower than the basic rate which is charged on many other forms of interest.

AN EXPENDITURE TAX

Proponents of tax simplification sometimes search for an answer in a complete change of the tax base. This may be misleading as they can usually recount the theoretical advantages but may not be able to foresee the complications that will arise in practice. One such idea which has been discussed very widely in recent years is the expenditure tax.

The idea of an expenditure tax was developed in some detail by the Meade Committee in 1978[18], following on earlier work by Kaldor.[19] It has not yet been adopted but it continues to fascinate those who seek solutions to present difficulties.

An expenditure tax is a direct tax on individuals and could be progressive in structure, probably on an annual basis. The main difference compared with an income tax is that it would be levied on total expenditure, not on total income. The basis of it will become clearer if we look at the equation of personal cash flows:

Income + Dis-saving + Other receipts = Expenditure + Savings + Tax paid.

Many people spend the whole of their income as soon as they receive it and so they would find no difference in their tax bill, but the nominal rate of tax would have to be expressed on the expenditure net of the tax itself. Thus a 25% tax on income, with the income apart from the tax being spent, would become an expenditure tax of 25/75 = 33⅓%.

If some of the income was saved the tax base would be reduced. Thus personal savings would be made out of gross income and not, as now, out of net of tax income. If the other receipts included items such as inherited wealth or gifts received no problem would arise if the sum received was reinvested as the two transactions would cancel out in the calculation of the tax base. If, however, some of the receipts were spent on consumption items extra tax would become due. In the case of business profits it could be assumed in most cases that any income left in the business constituted savings so the only figure required in calculating tax liability would be drawings.

There would be no need for the taxpayer to record individual expenditures as the total of these could be derived from the figures for cash income, savings and so on. It has been suggested that savings would be treated as such only if they were invested in registered assets. Thus working balances in bank current accounts, building societies and so on would be ignored. This approach would have the added advantage that by using unregistered assets for short periods people could smooth the size of their taxable net expenditure from year to year.

For the many people who spend the whole of their income the economic affects of an expenditure tax do not appear to differ from a tax on income. It is possible that a nominally higher rate of tax imposed on a net-of-tax basis would be perceived as a higher marginal rate and have more impact in terms of the substitution effect. On the other hand any scheme for making provisional tax deductions from employment income would have to use the tax inclusive rate, i.e. 25% rather than the 33⅓% used in the example above.

The main discussion about the economic effects of an expenditure tax has concentrated on its effect on savings. The first point to make is that there would no longer be an incentive to choose particular forms of savings (apart from the effect of non-registration of some assets). All would be treated alike and distortions in the choice of savings would be eliminated. Thus if savings are made for retirement, any cash invested, and investment income therefrom ploughed back into the fund, would be free of tax. Only the final withdrawals, whether of capital or of income, would attract tax and then only as they are spent.

The second point is whether the general level of savings would be affected. The answer to this question is uncertain. It may look at first as if the ability to reduce tax liability by saving may encourage it to take place. It depends on the motivation to save. If there is a savings target no change will occur. Indeed if the target plan envisages building up the fund by reinvestment of income earned on the fund an expenditure tax may make it easier to reach the target while investing less each year out of the primary income. On the other hand if investment plans envisage some dis-saving after retirement the tax regime will then be harsher and the savings target will have to be raised to achieve the same future spending power.

It has also been argued that an expenditure tax would be easier and cheaper to administer than an equal-yield tax on income. However, it may have its own problems too, and the most difficult of these seem to lie in the transition from an income tax. We cannot cover them in detail but the following points indicate their general nature.

1. Expenditure could be met by dis-saving from assets which were concealed at the commencement of the expenditure tax, while new declared investments could be used to reduce the apparent expenditure of the same year.
2. There would be serious disruption in the institutional savings markets in so far as the dominant institutions (pension funds, life assurance companies) would no longer possess a relative advantage in attracting savings. Tax capitalization effects would change and people would receive windfall gains and suffer windfall losses as a result. These effects would occur when the financial markets responded to the expectation that the expenditure tax was going to be imposed.
3. There could be strong objections to one particular effect. A family with several children will have a high level of expenditure and will thereby incur a higher tax bill than the family or individual with no children. This could lead to a situation in which families would live in a country which taxes income when their expenditure is heavy and vice-versa. Furthermore, international tax compatability would suffer if only one country adopts an expenditure tax.

4. There would no longer be any need to adjust the tax base for general price inflation as expenditure is always current cash, whereas the income calculation may depend, for instance, on the purchase of wasting assets in past years. Nor would there be any need to try to differentiate between capital and income transactions in business accounts. However, not all apportionments would disappear. The difficult borderline between business or employment expenditure and private expenditure would be just as important as it is now and it would still be necessary to consider whether non-cash benefits, such as private use of a company car, should be taxed as expenditure. (See Chapter 5 for a discussion of this.)

It should now be apparent that an expenditure tax is an interesting proposal which would simplify some aspects of the existing IT and remove some of the economic problems and uncertainties. Nevertheless, complexities would remain, including the essence of the family taxation problem which we shall be looking at in the next chapter. The problems of the transition and of international compatibility may turn out to be insoluble.

TECHNICAL NOTES

Technical Note 3.1 Income and substitution effects

The line AB in Fig. 3.1 shows the choice between work (earnings) and leisure. At maximum earnings OA there will be no leisure, and at maximum leisure OB there will be no earnings. If we draw in the indifference curve I_1 tangential to AB we get the preferred position where earnings are OE_1 and leisure is OL_1.

When a proportional tax is imposed on earnings at a rate of 30% the choice available is then shown by the line A_1B. The worker's choice must now lie on an inferior indifference curve I_2 and the new preference gives earnings (after tax) of OE_2 and leisure is OL_2. Leisure is reduced in amount by L_1L_2. Thus in this example the income effect has dominated to produce an increase in the work that will be done as a result of the tax.

The diagram can be used to separate the income and substitution effects. If the worker is to remain as well off as before he must remain on I_1. However, the rate of substitution between income and leisure has changed and this is represented by the slope of the choice line. The new slope is represented by CD and where this touches I_1 gives us earnings of OE_3 and leisure of OL_3. Line CD is, of course, parallel to A_1B.

OE_3 and OL_3 isolate the substitution effect and they show that leisure increases by L_1L_3. Then the income is reduced and produces an income effect which is measured by L_2L_3. Clearly the outcome in any case depends on the slopes of AB and A_1B and on the shape of the indifference curves.

Technical Note 3.2 Increased thresholds or lower tax rates?

Figure 3.2 shows a system of personal taxation in which the threshold is at £2500 (i.e. OT_1) and tax is payable at 30% thereafter. Two possible changes are being considered, both with the same revenue cost:

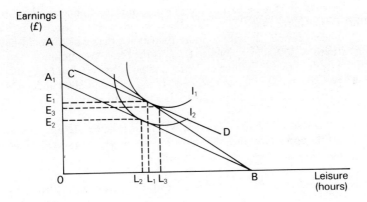

Fig. 3.1 Income and distribution effects.

1. Increase the threshold to £3 500 (i.e. OT_2), or
2. Insert a lower rate of tax of 15% above T_1 while keeping the threshold unchanged.

The upper limit of the 30% band and the higher rate bands are not being altered. The first question is where will the upper end of the reduced tax rate band be placed if the tax revenue is to be the same as under both schemes?

(a) Consider first T_3 which places the upper end at £4 500, i.e. $T_1T_2 = T_2T_3$. This will affect taxpayers and potential taxpayers as follows:

   (i) People in the range OT_1 will not be affected, they pay no tax.
   (ii) People in the range T_1T_2 will be worse off under scheme (2) as they will

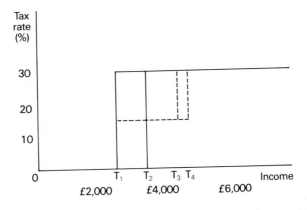

Fig. 3.2 Effect of increased thresholds/lower tax rates.

pay tax at 15% on part of their income instead of none at all.

(iii) People in the range T_2T_3 will also be worse off as the income taxed at 15% under scheme (2) will be more than twice that which would have been taxed at 30% under scheme (1). T_3 is the break-even point.

(iv) People above T_3 will be no better and no worse off. Up to T_3 they would pay 30% on £1 000 under scheme (1) and 15% on £2 000 under scheme (2). Above T_3 they would be taxed at 30% in both cases.

It must follow therefore that as nobody is better off and some are worse off the upper limit must be above T_3, otherwise the tax yield would rise (if no behavioural consequences ensue).

(b) Now consider the effect of the upper end of the reduced rate being at T_4.

(i) People in the range OT_1 will again be unaffected (no tax).

(ii) People in the ranges T_1T_2 and T_2T_3 will still be worse off under scheme (2) as they were under (a).

(iii) People in the range T_3T_4 will be better off to the extent of 15% of the excess of their income over T_3.

(iv) People above T_4 will all be better off under scheme (2) to the extent of 15% of T_3T_4.

(c) *Conclusion.* Compared with an increase in the general threshold a reduced rate scheme leaves the poor worse off and the rich better off. Assuming there are more people above T_4 than below it the relief to the rich will be trivial but the burden on the poor may be significant. Given the low threshold in the UK those who suffer would be mostly part-time workers, juveniles and pensioners.

NOTES AND REFERENCES

1. For a full discussion, see Lewis, A., *The Psychology of Taxation*, Martin Robertson, Oxford (1982).

2. Smith, A., *An Enquiry into the Nature and Causes of the Wealth of Nations*, Book V, Chapter II, Part II, Para. 3, Clarendon Press, Oxford (1776, reprinted 1976).

3. Maslow, A.H., *Motivation and Personality*, Harper and Row, New York (1954). In Chapter 5 (page 82) he writes 'A person who is lacking food, safety, love and esteem would most probably hunger for food more strongly than anything else.'

4. Brown, C.V. and Jackson, P.M., *Public Sector Economics*, Martin Robertson, Oxford (1982), at pp. 62–67.

5. For a wide ranging discussion see Pen, J., *Income Distribution*, Pelican, London (1974).

6. In 1938/39 a threshold of £125 on earned income; in 1986/87 a threshold of £2335 on all income.

7. *Revenue Statistics of OECD Member Countries, 1965–82*, OECD, Paris (1983), at Table 6.

8. For a useful discussion of the evidence see Brown, C.V., *Taxation and the Incentive to Work*, Oxford University Press, Oxford (1983).

9. For a fuller discussion see Chapter II of Kaldor, N., *An Expenditure Tax*, Allen & Unwin, London (1955).

10. Family Income Supplement is withdrawn at a marginal rate of 50%; rent and rates rebates at a combined rate of 16½%.

11. See Chapter 8 of Kay, J.A. and King, M.A., *The British Tax System*, Oxford University Press, Oxford (1983).
12. See especially University of Wisconsin Institute for Research on Poverty, *Final Report of the New Jersey Graduated Work Incentive Experiment in New Jersey and Pensylvania*, University of Wisconsin (1973).
13. Green Paper, *Proposals for a Tax Credit System*, Cmnd. 5116, HMSO, London (1972).
14. Board of Inland Revenue, *Report for the Year Ended 31st December 1985*, 128th Report, Cmnd. 9831, HMSO, London (1986).
15. *Inland Revenue Statistics, 1984*, HMSO, London (1985).
16. Ss. 26–27 and 8th Schedule, Finance Act 1984.
17. For a full account see Sandford, C.T., *Hidden Costs of Taxation*, Institute for Fiscal Studies, London (1973).
18. Institute for Fiscal Studies, *The Structure and Reform of Direct Taxation*, George Allen & Unwin, London (1978).
19. See note 9 above.

EXERCISES AND DISCUSSION TOPICS

1. It is widely accepted that income should be taxed on a progressive basis.
   (a) Explain what is implied by the word 'progressive', and
   (b) Discuss the *disadvantages* of this pattern of taxation.
2. A home owner in the UK is allowed tax relief on interest paid on loans up to £30 000 when these are obtained to enable him/her to buy or improve the dwelling house. Thus interest which would be a nominal 12% actually costs 12 (1–0.29)% for a basic rate taxpayer in 1986/87 and 12 (1–0.60)% for those with high incomes.

   Now suppose that this relief was suddenly withdrawn. Ignoring any electoral consequences for the government of the day, what effect would you expect this decision to have on home owners and on the housing market?
3. You are employed currently as your company's branch manager in Manchester at a salary of £20 000 per annum (plus pension benefits). Your employer offers you the job of managing the Bristol branch at a salary of £25 000. That branch has performed very poorly recently and the manager has just been dismissed.

   What factors, financial and otherwise, would enter into your decision to accept the offer? In the light of your analysis consider the possible effects of taxation on your decision.
4. You have a sum of £10 000 which is to be invested for five years, after which it will be required for another purpose. Two possibilities attract you, both of which will guarantee the return of the original investment in full. The first consists of National Savings Certificates (32nd Issue) which produce a tax-free return of 8.75% per annum compound payable at the end of the five years. The second is a 12% Treasury stock available for purchase at par value and redeemable in five years' time.

   Which investment would you choose:
   (a) if you are not liable to income tax at all,
   (b) if you pay income tax at the basic rate,
   (c) if you pay income tax at the top rate?
5. Discuss the extent to which the burden of administrative and compliance costs of a tax system depends on the nature of the taxes being levied.

4   Taxation of the family

In Chapter 2 we saw how income tax (IT) is imposed on individuals in the UK and discussed some of the points that have to be considered in the design of such a tax. In this chapter we shall extend the discussion to consider the complications that arise when the system tries to make provision for the family situation. As in Chapter 2 we start with a description of the UK system as it exists.

THE UK SYSTEM

The UK's system of family taxation has its roots in the increasingly outdated idea of the husband as the breadwinner and the wife as the dependant housekeeper. Thus the unit of taxation is a household consisting of husband and wife together.[1] We will look first of all at three consequences of this approach.

The first consequence lies in the provision of information. We have seen that the IT system depends heavily on the provision of information by the taxpayer, mostly by means of the annual return form. In the case of married couples living together the legal responsibility is placed wholly upon the husband irrespective of the size of the income received by his wife.[2] Thus a husband who has no income and is supported by a working wife finds himself in the strange position of being responsible for reporting her income to the tax office.

It would be possible to tax husband and wife jointly while requiring them to complete separate return forms or requiring both of them to sign a joint return form. In either case both would have some knowledge of the other's income and many people would regard this result as preferable to the present one where knowledge travels one way only, the husband being able to keep his income secret from his wife.[3]

This one-way system gives rise to another problem. A wife who, for whatever reason, wishes to keep secret from her husband a 'nest-egg' that she has saved or acquired is confined in practice to a limited range of tax exempt investments such as National Savings Certificates. If she puts her money in taxable investments not only is she contributing to a false declaration by her husband, she is at risk that her savings will be disclosed to the tax office by the institution concerned.[4] Once this happens the disclosure is likely to reach her husband as the tax office ferrets out the existence of the undeclared income. This problem cannot be overcome unless the idea of taxing household units is abandoned.

The second consequence of joint taxation arises from the fact that the incomes of both spouses are aggregated. This may require some reconsideration of the width of the tax rate bands which are to be applied. Two incomes taxed separately may not go beyond the basic rate band, whereas if combined they may extend well into the higher rate bands. Thus income aggregation has the potential to tax married couples more heavily than two single people with the same incomes. In fact, as we shall see, this does not happen in the UK so far as earned income is concerned because of some special reliefs, but it does happen with investment incomes. Fortunately, the very broad basic rate band helps to limit the damage.

The third consequence concerns the size of the threshold following aggregation. The UK's approach has been to give a married man a higher threshold than a single man on the grounds that the married man has financial responsibility for his spouse as well as for himself.[5] However, there does seem to be a belief in government circles that a married couple can live together more cheaply than two single people living separately as the threshold for a married man is increased by only 56% (in 1986/87) compared with that for a single man or woman. The effect is illustrated in Example 4.1 at the end of the chapter.

Entitlement to the higher threshold, which in formal terms belongs to the husband, depends on the existence of a legal marriage and on the married couple either living together or on the husband wholly maintaining the wife.[6] Maintenance, for this purpose, does not include support in the form of payments under a court order or a legally enforceable agreement. This point will be covered on p. 61 when we deal with divorce and separation.

At one time the higher threshold was given even if the marriage took place on the last day of the tax year (5 April). This produced a heavy workload for clergymen and registrars over the last two weeks or so of that year. The position now is that in the year of marriage the extra relief is given pro rata on a month by month basis.[7] No such pro rata limitation is considered necessary on the death of the wife, or on divorce or separation, except that the man cannot receive more than one full enhancement in any one tax year.

A specially increased threshold for single people who are beyond normal retirement age was explained in Chapter 2 (and Example 2.2). A similarly increased threshold is given to married couples where either reaches the age of 65 during the tax year.[8] The calculation is shown in Example 4.2.

In addition to the higher threshold itself the possible work disincentive effect of aggregating the earned incomes of spouses led to the introduction of an additional threshold in the taxation of a wife's earned income. When she has such income a separate threshold equal to the single person's threshold (or such lesser amount as is needed to cover the earnings if they are less than the threshold) is given against that income. There is no consequential reduction in the husband's enhanced threshold so the effect can be to produce a combined threshold more than 250% of that given to a single person.[9]

Clearly the size of this combined threshold cannot be justified on equity grounds. The main reason why it was introduced was to give married women a tax-free slice of income which might encourage them to join the labour force. One odd effect of this additional threshold is that if the husband has no income of his own his threshold (as a married man) is still available against the combined earnings (i.e. his wife's) as well as her extra threshold. When the position is reversed and his is the only earned income, then he is entitled only to the normal enhanced threshold as a married man. Examples 4.3(a) and (b) show the effect of this anomaly.

Given the obvious benefit of the wife's extra threshold a restrictive definition of 'wife's earnings' was introduced. The main restriction is that the relief is not available against a wife's company or state pension or allowances where that income results from her husband's work or services. Pensions and allowances which result from the wife's own work do qualify.

This extra allowance did not solve all of the problems which arose. We have commented already that income aggregation may result in the combined incomes being pushed into the higher rate bands. Although this affects only a minority of taxpayers, because the basic rate band covers income up to at least double the average level of industrial earnings, where it does occur it would very quickly offset the benefit of the wife's extra threshold.

This problem was overcome by the introduction of the 'wife's earnings option'. Under this option the husband loses his enhanced threshold as a married man, but the wife's earnings are then taxed as if they belonged to a single person, thereby attracting a complete second set of rate bands so far as necessary to cover those earnings.[10] It should be noted that this option does not apply to investment income which is still aggregated and taxed as if it belonged to the husband. Example 4.4 shows how this relief works.

Whether this option should be chosen depends both on the aggregate earnings and on the way it is divided between husband and wife. To take an extreme example, a combined income of £30 000 divided equally would make the option favourable in 1986/87, but if the same total includes wife's earnings below her extra threshold limit then it would not. The break-even points can be plotted for each tax year on a graph with the two incomes plotted along its horizontal and vertical axes.[11]

There is a further option which modifies the system described so far but it is little used, partly because it is rather complicated. The option is called 'separate assessment' and enables each spouse to submit their own return of income for the year and makes each of them responsible for the tax due on that income. Both must agree for the option to operate.[12]

Under separate assessment the total tax due is calculated in exactly the same way as has been described already but the tax is then apportioned between the spouses in accordance with statutory rules. Apart from some computational and administrative complexity two disadvantages remain.

1. Both spouses can deduce from their own tax liability the size of the other's income because of the way the tax is apportioned. This may be regarded as an improvement on only the husband having the information. The nature of the income is not revealed.
2. Neither spouse possesses the information needed to check the accuracy of the total tax calculation unless they have full details of the other spouse's circumstances. It is not unknown in such cases for them to ask a third party, such as a professional adviser, to do this check for them without disclosing information to either spouse about the other's affairs.

So far the discussion has been concerned with a system which stems from the idea of the dependant spouse. We will now go on to consider other dependants, including children, whether they arise from the marriage or not. Reliefs will be dealt with only in outline.[13]

For many decades it was thought that the cost of feeding and otherwise maintaining children should be dealt with by reducing the tax payable by their parents. These reliefs took into account the responsibilities of unmarried, divorced, adoptive and step-parents. As we saw on p. 22 these views have changed and in the UK child maintenance is now dealt with by means of weekly cash payments under the social security system.

There is another way in which the existence of children may affect tax liability. Children may be entitled to income in their own right. If so they are taxed like adults with an initial threshold of the same amount as any other unmarried person. This means that if the family's income belongs partly to the children the total tax liability will be lower than that of a family which has the same total income belonging wholly to the parents. Such a tax reduction cannot be achieved artificially by transferring some of the income to the children as such transfers, whether by deed of covenant or by the gift of income producing assets, from parents to minor unmarried children are made ineffective.[14]

Where parents have to support their children after they have reached the age of 18 years (or, if married, younger than that) they can do so either by an outright gift of an income producing asset or, more cautiously, by means of a deed of covenant which must be irrevocable for a period of at least six years. Usually they are valid for seven years.[15] As we saw in Chapter 2 the effect of the deed is to reduce the parents' taxable income and pass some of it to the child who, it may be assumed, can claim back the IT deducted at source against the tax exempt threshold. The fact that student grants are not taxable as income facilitates this procedure.[16] See Example 2.5 again.

Arrangements may be made, even for minor unmarried children, by grandparents and other relatives. With some ingenuity deeds of covenant can be a remarkably flexible instrument. The main traps in this sort of exercise are:

1. If the recipient's income already exceeds the tax threshold there is no tax saving in transferring income this way because the relief to the donor is limited to the basic rate of tax only.
2. In some cases the gifted income, being legally the income of the recipient, may affect entitlement to social security benefits.

More complicated arrangements may also be made under which income is accumulated in a trust, but that is beyond the scope of this book.

Turning now to the miscellaneous reliefs, two situations have been recognized in which a single person becomes entitled to the same higher threshold as a married man. The first occurs when there is a child or children under the age of 16 years or in full-time education. The relief is then available to widows, widowers and single parents. The relief does not vary with the number of children but may be claimed by someone other than the child's own parent.[17]

The second situation is that of the bereaved widow who becomes entitled to the higher threshold in the year of her husband's death and the following year, provided the husband was himself entitled to that threshold.[18] Thus in the year of his death the husband's income (which includes his wife's) up to the date of death gets the benefit of the higher threshold and the income for the rest of that year (the widow's) also gets that benefit (see example 4.5). No doubt this relief is intended to reflect the continuing costs of a household set up for two people.

Finally there are some smaller reliefs designed to help in special cases of potential hardship. One is available to registered blind people and reflects the additional costs incurred as a result of their disability. Like the others it takes the form of a small increase in the threshold.[19]

The smallest reliefs (see Appendix for amounts) relate to three situations. The first is for the maintenance of a dependant relative who is incapacitated, old, or the claimant's (or his wife's) widowed, divorced or separated mother. The second reflects the cost to a widow or widower of employing a housekeeper. Finally, someone who is aged or infirm may claim relief if dependent on the services of a resident son or daughter. All of these reliefs have their own detailed requirements, including rules to prevent overlapping or double claims.[20]

DIVORCE AND SEPARATION

Any tax system which treats a married couple as a unit must raise the question of what happens when that unit is divided by divorce or permanent separation. The separated husband can hardly be expected to know the details of his wife's income! Divorce and separation raise issues that do not arise on marriage and we will look at two aspects, the actual break-up of the marriage and the continuing situation thereafter.

Divorce is often preceded by a formal or informal separation. The timing is important as from the date of *permanent* separation the parties can no longer be taxed as if 'living together'. This has two consequences.

1. The husband is no longer entitled to the higher threshold after the end of the tax year concerned, unless he is wholly maintaining his wife otherwise than under a formal deed or court order.
2. The couple are no longer treated as a tax unit and their tax liabilities will henceforth be their own affairs, both for reporting income and for paying the tax due.

These consequences are quite straightforward except for the tax year in which separation takes place. The year has to be divided into two parts, before and after separation. The income of the husband for the whole year is aggregated with so much of his wife's as arises before the separation and this total is then taxed as if it was the income of a married couple for the whole year. The wife's income for the rest of the year is then taxed as if it were the income of a single woman for the whole year.[21] Thus it is possible for the wife's income to receive the benefit of two thresholds and two tax rate bands in one year (see Example 4.6). One could envisage this benefit being withdrawn if divorce becomes very common or if the situation is seen to be exploited. For 1986/87 the potential tax saving for many people would be of the order of £677.

Following permanent separation and/or divorce it is usually necessary for financial arrangements to be made between the disaffected partners. It may be the case that following separation and before divorce the husband will continue to support his wife on an informal basis, assuming she has insufficient income of her own. In these circumstances he may be able to qualify for the higher threshold, but only if he is 'wholly maintaining' his separated wife. He will not be so entitled after the end of the tax year in which divorce takes place. The wife will not be taxable on any such payments.

Where continuing financial support is then appropriate it will be arranged under a formal, legally enforceable, agreement or may be the subject of a court order. The result of either arrangement is that the payments reduce the income of the payer for tax purposes but, assuming that this is the husband, he can no longer claim that he is wholly maintaining his wife as such payments do not qualify for that purpose. The payments are received by the other spouse as taxable income subject to the normal threshold. Unless the payments qualify as 'small maintenance payments' under a court order IT at the basic rate has to be deducted at source and accounted for to the tax collector.[22] The recipient may then be entitled to some repayment of the tax deducted. Payments may be made on a similar basis to or for the benefit of the children of the marriage.

The transfer of assets on divorce or separation may raise questions of capital gains tax (CGT) and inheritance tax (IHT) which will be reflected in later chapters. Any income arising on such assets will belong to the receiving spouse as soon as those assets have been transferred effectively.

OTHER SYSTEMS OF FAMILY TAXATION

Now that we have looked at the UK system of family taxation it is time to see it in the context of other systems. This is particularly important because the UK system is a hybrid and the impact of the arguments that will be discussed on pp. 64–6 can only be appreciated if this broader context is made clear.

We have touched on some of the characteristics of a 'pure' unit, or joint taxation, system. Its essential features are that the incomes of the spouses are aggregated and the tax threshold and rate bands in a progressive system are then applied to the aggregate. The effect of this depends to some extent on the design of the underlying system and in particular the relative sizes of the thresholds for single and married people and the pattern of the tax rate bands. However, we can demonstrate the main characteristics if we take a very simple and hypothetical unit system.

	Single £	Married £
Income	10 000	20 000
Threshold	4 000	8 000
Taxable income	£6 000	£12 000
Tax at 25%	1 500	3 000

By considering this example various propositions can be derived.

1. Once they are married the proportions of total income belonging to each spouse can vary without altering the tax liability.
2. If the married threshold is twice the single threshold and both partners have income above the single threshold the fact of marriage will not alter tax liability unless higher rates of tax come into the picture (in which case marriage will increase liability).
3. If one partner to the marriage has no income marriage will reduce tax liability so long as the married threshold is greater than the single threshold.

4. If the married threshold is less then twice the single threshold marriage will always produce greater tax liability so long as both partners have income above the single threshold.

5. If one spouse decides to start work to add to the family income those earnings will pay tax from the first £ at the top rate already being paid on the other income (which explains the special relief for wives' earning in the UK).

A variant of the unit system is the quotient system. This is an attempt to overcome the effects of aggregating two incomes where tax liability at higher rates would be the result. It is used in France and in the USA.[23] Under this system the incomes are aggregated but are then taxed as if the combined total represented equal incomes of two single people. Again we can look at a simple, hypothetical, example.

		£
Income:	Husband	15 000
	Wife	5 000
	total	20 000
One half thereof		10 000
Single threshold		4 000
Taxable income		6 000
Tax (say): £5 000 at 25%		1 250
£1 000 at 40%		400
Total tax		1 650× 2 = £3 300

In France the quotient system has been extended to include minor children. Thus whereas the quotient for husband and wife is 2, that for husband, wife and one child is 2½. This means that where the child has no income of its own the system can provide relief from tax both in terms of an increased threshold and of reduced liability at the higher rates.

What, then, is the effect of the quotient system? The propositions (1) to (5) stated above continue to apply except that (4) is no longer relevant and (2) should be modified to state that marriage may reduce tax liability if higher rates of tax were payable by one or both of the partners before marriage and their incomes are not equal. This happens because part of the higher income is, in effect, added to the lower income and may then fall into a lower rate band.

Before we leave the quotient system we should note one problem which arises to a slightly lesser degree in the pure unit system as well. One consequence of proposition (3) is that on the death of a spouse who contributes little or no income to the family the income will continue largely or wholly unchanged but tax liability may rise sharply. This problem will be less severe in the case of separation and divorce as there is then likely, as we have just seen, to be some transfer of income as part of the settlement. In the case of death the surviving partner will often wish to maintain the same household arrangements, at least for a while.

One solution that has been employed to deal with this problem is to continue to tax the income of the surviving spouse on a 'married' basis for a limited period after bereavement. Indeed we have seen already that the UK system provides some relief to the widow for the year of her husband's death and the following year. There seems to be an equal case for similar treatment of the widower where the present benefit is confined to the year of his wife's death only.

At the opposite end of the spectrum to unit taxation lies individual taxation. Support for this has grown in recent years as it has become more fashionable to argue that married women, having become more equal in economic and social terms, should be treated as independent-earner persons for tax purposes.[24] This would mean that the fact of marriage would become irrelevant to the calculation of tax liability and everyone would be taxed solely on their own income. The arguments favouring individual taxation may also reflect a changing social structure in which legal marriage is not the only situation in which an enduring heterosexual relationship may exist. Others branches of the law may be changing to reflect this social development.

Thus the arguments concern the social and economic factors which the tax system should reflect and they depend very heavily on value judgements. We will look first at the financial consequences of changing the system to independent taxation and then go on to look at some of the underlying issues.

The financial consequences of independent taxation can again be stated in a series of propositions.

1. The fact of marriage in itself has no effect on tax liability.
2. Where two household incomes (whether married householders or not) are the same in aggregate but are contributed in different proportions the total tax liability may differ.
3. Where one spouse decides to work to add to the family income he or she will have the benefit of a new threshold and of a full band of taxable income below the higher rates.
4. The tax system does not distinguish between a single person and a married person with a dependent spouse (for whatever reason that dependancy exists).

It will be appreciated that the present UK system, because it is a hybrid, also has the attributes of propositions (2) and (3) so far as a wife's earned income is concerned.

In the light of this account of individual taxation it is interesting to consider what would be the effects if the present UK system was converted to it. Three issues arise.

1. *Investment income.* At present all investment income of the spouses is aggregated. If it was allocated to its true owners the tax yield would fall. For instance, a non-working wife would have the benefit of a single person's threshold against it whereas none is available under the present system. Probably of equal importance is the opportunity it would provide for the spouse with the higher income and tax rates to transfer assets to the other spouse and thereby reduce the rate of tax on the income arising. Because of this possibility it was suggested in the 1980 Green Paper that a system of joint (unit) taxation could be retained for investment income only.[25] Presumably unmarried couples are less willing to transfer assets in this way until the property rights of the parties in a divorce are extended to other joint households.
2. *The two-earner family.* We saw on p. 57 that in this situation many married couples enjoy over 250% of the single person's threshold. There seems to be no particular reason why the relief should exceed 200%. The present situation arose

largely out of wartime conditions, in particular the need to encourage married women to join the labour force, and it has since been justified as being easier to administer.[26] Under individual taxation neither of these reasons would have any force.

3. *The one-earner family.* This is the greatest problem of the three and possible solutions tend to descend into a fog of administrative and legislative complexity. Certain cases can be dealt with fairly easily. Marriages where one spouse stays at home to look after children can be dealt with by an enhanced cash payment for each child funded out of the increased tax yield which would result from the withdrawal of the higher threshold. Working mothers could still choose to spend all or part of this increased benefit on child-care facilities. Another group who need be no worse off are pensioners. In so far as the pension reflects the existence of a dependent spouse that part of it could be deemed to be income of that spouse. This would attract the benefit of a joint threshold greater than the single person's, possibly twice as much, and may even eliminate the need for a special age allowance. This leaves the non-working spouse and especially the one (typically the wife) who does not work because she no longer finds it easy to find a job, or has elderly relatives who are partially or intermittently dependent on her. One possibility is to provide a larger threshold for the husband whose wife does not use her own threshold. This adds to the administrative complication and destroys the principle of independent taxation, but is the approach favoured by the UK government at the time of writing.[27]

It will be seen from this brief account that change is not easy. Some people would be worse off, relatively if not absolutely, under a new regime and this could be unpopular politically. It may be that changes would have to introduced gradually but, one hopes, within the context of a long-term plan.

CRITERIA TO BE APPLIED TO FAMILY TAXATION

We looked at some of the general criteria affecting income taxes in Chapter 3. These can now be extended to family taxation in the various forms that have just been described. They will show that no design can be ideal and that policy becomes a question of reconciling conflicting issues to produce an acceptable compromise.

Horizontal equity requires that people in a similar situation should be treated alike. Unfortunately in family taxation as elsewhere it may not be easy to define what is a 'similar situation'. The first question is whether marriage is relevant at all. Is there any economic difference between a married couple and an unmarried household? If not, then individual taxation satisfies this criterion.

More difficult is the income split in a joint household. If the joint income is, say, £20 000 a year, does it matter whose income it is? It can be argued that if it is earned income it does. If it is derived from both spouses or partners working full-time the incidental costs incurred (travelling, clothing, meals out, help in the home) may well be greater but they are not tax deductible as such. If there is only one earner then the other person may have more time for household tasks and there may be more time and energy to enjoy the available leisure. This argument may seem to bend towards individual taxation but perhaps that goes too far. What does seem to be clear is that the UK system which taxes one-earner couples differently according to which of them earns the income cannot be justified on any grounds.

The question of vertical equity brings in the same issues as it depends on the definition of what is meant by the words 'better off'. A married couple taxed individually can arrange to transfer their assets so as to reduce tax liability more easily than two single people (see Example 4.7). This seems to lead to the conclusion that they should be deprived of this possibility either by joint taxation or by legislation designed to prevent such transfers being effective. It does seem likely that such legislation would be neither very simple nor very effective and this fact leads us back to some form of unit taxation. The liability of the married couple, as compared with unmarried couples, would then depend on how the assets of the latter were distributed between them. It is of course part of the concept lying behind individual taxation that people are to be treated as individuals and in so far as they choose to pool their household resources that is irrelevant to their tax liability.

Turning now to economic efficiency, the special factor in family taxation concerns the effect of the system on the incentive or disincentive for the so-called secondary earner. The argument is directed at the position of the spouse (often the wife) whose earnings would be supplementary so far as the joint household is concerned. If extra costs and extra effort are involved in starting work and if the basic needs of the family are satisfied by the income of the primary earner the economic incentive to start work may be low. In other words the elasticity of supply for this type of labour is high.

In these circumstances a system which imposes tax immediately at the family's highest marginal rate is more likely to have a significant disincentive effect. Thus either individual taxation or the UK's current hybrid system may be seen to have good characteristics if what is desired is to avoid discouraging secondary earners. Of course it is possible to envisage a national policy which seeks to impose such discouragement. Unit and quotient systems would then be more appropriate.

Simplicity and costs of administration may be affected as well. Although unit systems mean that the incomes of two people can be dealt with singly, thereby reducing the work load, it is still necessary to co-ordinate the information. Thus under the UK arrangements the wife's earnings are dealt with by reference to her place of work while the administration of that aspect of the joint incomes depends on information held in respect of her husband who may well work elsewhere. With individual taxation this co-ordination would not be necessary.[27] On the other hand individual taxation would require two tax returns instead of one.

However, as we have seen, individual taxation might give rise to other problems. Legislation might be considered necessary in respect of transfers of investment income. Reliefs might be required for particular circumstances, such as the wife who has a good reason for not working and is dependant on her husband. Once these factors enter into individual taxation it becomes more complex and more expensive to administer.[28]

Social factors cannot be ignored. It may be that in a country at a particular time there is a desire either to encourage or discourage marriage by using the tax system. Many people would argue that the tax effect would have to be substantial before it had any real social influence anyway. Nevertheless, governments are entitled to feel that, in order to signal their intentions, the tax system should be either neutral to marriage or at least consistent with prevailing social values.

Individual taxation, unless it is modified to deal with the case of the dependent spouse, would be neutral to marriage. The present UK system favours marriage for the most part but can act against marriage for well-to-do couples with substantial investment income.[29] Other systems will vary in their effect according to the thresholds and tax rate bands and to the circumstances of the couple concerned. There is no universal truth.

Another social factor which many see as being important is privacy. As we have seen, the present UK system gives the husband privacy about his financial affairs but his wife has to reveal all relevant financial information to him. It seems very difficult indeed to justify this attitude against current social habits. However, equal rights in this respect do not depend just on the tax system. It would be easy to devise a unit system in which both partners have full access to information about each other.

Only individual taxation, however, would ensure that both partners could have complete privacy from each other if that is their wish. Merely separating information provision and tax payment in a unit system (as in the UK's separate assessment option) does not achieve this aim because the tax due depends in part on the income of the other spouse and this can be deduced from the calculations that have to be made.

EXAMPLES

The calculations in Examples 4.1–4.6 are based on UK tax rates for 1986/87. For other years see Appendix.

Example 4.1 Higher threshold

	Single £	Married £
Income	10 000	10 000
Personal relief	2 335	3 655
Taxable income	£7 665	£6 345
Tax at 29%	2 222.85	1840.05
Tax saved	£382.80	

Example 4.2 Age relief

	Single £	Married £
Income	5 000	5 000
Age relief	2 850	4 505
Taxable income	£2 150.50	£495
Tax at 29%	623.50	143.55
Tax saved	£479.95	
Income	10 000	10 000
Age relief	2 450*	4 105*

Taxable income	£7550	£5895
Tax at 29%	2189.50	1709.55
Tax saved	£479.95	

*Reduced by ⅔rds of the excess of income over £9400 – but not so as to reduce it below the normal personal reliefs of £2335 single and £3655 married.

Example 4.3 Wife's earnings

		Husband £	Wife £	Total £
(a)	Earnings	10000	1000	11000
	Reliefs	3655	1000	4655
	Taxable income	£6345	£0	£6845
	Tax at 29%	1840.05	0	1840.05
(b)	Earnings	0	11000	11000
	Personal reliefs	3655*	5990*	5990
	Taxable income	£0	£5010	£5010
	Tax at 29%	0	1452.90	1452.90

*Husband's relief of £3655 set against wife's earnings in addition to the wife's earnings relief of £2335

Tax reduction (a) – (b) is £387.15.

Example 4.4 Wife's earnings option

	Husband £	Wife's earnings £	Total £
Normal basis:			
Earnings	20000	10000	30000
Investment income:			
Husband	1000		1000
Wife	2000		2000
Total income	23000	10000	33000
Personal reliefs	3655	2335	5990
Taxable income	£19345	£7665	£27010
Tax at 29% (on £17200)			4988
at 40% (on £3000)			1200

at 45% (on £5 200)			2 340
at 50% (on £1 610)			805
Total tax			£9 333

Exercise the option:

Total income as above	23 000	10 000	33 000
Personal reliefs	2 335	2 335	4 670
Taxable income	£20 665	£7 665	£28 3:0
Tax at 29% (on £17 200/7 665)	4 988	2 222.85	7 210.85
at 40% (on £3 000/0)	1 200	—	1 200
at 45% (on £2 460/0)	207	—	207
Total tax	£6 395	£2 222.85	£8 617.85
Tax saved		£913.75	

Example 4.5 Year of husband's death

	Before death £	After death £
Husband's income	10 000	0
Wife's earnings	4 000	6 000
Total income	£14 000	£6 000
Personal reliefs:		
Married man	3 655	
Wife's earnings	2 335	
Single woman		2 335
Widow's bereavement		1 320
Taxable income	£8 010	£2 345
Tax at 29%	2 322.90	680.05

Example 4.6 Year of separation (earned income)

	Husband £	Wife £
Husband's income, whole year	15 000	—
Wife's income: before separation	4 000	—
after separation		6 000
Total income	£19 000	£6 000
Personal reliefs:		
Married man	3 655	
Wife's earnings	2 335	

Wife as if single		2 335
Taxable income	£13 010	£3 665
Tax at 29%	3 772.90	1 062.85

Example 4.7 Individual taxation (hypothetical)

Assume that the personal relief is £2 500 each and that tax is charged at 25% on £20 000 and 40% thereafter.

		His £	Hers £
(a)	**Unmarried couple:**		
	Earnings	20 000	1 000
	Investment income	5 000	0
	Total incomes	25 000	1 000
	Personal reliefs	2 500	2 500
	Taxable income	£22 500	£0
	Tax at 25% (on £20 000)	5 000	0
	at 40% (on £2 500)	1 000	0
	Total tax due	£6 000	£0
(b)	**Married couple, assets transferred to wife:**		
	Earnings	20 000	1 000
	Investment income	1 000	4 000
	Total incomes	21 000	5 000
	Personal reliefs	2 500	2 500
	Taxable income	£18 500	£2 500
	Tax at 25%	4 625	625
	Tax saving compared with (a)	£750	

Note: The tax saging consists of:

	£
Use of personal relief by 'her' (£1 500 at 25%)	375
Removal of income from higher rate (£2 500 at 15%)	375
	£750

NOTES AND REFERENCES

1. Ss. 37 and 42, Taxes Act 1970.
2. S. 37, Taxes Act 1970, deems the wife's income to be that of the husband whose responsibility under S. 8, Taxes Management Act 1970, is thereby extended.
3. See Green Papers, *The Taxation of Husband and Wife*, Cmnd. 8093, HMSO, London (1980), at paras. 7, 25, 48 and 73; *The Reform of Personal Taxation*, Cmnd. 9756, HMSO,

London (1986), at Chapter 2; and Equal Opportunities Commission, *Income Tax and Sex Discrimination*, EOC, Manchester (1978), at Chapter 4.

4. As a result of the Inland Revenue's powers to obtain information under SS.17–18, Taxes Management Act 1970, for instance. See the contents of Chapter 14 of this book for a discussion of this topic.
5. See para.14 of the 1980 Green Paper referenced in note 3 above.
6. S.8(1), Taxes Act 1970.
7. S.8(2), Taxes Act 1970.
8. S.31(1), Finance (No.2) Act 1975 (as amended in respect of the money amounts).
9. S.8(2), Taxes Act 1970.
10. S.23 and 4th Schedule, Finance Act 1971.
11. 'Which' Tax Saving Guide, Consumers Association, London (March 1987).
12. Ss.38–39, Taxes Act 1970.
13. Details are provided in the notes enclosed with return forms issued to individuals each year by the Inland Revenue.
14. Ss.437 and 444, Taxes Act 1970.
15. S.434, Taxes Act 1970.
16. S.375, Taxes Act 1970.
17. S.14, Taxes Act 1970.
18. S.23, Finance Act 1980.
19. S.18, Taxes Act 1970.
20. Ss.12 and 16–17, Taxes Act 1970.
21. This position follows from the terms of the aggregation provision, S.37, Taxes Act 1970. See also s.42 of that Act.
22. S.65, Taxes Act 1970.
23. Halpern, L., *Taxes in France*, 3rd edn., Butterworths, London (1980), at paras.660–665; and Gattney, D.J., Skadden D.H. and Wheeler, J.E., *Principles of Federal Income Taxation*, McGraw-Hill, New York (1982), at pages 11–12.
24. See for instance the report of the Equal Opportunities Commission and the Forward and Chapter 1 of the 1980 Green paper, both referenced at note 3 above.
25. 1980 Green Paper (see note 3 above) at para.87.
26. *Ibid.*, para.15, and The Royal Commission on the Taxation of Profits and Income, *Second Report*, Cmd.9105, HMSO, London (1954) at para.130.
27. 1986 Green Paper, referenced at note 3 above.
28. 1980 Green Paper, referenced at note 3 above, at para.130.
29. It also favours unmarried couples who have borrowed more than £30000 to buy their home as the loan interest limit then applies to them separately. See p.27 for details of this relief.

EXERCISES AND DISCUSSION TOPICS

1. Mr and Mrs Taylor are aged 67 and 68 years respectively. In the year ended 5 April 1987 their assessable income was as follows:

	£
Mr Taylor:	
State retirement pension	3187
Pension from former employer (net)	4877
(£723 tax deducted under PAYE)	
Dividends from UK companies (excluding tax credits)	35

Interest on debentures (net)	49
National Savings Bank interest (ordinary account)	99
Building society interest	210
Mrs Taylor:	
Building society interest	315
Bank deposit interest	45
Rent from unfurnished house	1 254

In 1981 Mr Taylor covenanted to pay his local church, for a period of seven years, an annual sum of £200 (gross).

Required:

A computation of Mr and Mrs Taylor's tax liability for 1986/87.

Note: The first £70 of interest on a National Savings Bank ordinary deposit is tax exempt. Husband and wife have separate exemptions.

ICSA, June 1985 (Question updated and capital gains tax point excluded.)

2. Mr Edwards, a married man aged 45, started in business as a retail tobacconist in 1976. He ceased to trade on 28 February 1987, his recent operating results, adjusted for tax purposes being:

		£
Year ended 30 April 1983	Profit	12 100
Year ended 30 April 1984	Profit	11 200
Year ended 30 April 1985	Profit	11 216
Year ended 30 April 1986	Profit	11 100
Ten months ended 28 February 1987	Profit	10 250

Additional information relevant to his tax affairs, and those of his wife, is as follows:

(a) In 1986/87 he paid allowable mortgage interest of £2 750 net of basic rate tax and a retirement annuity premium of £2 000.
(b) On 6 March 1987 he commenced employment as a sales representative and his gross earnings up to 5 April 1987 amounted to £740.
(c) The couple have a joint ordinary account with the National Savings Bank which they opened in August 1985. Interest has been:

	£
1985/86	132
1986/87	183

(d) Mrs Edwards earned a salary of £15 200 between 6 April 1986 and 31 January 1987. On 1 February she started her own business as a chiropodist; agreed profits for the nine months to 31 October 1987 were £14 860.
(e) In 1986/87 Mrs Edwards received investment income as follows:

	£
Dividends from UK companies	710
Debenture stock interest (net)	426

(f) In 1983 Mrs Edwards covenanted to pay a national charity, for a period of 4 years, an annual sum of £100 (gross).

Three years ago the couple elected to have Mrs Edward's earnings separately assessed and the election has not been revoked.

Required:
   Computations of the tax liabilities of Mr Edwards and Mrs Edward for 1986/87.

ICSA, December 1985 (Question updated.)

3. Richard White and Jane Stone were married on 20 June 1985. Mr White has the child from his previous marriage living with him. Mr and Mrs White received the following income:

	Mr White		Mrs White	
	1985/86	1986/87	1985/86	1986/87
	£	£	£	£
Salary (gross)	16000	17000	8000	8500
(*note*: tax deducted)	3854	4064	899	989
Dividends	700	781	2100	2059
Building society interest*	210	142	350	426
Bank interest*	70	213	35	71
Life assurance gain	4150			

   *Received net.

Mr White pays a subscription of £70 (net) under deed of covenant to a national charity. Mrs White pays mortgage interest of £4000 per year (gross, MIRAS not applied) on a loan of £40000 on her house. She went to live in Mr White's house on her marriage and immediately put her house up for sale. Unfortunately she was unable to sell the house until April 1987. The life assurance gain arose on the maturity of a qualifying unit-linked life assurance policy, taken out in 1972.

Required:
(a) Compute the net tax payable by Mr and Mrs White for 1985/86 and 1986/87.
(b) Show whether the wife's earnings election is beneficial for 1986/87.

IoT, Associateship Intermediate Examination, May 1986 (Question updated.)

4. Describe and illustrate the criteria which need to be considered when policy decisions about the taxation of married couples are being made.
5. It has been suggested that the tax system can be used to discourage married women from seeking work. Explain how this may arise and discuss the effects, in this respect, of the various systems that may be used for taxing married couples.

5 The taxation of quasi-incomes

In this chapter we shall look beyond the rather narrow idea of income as a regular cash flow of wages, rents, dividends and trading profits. The reasons why it is necessary to do this will be considered on p. 78 et seq. but we will start with an introduction to capital gains tax (CGT) as it now exists in the UK.

CAPITAL GAINS TAX (CGT) IN THE UK

CGT is imposed on the gains realized on the disposal of assets of all kinds, land, buildings, other physical assets, financial investments and other legal rights which have monetary value.[1] These transactions can be distinguished from the income derived by a trader from the purchase and sale of goods by the fact that they do not amount to a regular trading activity. Thus a property developer buys and sells land to produce the profits of his trade whereas the owner of a property let to a tenant receives his income in the form of rent (less outgoings). He will become liable to CGT, not IT, if he sells the property at a profit. It is the nature of the transactions, not the nature of the assets bought and sold, which determines the distinction between income and gains, but at the borderline it is not an easy one to make.

The first sentence of of the previous paragraph, it will be observed, used the word 'disposal' rather than 'sale'. This is because of the fact that although the tax is imposed on realized gains these are not confined to gains resulting from sales for value received. The gift of an asset, or its sale at an artificially low value, is taxed as if it had been a sale for full value subject only to an election available to individuals and trustees whereby the liability can be deferred until the recipient or donee disposes of the asset subsequently.[2] At one time death was treated as producing realization of all the assets owned by the deceased but this is no longer the case. Even so, the inheritors are still allowed to calculate their future gains as if they had bought the assets at the current market value as of the date of the death which produced their inheritance.

CGT is imposed on assets of all kinds unless they are specifically exempt, and on capital sums derived from assets even if the payer does not acquire an asset.[3] This can lead to some unexpected situations. Where a company director paid £50000 to his employing company to release him from his contract it was held that the company must have had a legal right (an asset) to which the payment could be related. The director, of course, merely got rid of an obligation, he acquired no asset.[4]

Another example of the care that is needed in dealing with transactions which may be caught by CGT lies in the legislation about value shifting.[5] A change in the voting rights of shareholders which results in loss of control of the company by one of them will reduce the value of his shares without necessarily increasing the value of the others. Nevertheless it may lead to a CGT liability.[6]

The basic calculation of a capital gain is quite simple but there are many complications in particular circumstances. The simple calculation involves a comparison between the original cost of the asset and the net proceeds on disposal. Costs that are incidental to purchase and sale are deductible, as well as the cost of any improvement made to the asset while it is owned. No deduction is allowed for normal maintenance and repair costs. However, where the asset is used in a trade, or is let, these costs would have been deductible in arriving at the taxable income year by year.[7]

Sometimes only part of an asset is sold. The calculation then requires identification of the apportioned part of the original costs which will be deducted from the disposal proceeds.[8] This is calculated as follows:

$$\text{Full cost} \times \frac{A}{A+B}$$

where A = disposal proceeds (or market value if given away), and
      B = current market value of the part unsold.

A full calculation is shown in Example 5.1

The calculations may result in a loss rather than a gain. Capital losses can be set off against gains on other assets disposed of in the same tax year, and if not so used can be carried forward to be set against the net gains of the next available year.[9] It should be appreciated that in so far as the owner has control over realization and its timing he can ensure that full benefit is taken of any loss as soon as possible.

CGT may be levied on gains which have accrued over very many years and which owe more to rises in the general price level than to an increase in real wealth. The government has accepted the argument that only real gains should be taxed and from April 1982 a form of indexation relief was introduced. Originally this was not applied for the first year of ownership but since 1985 the whole of the gain from 1982 has been indexed.[10] It should be noted that in the case of assets owned before April 1982 only the gain since that time is indexed, the adjustment being applied to the value as of the beginning of April 1982 (or to the actual cost if greater).

The principle of indexation can be demonstrated in a simple, hypothetical example as follows (but then see Example 5.2 for a more detailed calculation). If an asset was purchased in 1980 for £5000 and sold in 1987 for £12000 the overall gain would be £7000. However, if the asset was worth £10000 in April 1982 and the general price rise between that month and the date of sale was 15% the gain would be reduced by £1500. Thus we get:

	£	£
Sale proceeds		12000
Cost (1980)	5000	
Indexation (10000 × 0.15)	1500	6500
Chargeable gain		£5500

The indexation adjustment is applied to the calculation even if it creates or increases a loss. Official monthly index numbers are published, based on the RPI, and these are shown in the Appendix.

Many assets are acquired in the expectation that they will lose value because of some inherent characteristic. Machinery and buildings wear out, leases and other legal rights have a finite life and so on. As we shall see in Chapter 9 the use of wasting assets may attract depreciation relief in calculating trading profits and other income, but where CGT may arise on the disposal of such assets special rules have been devised.[11] These rules operate as follows.

1. Where there is a loss of value and that loss is covered by a depreciation allowance the loss is ignored for CGT purposes but there could still be a chargeable gain if, in the end, the asset is sold for more than it cost. (In the latter case the depreciation allowance would normally be withdrawn.)
2. Where there is an inherent loss of value not covered by other reliefs the calculation of the capital gain or loss is based on an apportioned part of the original cost. In the case of wasting assets other than leases of land and buildings the cost is written off evenly over the expected asset life.

Thus, ignoring indexation, we might get the following calculation for an asset with a 10 year life if sold after 6 years:

	£	£
Sale proceeds		10 000
less: Original cost	18 000	
less: Wasting element 6/10	10 800	7 200
Chargeable gain		£2 800

It will be seen that there is a chargeable gain even though the asset was sold for £8 000 less than it cost. This gain would be reduced by indexation relief applied to the allowable cost.

For leases of land and buildings the wasting formula is altered to give an assumed curved line loss of value over the last 50 years of the total life. There is no wasting factor while the lease still has more than 50 years to run. The formula is based on annual index numbers which are reproduced at the end of this chapter.[12] Using the same figures as in the previous example we get:

	£	£
Sale proceeds		10 000
less: Original cost	18 000	
less: wasting element:		
$18\,000 \times \dfrac{(46.695 - 21.938)}{46.695}$	9 526	8 474
Chargeable gain		£1 526

It will be seen that as the wastage increases year by year the wasting element is smaller than it was with the even spread used in the first calculation. The added effect of indexation is shown in Example 5.3.

CGT was first introduced into the UK from April 1965 and was not retrospective so it did not apply to gains accruing before that month. As the elapsed time since its introduction has moved beyond 20 years the number of pre-1965 assets still held by the same owners has declined but enough of them exist to make a brief reference to the calculation rules necessary.[13]

The calculation of gains on pre-1965 assets is based on the April 1965 value of the asset. For quoted shares and securities there will be a known market value as at 5 April 1965 and this is the one that is used. There may still be some problems in adjusting this value figure for subsequent bonus and rights issues and for shares exchanged in take-over operations. There have to be rules, too, for identifying which shares have been sold out of a holding of shares of the same company which were acquired at different times and which are being sold piecemeal. Examples 5.4 and 5.5 show how these rules work.

For many other assets the April 1965 market value is not so easily ascertained and the approach to these is to treat any gain as accruing evenly over the full period of ownership. Thus if land was purchased in 1962 for £50 000 and sold in 1987 for £300 000 the annual increase in value would be £10 000 and the value in 1965 treated as £80 000. (In practice the calculation takes parts of years into account.) Clearly the owner would prefer to use the actual value in 1965 if it exceeded £80 000 and this option is available – but he will have to provide good evidence for the alternative figure.

As with IT, CGT is only payable by an individual if the net gains (gains less losses) for a tax year exceed the threshold for that year. The level set for this threshold is high enough to exclude most small savers from liability but it can still catch the individual who has invested in a property and then sells it after many years of ownership. Gains above the threshold are taxed at a flat rate (see Appendix).

The taxation of gains realized by a husband and wife is consistent with the current treatment of their investment income as described in Chapter 4. They are treated as one unit and asset transfers between them are deemed to be at a price which produces neither chargeable gain nor allowable loss. They share one threshold and if either of them sells an asset acquired from the other spouse the deemed price at the time of the transfer between them is the figure to be used in calculating the gain or loss.[14]

In one special case the threshold is, in effect, increased. The owner of a business, having decided to sell it in order to retire, could find himself disadvantaged by a very high CGT liability on the disposal of assets which he may have owned for many years. This burden is reduced by retirement relief on business assets provided the business has been operated by him for at least one year and he is at least 60 years old (or retiring because of ill health if younger). The relief is on a sliding scale which relates to the qualifying conditions. These conditions are detailed and complicated and need to be met precisely. They may apply also to partners and to the owner/managers of private companies.[15]

Having seen in broad outline how the gains are calculated we can now turn to those transactions which are exempted from the tax. This means too that any losses suffered on them are not relieved. Exempt assets can be put into two categories, those exempted for policy reasons and those exempted for administrative reasons. The former group include the following.

1. *Owner-occupied residences.* This exemption is consistent with the IT relief for

mortgage interest but has an additional justification in that it removes a possible inhibition on labour mobility which could arise if moving jobs involved paying CGT on a change of house. The exemption extends to one further house per married couple or single person if that house is occupied by dependent relatives. Detailed rules cover such matters as overlapping ownership when a sale is delayed, choice of the exempt residence if two are owned and occupied concurrently, temporary absences from home and apportionment of the gain where part of the period of ownership does not qualify for the exemption. Problems may arise too where the house is occupied together with extensive grounds and parts of the grounds are sold separately.[16]

2. *Government securities and national savings.* An exemption is given for gains on government (gilt-edged) stocks[17] mainly because when CGT was introduced the government would have been open to the accusation that it had changed the terms of its contracts with the lenders unilaterally. The exemption now applies to certain company loan stocks. Many forms of national savings (SAYE, savings certificates and premium bonds) are issued on terms whereby they are exempt from CGT as well as IT.[18] This enables the government to issue them competitively at low nominal rates of interest.

3. *Life assurance polices.* The proceeds are exempt in the hands of the original beneficial owner but only because the underlying funds have been taxed already in the hands of the insurance company.[19]

4. *Gifts of assets of national, historic or scientific interest.* This ties up with a similar exemption from inheritance tax (Chapter 6) and is designed to encourage people to make such gifts for the benefit of the nation.[20]

5. *Prizes and betting winnings.* Prizes in general might not be worth bothering about but a tax on betting winnings could produce claims for relief on losses amounting in total to more than the gains (assuming that bookmaking is profitable).[21]

6. *Compensation or damages for personal or professional wrong or injury.* It would seem unjust to tax, say, the victim of a road accident on the compensation received for pain and suffering or the victim of an unpleasant libel on the recompense received. However, where compensation is paid for loss of earnings the amount awarded will allow for the fact that it is not taxable whereas the lost earnings would have been, and so the benefit of the exemption may go largely to the person paying the damages.[22]

The exemptions for administrative reasons arise largely from the fact that many small transactions take place, often between private individuals, and it would be neither practical nor cost effective to seek to tax them. The exempt assets include the following.

1. *Chattels which are wasting assets (unless used in a business).* These include all sorts of domestic appliances.[23]

2. *Non-wasting and business chattels (even if wasting – see 1) with a disposal value not exceeding £3 000.* This can cover items such as antique furniture. Where the value slightly exceeds £3 000 the liability is limited to a fraction of the excess. Arguments can arise as to whether chattels form part of a set or group which taken together is worth more than £3 000.[24]

3. *Currency for own maintenance abroad.* Losses are quite likely to outweigh any gains and amounts tend to be quite small.[25]

In the normal case, when an asset is sold for cash it is appropriate to charge the tax at that point. However, we have noted that a disposal may take place in the technical sense (a gift, for instance) without any cash being received. Such cases can receive the benefit of relief whereby the gain is 'rolled over' so that payment of the tax is delayed. We will look at three such cases.

1. When an asset is given away the donor realizes no cash from the transaction but becomes liable to CGT on the disposal. The problem of cash availability can be solved if both parties, donor and donee, make a joint election whereby the chargeable gain is deducted from the base value acquired by the donee.[26] Thus the donee would pay the tax but not until he disposes of the asset. Such an election would be pointless if the donor's gains for the year were within the CGT threshold. The detailed rules are devised so as to ensure that this relief cannot be given to the donor if the donee is in a position to avoid paying the tax in due course.

2. When one company acquires another the arrangement will often include an invitation to the shareholders in the victim company to accept shares and securities in the bidding company in return for their existing holdings. If they accept, those shareholders will have disposed of their original shares, not for cash but for new financial rights. In these circumstances the shareholders are treated as if they still owned the old shares at the old cost.[27] There is no calculated gain to 'roll over', but the original asset has, in effect, taken on a new name.

3. From an economic efficiency viewpoint the third case may be the most important. Managers may sell business assets in order to develop their business through the use of new, bigger and better assets. In those circumstances there is no need for the business to pay CGT on the old assets when they are sold. The gain is calculated and then deducted from the base cost of the new assets.[28] If the whole of the sum realized from the sale is not used for a qualifying purchase the CGT must be paid on that unused part of the sum or on the computed gain if less (see Example 5.6). The point of this relief is to ensure that businesses will not be inhibited in their expansion plans by the crystallization of a CGT liability. Again detailed rules must be satisfied but they are quite realistic in allowing for such probabilities as the new assets being acquired before the old ones are sold.

One of the reasons for the introduction of CGT was a belief that the existing definition of income left open too many tax-free avenues for increasing wealth. It was argued that income as defined in the Schedules was an incomplete measure of ability to pay (an equity argument) and tended to result in funds being sidetracked into tax-free investments (an economic efficiency argument). However, CGT deals with only one aspect of the income definition problem and we will now examine some of the others.

THE DEFINITION OF INCOME

We saw in Chapter 2 that income is defined in the UK by means of a list, viz. the Schedules and Cases. The legislation contains no general definition to which reference can be made or which supplies an underlying logic to the process of taxing income. If we search for a general definition the one most commonly quoted is that proposed by J.R. Hicks:

'Income is what a man can spend and still expect to be as well off at the end of the accounting period as he was at the beginning.'[29]

This definition raises some problems, especially as it depends on expectations, not hindsight, and requires a calculation of 'well-offness'. It would imply that gifts and inheritances would be taxed as part of income, a topic we shall look at in Chapter 6. It is, however, clear that it covers the kinds of income that are taxed already, wages, rents, dividends, trading profit and so on. Its possible effects in other situations will be seen if we consider three of them.

The first one relates to the ownership of assets. If an asset rises in value than the owner's 'well-offness' will be increased and that increase will, on the Hicks basis, be available to be spent. Thus it would be income. Note that it would be income of the period in which the rise in value took place, not when it was realized. Thus a decision to realize it would not affect tax liability. It can be argued that if the asset was not sold there would be no cash to pay the tax but this could be overcome by allowing deferral of the tax payment subject to an interest charge on the unpaid tax. The annual valuation problems would be formidable.

The second situation relates to the cash flow from an investment. If there is an investment of £100 at the beginning of the period and interest of £12 is received the income element under Hicks depends on the value of the investment at the end of the period. If its value in money terms is still £100 (e.g. a bank deposit) but because of rising prices the equivalent of the original 'well-offness' is £105 we find that the income is only £7. Many people would argue that this is more reasonable, albeit more complex, than the existing treatment as a high rate of interest reflects inflationary expectations.

Thirdly we must look at what is implied by the word 'spend'. It is apparent that Hicks had personal consumption in mind rather than spending which is undertaken to produce current or future income. Presumably business costs are not included but this leaves a hazy borderline if the spending has a dual purpose. Another problem lies with betting. If the bets placed are to be treated as spending then the gross winnings are income, which seems unfair if the income is to be taxed in full. If, however, the spending is the net cost (losses less wins) then betting is irrelevant to the income calculation as it then represents the result of one of the many choices available between spending to consume and spending to increase wealth. The latter is itself potential spending (i.e. it could be spent on consumption) and it should be remembered that the Hicks definition includes both actual and potential spending – 'what a man *can* spend'.

One attempt to use a Hicksian definition of income is found in the idea of a comprehensive income tax (CIT) which we will now consider. CIT has been discussed widely at various times and particularly in the report of the Canadian Royal Commission in 1966.[30] Its concept is that tax shall be levied annually on all accretions to economic power. All such accretions would be taxed at the same rate so that people would not gain or lose relatively just because their accretions came in one form rather than another. The ideal is one tax imposed on an annual total of income, accrued gains, windfalls and gifts and inheritances received.

The main advantage claimed for CIT, apart from the non-discriminatory treatment of all accretions, is that with a wider tax base the rate of tax could be reduced at the margin, thereby mitigating the impact on the economy of the substitution effect. It would replace or substantially reduce any existing tax on gifts and inheritances, but as we have seen the yield of these in the UK is quite small.

At first sight the idea of CIT is attractive, especially as it would reduce the economic distortions caused by the existence of different taxes at different rates. Unfortunately there are some serious problems which have prevented it from being adopted.[31] They include the following.

1. It would in practice be difficult and costly to calculate the annual rise in the value of many assets other than quoted shares and securities. This could be overcome by basing the tax on realized gains (treating death as a realization) and adding an interest element to remove the benefit of deferral. This could be done mathematically with an assumed straight-line growth in value, or a compounded constant rate of growth, the interest element being applied to each year's assumed gain or to the tax thereon.
2. There is a question whether the increase in the value of certain intangible assets such as pension rights and the value of increased skills (i.e. future earning capacity) should or could be brought into the tax net.
3. Comprehensive income could fluctuate widely from year to year. This would imply either the removal of progression from the tax system in favour of a proportional tax, or some averaging formula such as a five year moving average.
4. It raises the question of how profits retained by companies should be treated in taxing their shareholders (discussed further in Chapter 8).
5. It does nothing to deal with the problems created by the existence of general price inflation. We have seen that the present UK system is partly indexed. It seems that if CIT was adopted indexation would have to be all or nothing. If the former it would be complex, if the latter the result would be unfair.

However unlikely it may be that an attempt will be made to introduce CIT the concept is important because it brings out the features of one theoretical model and helps us to see more clearly some of the defects of the present arrangements, particularly in their effect on investment decisions.

Returning now to those arrangements, we noted in Chapter 3 that the rewards for personal financial investment may be taxed or untaxed and that the price of investments can be affected by these tax differentials (tax capitalization). One reason for widening the scope of IT to all accretions of spending power is to overcome the present situation in which investment decisions are distorted because of differences in the taxation effect. Let us now look at three aspects of this.

The first concerns differences between people. In the tax capitalization example on p. 45 we assumed an IT rate of 50% for both investments. This was convenient for a simple illustration but the true position is more complicated because people's IT rates differ, as do, in effect, their CGT rates (because of the large threshold). We will again assume two investment opportunities but this time the prices reflect tax capitalization. They are:

1. £100 (nominal) of loan stock, cost £105, interest 15% nominal, redemption in two years at £100
2. Ordinary shares, cost £105, dividends £5 per year, expected selling price in two years £115.

Now consider the tax position of three potential investors:

1. X is tax exempt.
2. Y pays IT at 29% but is below the CGT threshold.
3. Z pays IT at 50% and expects to be above the CGT threshold (tax at 30%).

Their rewards would be as follows if we ignore the time value of money and indexation of capital gains:

	X £	Y £	Z £
Loan stock:			
Interest (2 years)	30	30	30
less: Tax	—	8.7	15
	30	21.3	15
less:			
Loss on redemption (105 – 100)			
(assume no CGT relief)	(5)	(5)	(5)
	£25	£16.3	£10
Ordinary shares:			
Dividends (2 years)	10	10	10
less: Tax	—	2.9	5
	10	7.1	5
Capital gain (115–105)	10	10	10
less: CGT	— 10	— 10	3 7
	£20	£17.1	£12

It seems clear from these figures that X will buy the loan stock, Z will buy ordinary shares and Y will tend to buy the ordinary shares unless the risk category favours loan stock.

Three conclusions can be drawn from the example, all of which are valid in the real world.

1. Any particular type of investment is likely to attract investors of one tax category and those investors will therefore dominate the market in that security. Thus high coupon loan stocks will tend to attract investment only from tax exempt investors of whom the largest category in the UK consists of the pension funds. This leads to fragmentation of capital markets.
2. An organization, whether a business or a public authority, must take into account who is likely to provide funds and issue the appropriate kinds of financial instrument when raising those funds.
3. Because the ordinary shares are relatively more attractive to Z than to Y and the market price reflects that fact, Y should not invest solely to minimize his tax liability. The correct policy is to maximize net of tax returns. If Y decides to buy

shares it is because the return is £17.1 compared with £16.3 for the loan stock, not because the tax is £2.9 instead of £8.7.

The second of the three aspects concerns the relief for savings. We have seen that some types of savings are favoured and that, in particular, income invested in an approved pension scheme is effectively relieved from tax liability. We have seen too that under an expenditure tax this kind of special, and therefore distortionary, treatment would be eliminated by removing net savings from the tax base altogether. An alternative approach would be to tax all income without regard to savings of any kind. Thus under CIT there would be no relief for personal savings of any kind and they would no longer be channelled into particular forms of saving. It is arguable that the volume of savings would not be affected (especially if the marginal tax rate fell) and that the capital markets would work more efficiently in allocating funds to the most productive investments.

The present UK approach is typified by the Business Expansion Scheme (BES). Under this scheme amounts invested in small businesses can be deducted from the income of the investor for IT purposes.[32] Thus for a 60% IT rate payer an investment of £10 000 can be made at a cost of £4 000. The idea behind the scheme is that it encourages investment in risky businesses in the belief that they are the main sources of those new ideas which when developed will ensure better economic growth in general.

There are some problems with this approach, even if the legislation can be made watertight.

1. The scheme cannot exclude projects which would have taken place anyway, although their precise source of finance may be altered. To this extent the tax relief, which reduces the yield, is wasted.
2. The scheme may facilitate the development of projects with a very low rate of return for which there is no good economic case. In the example quoted above the investor may be quite content with a return of £8 000 after five years (the minimum period) and the benefit of the tax relief may, in effect, have been enjoyed by entrepreneurs who received salaries which were unjustified by the work done.

The ideal solution would seem to lie in the development of a capital market which is ready to provide funds to all deserving enterprises rather than creating further fragmentation by special tax reliefs. The BES has the further disadvantage that it complicates the tax system system especially as it has been found very difficult to define the approved categories in a way which excludes unintended beneficiaries.[33]

A third aspect which arises from the narrow definition of income is the way in which the tax burden on the rewards of investment may be reduced by the use of tax shelters. We have seen already that there are different rates of tax on income and gains and that investments are exempt from tax (some national savings) or are taxed in a special way (building societies and banks). These factors should affect the investment decisions of taxpayers of all kinds and of those who pay no tax at all. In the case of higher rate taxpayers the optimum investment policy faces even wider opportunities because of the existence of tax shelters. In one sense an investment in ordinary shares uses the company as a tax shelter, profits retained in the company adding unrealized value to the shares while suffering only the company's tax rate at a maximum of 35%. The benefit of the pension fund exemption is also greater for the high rate taxpayer as the fund can reinvest 100% of its investment income whereas he could only reinvest 40% of his (if he pays IT at the top rate of 60%).

The point of these and of many other tax shelters is that the income received by the institution on its invested funds is not allocated immediately to the individual and must therefore be taxed, if at all, at some general overall rate. A common example is the use of endowment policies with life assurance companies. Funds are placed in the hands of the company to be accumulated (subject to a deduction for the cost of providing cover for early death) over a period of some years. At the end of the agreed period the accumulated funds are returned to the investor and no further tax is due from him. The benefit may be considerable as the company pays tax on its investment income at a rate of 35%,[34] a significant advantage when compared with IT at 60%. Of course, if the earlier discussion is borne in mind it will be appreciated that the investments chosen by the insurance company would not be the same as those which would have been chosen by the investor if he had invested directly, and indeed this may add a little to the advantage obtained.

The advantage of tax shelters could be exploited by the use of very short-term contracts which have the effect of giving the investor the benefit of the lower tax rates almost on a year-by-year basis because he realizes his tax-free entitlement frequently. However, this idea has been restricted by legislation which requires the term of the investment to be for a minimum period, failing which higher rate tax is charged.[35]

More sophisticated tax shelters have been devised, using in particular the opportunity to invest funds abroad. Some of them have been countered by legislation but opportunities still remain. These are beyond the scope of this book.

NON-MONETARY BENEFITS – EMPLOYEES

The discussion so far has been concerned with monetary benefits and the possibility of taxing them when they arise other than as 'income' paid directly to the individual recipient. However, not all taxable benefits come in monetary form and in this section and the next we will look at some of these non-monetary benefits as part of our general theme of expanding the definition of income beyond the simple idea of a regular annual cash flow.

The first group of such benefits are those received by employees. Although they receive their main reward in the form of cash the desire to avoid paying tax has led to the development of other forms of reward, not all of which have been successful from a tax saving point of view. The potential value of such devices is emphasized by the clear decisions of the courts many years ago that cash payments for doing a job are taxable whether received from the employer or from elsewhere (e.g. tips, contractual rights to collections from spectators and so on).[36]

Originally the general question of non-monetary benefits was considered by the courts when employees appealed against the Inland Revenue's attempts to tax them. The principle laid down by the courts was that the value of such benefits was taxable if it was 'money's worth', a phrase which means that it was convertible into cash or represented payment by the employer of the employee's own liability.

An example of a benefit convertible into cash can be found in a scheme under which employees were given the right to use a company car for their own private purposes. The car could not be used to produce cash directly (it could not be hired to another person) but the court decided that the benefit was taxable because the cash wages of those employees who had cars were reduced below the normal level and would be restored to their full amount if the car was surrendered.[37]

In another case the value of a new suit provided by the employer (and supplied directly by a tailor whose contract was with the company not the employee) was held to be assessable to tax but only to the extent of the realizable value, a mere fraction of its cost.[38] In an earlier case an employer agreed to pay wages 'free of tax'. It was held that the employer was paying the employee's own liability for him and so the taxable income was the wage plus the tax due grossed up.[39] This meant that if the cash wage was £5 000 and the tax on £5 000 was £1 000 with a marginal rate of tax of 25% (say) above £5 000, the grossed up wage (W) liable to tax would be:

$$W = 5\,000 + 1\,000 \times \frac{100}{75} = £6\,333$$

	£
Tax thereon: on 5 000	1 000
on 1 333 at 25%	333
	£1 333

One of the main issues tackled in the case law was the provision of living accommodation for the employee. Often an employee has to live on the premises in order to do his job properly. This can apply to people such as caretakers, policemen and bank managers. The courts took the view that they were not 'beneficial occupiers', but occupied the accommodation merely as representatives of the employer who was the true 'occupier'. Thus they escaped tax on the benefit.[40] These principles have since been modified by legislation so that, for instance, the director of a hotel company may have to pay tax on the benefit he enjoys by living in part of the hotel rent free even though he is there to manage the hotel.[41]

Using the principles laid down by the courts employers still found it possible to devise non-monetary benefits which escaped tax liability and this led to legislation which was designed to restrict the tax advantages.[42] The legislation is directed at company directors and senior employees, leaving others to be dealt with under the case law principles on the assumption that only the former are likely to enjoy significant benefits. The main benefits caught by this legislation are as follows.

1. Company cars, the most common benefit, are treated as income of the user according to a scale of annual sums which vary with the type of car and the degree of business use (see Appendix).[43] Additional tax may also be due if the company pays for the petrol. It has been asserted that for most users the scale of benefits assessed does not reflect fully the value received.[44]
2. The provision of services and furniture, etc., in connection with living accommodation, the value assessed being the cost of the services plus 20% of the cost of assets supplied for use by the director or employee.[45]
3. The full value of any vouchers or credit cards supplied by the company and used by the employee.[46]

4. The cost of medical insurance paid by the company unless it is taken out to cover business trips abroad.[47]
5. Loans may be made to employees at a preferential rate, a common practice of banks and other financial institutions. In such cases there is a taxable benefit equal to the normal rate of interest less any interest actually paid by the employee, but this benefit is not taxed when the interest would have been tax deductible if it had been actually paid by the employee, on the purchase of his home for instance.[48]

Not all benefits are caught by the legislation and some are specifically excluded from it. A company can provide free or subsidized meals for all employees without them being treated as taxable benefits. The provision of pension rights is exempt, as will be apparent from the earlier discussion. Finally, it is possible for a company to issue its own shares to employees on favourable terms without adding to their taxable incomes provided it is done in conformity with legislative requirements and limitations.[49]

Thus it is clear that, whilst many non-monetary benefits are caught, advantage can be taken of the permitted exemptions and of the underestimation of the value of benefits. Nevertheless, in an ideal world it is better for the employee to have the cash to spend as he wishes. Benefits in kind leave him with no individual choice.[50] Perhaps he does not like the style of food served in the canteen and would prefer to eat elsewhere if he was given the cash.

One final form of employee benefit is hidden rather than non-monetary. A director, senior employee or salesman may be given cash to cover out of pocket expenses while travelling, entertaining and so on. If this money is given too generously it forms part of the reward for the job and the legislation seeks to ensure that any excess payments are taxed. It does this by placing the onus on the director or employee to show that the money received has been spent in such a way as to satisfy the Schedule E expenses rule.[51]

OTHER NON-MONETARY BENEFITS

We will now turn away from employee benefits to look at other types of non-monetary benefits. Here the issues are not so clear cut and they have produced a considerable amount of discussion and argument.

We will start with the owner-occupied house. The problem can be posed by means of a simplified example. We suppose that the potential house owner can either buy a house for £50 000 or pay rent of £5 000 per year. If he decides to buy we assume he will either sell investments which currently produce £5 000 per year, or borrow £50 000 at an interest rate of 10%, the interest being fully tax deductible (despite the present restriction in the UK). A tax rate of 40% will be used. The result is set out in Table 5.1

The rent is not tax deductible because it represents consumption out of taxed income, but then we find that purchase of the house is preferable either because the loan interest is tax deductible or because investments are realized and the loss of income on them is mitigated by the reduction in tax payable. Thus merely removing the tax relief for the interest paid does not remove the discrepancy between the buy and rent decisions.

Now it may be the deliberate policy of the government to encourage people to buy houses for their own occupation rather than pay rent, but there will always be those who prefer to rent, possibly for good economic and financial reasons such as having a

Table 5.1 Methods of financing accommodation

| | Buy House | | Rent house |
	Sell investments	Borrow	
	£	£	£
Investment income	0	5000	5000
less: tax	0	(2000)	(2000)
Net income (A)	£0	£3000	£3000
Interest paid	0	5000	0
less: Tax relief	0	(2000)	0
Rent paid (no tax relief)	0	0	5000
Net outgoings (B)	£0	£3000	£5000
Net 'cost' (B–A)	0	0	2000

job which involves frequent changes of location (chain store managers, for instance).

One device that could be introduced and which would remove the discrepancy would be to treat the house as producing a notional income on which the owner–occupier is taxable.[52] If ownership of the house was deemed to produce an income of £5000 the additional tax bill in the first two columns of Table 5.1 would result in all three cases having the same net cost. It would then be rational to allow a deduction for interest paid without restriction as the bigger the house and loan the bigger would be both the notional income and the actual deduction. Of course in practice the figures would not be so well balanced as they appear in Table 5.1, not least because of distortions in the market for rented housing and the effect of inflationary expectations on interest rates, but the basis of the argument should be clear.

Similar arguments can be used in respect of other assets which produce non-pecuniary benefits. If I sell investments in order to buy a yacht in which I hope to cruise around the Mediterranean each summer the opportunity cost of this piece of conspicuous consumption is reduced by the tax that is no longer payable on the investment income. In theory the same argument can be applied to motor cars and other assets used for leisure purposes but in practice it would only be possible to look at the more expensive items. Wherever the line was drawn equity would require that the cost of borrowing to buy the asset which was deemed to produce income would have to be deductible.[53]

Apart from the use by an employee of his employer's assets no tax charge on notional income is made in the UK at present although one did exist on owner–occupied housing until 1963, albeit the values used had become hopelessly out of date. The possibility of re-introduction seems to be remote, not least because of the effect of tax capitalization on the price of houses. Large numbers of people have entered into long-term commitments in the belief that the present system of liability and relief will continue.

The idea of income being deemed to exist where there is no cash flow is not confined to the ownership of assets. In a variety of circumstances people perform economically useful activities without receiving any reward. It has been observed in the courts that any attempt to treat as income the value of professional services provided free to charitable organizations would be neither practical nor desirable.[54]

Nevertheless the question does merit some further discussion and once again there is a problem of where to draw the line. Let us look at the effect of tax on decisions about house maintenance and decoration. This is undertaken to maintain or improve the value of an asset and is therefore both economically useful in general and valuable to the owner of the asset. Consider two ways in which it may be done, do-it-yourself (DIY) by the owner or the use of an independent builder and decorator who accounts properly for his tax liability. Either way there will be a cost of materials used, which we can assume to be identical, and a cost of labour which will differ between the two cases. If we assume also that the potential DIY owner would work longer hours in his normal job if he decided to pay a builder and decorator we might find a cost comparison as follows.

	DIY	Employ builder
	£	£
Loss of wages, say	1 000	
less: Tax thereon	290	
	£710	
Payment for labour etc.		1 000

We can now see that the financial cost to the owner is lower if he chooses DIY because of the tax payable on his extra wages. The tax revenue suffers twice, first by the loss of tax on the wages not earned and then on the builder's lost income. To put it another way there is a double tax penalty if you employ a builder and decorator.

It is hardly realistic to solve this problem by charging the house owner with tax on the value of his own work (which he may in any case regard as a form of leisure), but the example does bring out the scope for economic distortion and it may have the incidental effect of reducing the professional standards of workmanship on the nation's housing stock!

Two particular examples of this sort of activity throw light on some of the difficulties that may have to be overcome in designing a satisfactory tax system. The first is the subsistence farmer. In parts of the world an important part of a country's economy consists of the family farm or smallholding which produces a high proportion of the total consumption needs of the family, certainly so far as food is concerned. Such activity may produce very little cash income and this fact, combined with illiteracy, means that the calculation of a realistic income figure is impossible.

It will be appreciated that subsistence agriculture is no more than DIY on a large scale. If I operate a smallholding with the aim of producing most of my own food, some clothing, maintaining my dwelling and so on, then I will hope to make do with only a small cash income to pay for those things I have to buy in and to represent any surplus. Where such activity is common or predominant people can only be taxed, if at all, on an approximate basis, perhaps related to the amount and quality of the land they farm. This means that they are being taxed on notional income, not cash income.[55] In fact UK farmers were taxed in this way until 1948.

The second example is the non-working wife. It may be argued that her services to the household should be deemed to be rewarded as if she were an employed housekeeper. The effect of doing so depends to some extent on the design of the tax system as it affects married couples, but one consequence would be that it would be fairer to the single person who employs a housekeeper (full or part-time) and it would mean that in so far as the deemed income disappeared when the wife went out to work in paid employment she would not be inhibited from doing so by the need to pay a housekeeper in pre-tax terms out of her own net of tax wage. Again the discussion really relates to the idea that the wife has a tax incentive to 'do it herself' whereas economic optimization might suggest that her talents should be used where they are most effective, possibly not in household duties.

AN ANNUAL WEALTH TAX

Another idea which ties in with the preceding discussion was under active consideration in the UK a few years ago. This was an annual wealth tax, and it forms an appropriate topic with which to end this chapter.

The essential feature of the tax is that it is an annual tax and that it is based on an annual valuation of wealth. It need not be a confiscatory tax as it may replace all or part of an existing income tax on the cash flows resulting from the ownership of the assets concerned. Suppose, for instance, that I own assets worth £10000 and that these produce an income of £1000 per year. Under an income tax system the income is taxed at, say, 29% to give a liability of £290. Under an annual wealth tax levied at 2.9% of asset value the same tax would be payable. It is clear that in this example the two taxes have the same effect.

However, the wealth tax would have two features not present in an income tax.

1. It would relate the tax to asset value, not to income yield. Thus if the investment in the example consisted of ordinary shares with growth potential but paying a dividend of only 5% the wealth tax would impose a relatively greater burden than an income tax.
2. The wealth tax could be imposed on assets such as valuable pictures and antiques which produce no cash income. It would only be possible to levy an income tax in such cases if notional income was deemed to exist on the lines discussed in the previous section (e.g. on my Mediterranean yacht).

The imposition of wealth tax is a very contentious matter as will be apparent if we now summarize the arguments for and against.[56]

Arguments in favour of a wealth tax

1. An annual wealth tax replacing an income tax would reduce the distortion in investment decisions. Under an income tax any cash benefits are reduced by the tax whereas the non-monetary benefits (the pleasure and prestige of dining with antique silver) are enjoyed in full. Tax capitalization will have occurred so distorting the relative market prices.
2. A risky investment which turns out well may be taxed heavily if the reward consists of monetary income. Under a wealth tax future liability may be increased but the value of the asset in the earlier years would reflect the uncertainty about the outcome and would not be increased retrospectively. Thus the wealth tax would reduce some of the disincentive to risk-taking.

3. It has been argued that wealth is itself part of a person's taxable capacity and that equity requires that it be taken into account. Two people whose incomes are identical are not in a similar position if one has greater wealth than the other. It may be recognized that this argument is a variant on the idea adopted in the UK until 1984 whereby investment income was taxed more heavily than earned income.
4. A government which seeks to achieve some redistribution of income and wealth is likely to find an annual wealth tax a superior instrument to either IT or CGT. Under these taxes rich people find many alternative havens for their wealth when looking for ways to reduce their tax liability. It is widely recognized that high rates of IT alone have only a minimal redistributive effect on a well advised wealthy man.[57]

Arguments against a wealth tax

1. A re-distributive wealth tax could be very difficult to enforce except against those whose wealth was both 'visible' and confined to their home country. A very rich man with his investments spread worldwide would almost certainly escape by avoidance or evasion or both, even if there were currency and capital transfer controls round the borders of his home country. Thus the tax might hit the moderately rich harder than the very rich.
2. There are some quite difficult equity problems in defining the wealth that is to be taxed. These are discussed at greater length later in this section.
3. The tax would require an annual valuation of all personal wealth. For some people this would be easy enough, but for others it would be both subjective and expensive. Even such common assets as land and buildings, shares in family companies and jewellery would present valuation problems and they are by no means the most difficult.
4. Many valuable assets could be hidden quite easily. There would be a tendency to distort investment into assets such as jewellery and precious metals. In so far as these have world, rather than national, prices the tax capitalization effect would be small.
5. As the wealth tax would be imposed irrespective of cash income there could be difficulties in collecting the tax, especially if the main asset is illiquid or indivisible. Thus assets which are held to long-term maturity (forests, malt whisky) would be taxable but would produce no immediate cash flow. One solution might be to limit the tax to some proportion of total cash income but that destroys its main intention.
6. The combined effect of all these points is that the tax would be expensive to collect, both administratively and in terms of compliance costs. Attempts to reduce these costs by simplifying the tax and reducing its scope detract from the theoretical virtues described under the advantages above.

As was suggested in the second of the disadvantages above there are some very real difficulties in arriving at a satisfactory definition of wealth. Most people would say that they have a good idea of what is meant by wealth. These ideas are reinforced by knowledge of the existing taxes levied on wealth transfers when someone dies. However, those taxes relate to identifiable events which in themselves crystallize the nature and value of the assets concerned. An annual wealth tax lacks the benefit of this crystallization and we shall see the problem this creates if we look at three kinds of asset.

Trusts are legal devices whereby assets are held by trustees for the benefit of others. They do not exist solely for tax reasons. They may be set up so that assets can be administered on behalf of young children, or a man may wish to leave assets to his children but retain them in trust so that the income can be used to support his widow during her lifetime.

Some of the problems that would arise in taxing trust assets apply equally to the taxation of trust income. Tax laws seek to ensure that trusts are not used to hide assets and income from the full impact of the taxation liability which is intended to be levied on those who benefit from them. Thus in the case of a life tenant (the widow in the example given in the previous paragraph) it may be argued that the trust assets should be taxed under an annual wealth tax as if they belonged to her although she has no right of access to them.

More difficult is the trust which is discretionary in the sense that the trustees have power to distribute income to all or any of a group of beneficiaries. It cannot be said that anyone in that group is entitled at any time to either income or assets. If the wealth tax has a progressive structure it will be necessary to define a share in such assets, determined perhaps by the share of income received from the trust in the past year. Even that would not solve the problem if the trustees have power to add income to the trust capital and distribute none of it.

A second kind of problem asset is the pension fund. These now own a considerable proportion of the nation's financial assets so they cannot be dismissed as a trivial matter. As we have seen their expansion is itself the result of tax advantages. One effect of their growth is that the distribution of wealth in the UK is quite different if pension rights are taken into account.[58]

There is a strong equity argument for the inclusion of pension rights in the base for a wealth tax. If a man saves and invests in an informal way to provide for his retirement he would be liable to wealth tax on the assets so acquired. It follows that another man who saves through a formal scheme should likewise be taxed on his share of the assets of the scheme.

Unfortunately a pensioner's share of the assets in a pension fund cannot be easily or reliably calculated. The fund may have thousands of potential pensioners of varying ages and lengths of pensionable service. Some of them may leave their employer before they retire and lose all or part of their pension entitlement. Furthermore, the calculation of the present value of future pension rights depends on several variables such as the expected pension, duration of life, date of retirement and the discount rate to be used. It is easy to show that small changes in these assumptions can make a considerable difference to the final figure.

Thus the equity case for including the present value of future pension rights (including the state pension) seems to be clear, but the impossibility of arriving at an objective figure means that they could only be included in a wealth tax on some more or less arbitrary basis.

The third kind or problem asset presents the same difficulties as pension rights, only more so. The value of human capital is the present value of future earning power resulting from the acquisition of additional skills. The argument for including it in a wealth tax base runs as follows. If I have some spare cash I may invest it and would then have greater wealth and would have increased my expected future income as a result. One alternative is to use the cash to increase my skills (perhaps I decide to learn more about computers) and as a result I have again increased my expected future income. If equity is to be maintained both forms of wealth should be taxed.

It is clear that any such idea is fraught with practical difficulties. The cost of acquiring my new skills can be measured, but that is an input measure, not a measure of the resulting value (the output measure). Again that value will depend on the future expected flows suitably discounted. It is unlikely in the end that the concept of human capital will be taken seriously as a policy proposal.

A final point may be made. In the case of skills and pension rights no problem arises on valuations at the date of death as they must be zero. The difficulties relate only to an annual wealth tax and not to the other capital taxes to which we shall turn in the next chapter.

EXAMPLES

These examples are based on the tax rates and reliefs for 1986/87. For other years see Appendix.

Example 5.1 Part disposal

A bought a plot of land freehold for £50 000. Two years later he was approached by B who wished to acquire part of the plot and a price of £15 000 was agreed. By that time the rest of the plot was valued at £45 000.

Ignoring indexation (covered in Example 5.2 below) and incidental costs the chargeable gain would be:

		£
Sale proceeds		15 000
less: Cost × £50 000 × $\dfrac{£15,0000}{£15\,000 + £45\,000}$		12 500
Gain		£2 500

If this was A's only gain for the year no CGT liability would arise as the threshold is £6 300.

If the rest of the plot was sold later the unindexed cost would be taken as £50 000 – £12 500 = £37 500.

Example 5.2 Indexation

(a) *Asset acquired after March 1982.* C acquired an asset for £20 000 in June 1982 when the official index (see Appendix) stood at 322.9. He sold the asset for £24 000 in March 1986 when the index stood at 381.6.

	£	£
Proceeds		24 000
less: Cost	20 000	
Index factor:		
$20\,000 \times \dfrac{(381.6 - 322.9)}{322.9}$	3 640	23 640
Chargeable gain (subject to threshold)		£360

Note: The index number calculation produces a result of 0.18179, but this is rounded to 0.182 in accordance with s. 87 (4), Finance Act 1982.

(b) *Asset acquired before April 1982.* The facts are the same as in (a) except that the asset was purchased in June 1980 and its value in March 1982 was estimated at £22 000. The March 1982 index number is 313..4

	£	£
Proceeds		24 000
less: Cost	20 000	
Indexation factor:		
$22\,000 \times \dfrac{(381.6 - 313.4)}{313.4}$	4 796	24 796
Capital loss		£796

Indexation creates a loss which can be used against gains of the same or following years.

Example 5.3 Wasting assets with indexation

D acquired a 20 year lease on 25 March 1983 at a cost of £20 000. The lease was sold for £22 000 on 25 March 1986. The gain is calculated as follows:

	£	£
Sale proceeds		22 000
less: Cost	20 000	
Wasting element (deducted):		
$20\,000 \times \dfrac{(72.770 - 66.470)}{72.770}$	1 731	
	18 269	
Indexation (added):		
$18\,269 \times \dfrac{(381.6 - 327.9)}{327.9}$	2 996	21 265
Chargeable gain		£735

Note how the indexation factor is based on the allowable element of the original cost.

Example 5.4 Shares owned on 6 April 1965

E purchased 100 quoted ordinary shares in F plc at a price of £2.50 each on 1 April 1960. On 1 October 1968 F made a one-for-one bonus issue. E sold all of his shares for £5.20 each on 20 March 1986. The share price on 6 April 1965 was £2.25 and on 31 March 1982 was £3.80. Transaction costs have been ignored.

	£	£
Sale proceeds (200 × £5.20)		1040
Original cost (100 × 2.50)	250	
Value at 6.4.65	220	
Use option to take the higher price	250	
Indexation allowance:		
Value at 31.3.82 (200 × £3.80 = 760):		
$760 × \dfrac{(381.6 - 313.4)}{313.4}$	166	416
Chargeable gain		£624

Example 5.5 Identification of shares sold

G purchased shares in H plc as follows:-

1 March 1962	100 shares for	£800
20 March 1970	100 shares for	£1750
15 March 1983	100 shares for	£3400
14 March 1985	100 shaes for	£4200

On 20 March 1986 he sold 150 shares for £7100.

(a) Shares purchased on or after 1 April 1982 are pooled. Thus for the last two purchases we get:

	Number	Cost	Indexation (see notes below)	Pool value
		£	£	£
Cost 15.3.83	100	3400	558[1]	3958
Cost 14.4.85	100	4200	88[2]	4288
Value at 20.3.86	200			8246

Note 1: $3400 × \dfrac{(381.6 - 327.9)}{327.9} = 558$

Note 2: $4200 × \dfrac{(381.6 - 373.9)}{373.9} = 88$

(b) Share sales are identified with the last ones purchased but treating the post-April 1982 pool as one holding. Thus we get:

		£
Sale proceeds		7 100
less: Pool at 20.3.86 $\dfrac{(8\,246 \times 150)}{200}$		6 185
Chargeable gain		£915

The pool goes forward as (8 246 – 6 185) = £2 061 with further indexation for any later sale.

Example 5.6 Roll-over relief

J Ltd. sold the goodwill and freehold premises of one of its branches for £150 000. The chargeable gain is calculated at £72 000.

Three months later it purchased new freehold premises for £200 000.

The chargeable gain of £72 000 can be rolled over and the cost of the new premises is then deemed (for CGT purposes) to be £200 000 – £72 000 = £128 000.

If the new premises had cost only £125 000 and the rest of the sale proceeds of £150 000 used to finance working capital the rolled-over gain would have been restricted to £48 000, i.e. £72 000 – (£150 000 – £125 000), and CGT would have been payable on the balance of £25 000.

NOTES AND REFERENCES

1. S. 1 and Part II, CGT Act 1979.
2. S. 79, Finance Act 1980.
3. S. 20, CGT Act 1979.
4. *O'Brien* v. *Benson's Hosiery (Holdings) Ltd.* (1979) 53 TC 241, 3 All ER 652.
5. Ss. 25–26, CGT Act 1979.
6. *Floor* v. *Davis* (1979) 52 TC 609, 2 All ER 677.
7. Ss. 31–33, CGT Act 1979.
8. S. 35, CGT Act 1979.
9. Ss. 4, 5 and 29, CGT Act 1979. The losses brought forward are not to be used in so far as the gains are already covered by the annual threshold. Any balance not used is carried forward to the following year.
10. S. 68 and 19th Schedule, Finance Act 1985.
11. Ss. 37–39, CGT Act 1979.
12. 3rd Schedule, CGT Act 1979 – reproduced in Table 5.2.
13. 5th Schedule, CGT Act 1979.
14. Ss. 44–45, CGT Act 1979.
15. Ss. 124–125, CGT Act 1979, and Ss. 69–70 and 20th Schedule, Finance Act 1985. For a full exposition see Slevin, K. S., *Retirement Relief*, C.C.H. Editions, Bicester (1986).
16. Ss. 101–105, CGT Act 1979, and see *Varty* v. *Lynes* (1976) 51 TC 403, 3 All ER 447, and *Batey* v. *Wakefield* (1981) 55 TC 550, (1980) 1 All ER 61.
17. S. 67, CGT Act 1979, and s. 67, Finance Act 1985.

Table 5.2 Index numbers – leases

Years	Percentage	Years	Percentage
50 (or more)	100	25	81.100
49	99.657	24	79.622
48	99.289	23	78.055
47	98.902	22	76.399
46	98.490	21	74.635
45	98.059	20	72.770
44	97.595	19	70.791
43	97.107	18	68.697
42	96.593	17	66.470
41	96.041	16	64.116
40	95.457	15	61.617
39	94.842	14	58.971
38	94.189	13	56.167
37	93.497	12	53.191
36	92.761	11	50.038
35	91.981	10	46.695
34	91.156	9	43.154
33	90.280	8	39.399
32	89.354	7	35.414
31	88.371	6	31.195
30	87.330	5	26.722
29	86.226	4	21.983
28	85.053	3	16.959
27	83.816	2	11.629
26	82.496	1	5.983
		0	0

If the duration of the lease is not an exact number of years the percentage to be derived from the Table above shall be the percentage for the whole number of years plus one twelfth of the difference between that and the percentage for the next higher number of years for each odd month counting an odd 14 days or more as one month.

Source: Capital Gains Tax Act 1979, Schedule 3.

18. S.71, CGT Act 1979.
19. S.140, CGT Act 1979.
20. S.147, CGT Act 1979.
21. S.19 (4), CGT Act 1979.
22. S.19 (5), CGT Act 1979, and *British Transport Commission* v. *Gourlay* (1955) 3 All ER 796.
23. S.127, CGT Act 1979.
24. S.128, CGT Act 1979.
25. S.133, CGT Act 1979.
26. S.79, Finance Act 1980.
27. S.85, CGT Act 1979.
28. Ss.115–121, CGT Act 1979.
29. Hicks, J.R., *Value and Capital: An Enquirty into some Fundamental Principles of Economic Theory*, 2nd edn., Oxford University Press, Oxford (1946), at page 172.

30. *Report of the Royal Commission on Taxation*, Queen's Printer, Ottowa, Canada (1966).
31. See Chapter 7 of The Institute for Fiscal Studies, *The Structure and Reform of Direct Taxation* (The Meade Committee), Allen and Unwin, London (1978).
32. S.26 and 5th Schedule, Finance Act 1983, as amended.
33. For instance, 9th Schedule, Finance Act 1986, contains 21 paragraphs which aim to eliminate 'misuse' of the scheme as originally intended.
34. S.310, Taxes Act 1970, and S.18, Finance Act 1984.
35. The legislation is complex but its main effect is to charge higher rate tax (but not basic rate tax) on the gain received.
36. See, for instance, *Calvert* v. *Wainwright* (1947) 27 TC 475, 1 All ER 282, and *Moorhouse* v. *Dooland* (1954) 36 TC 1, 1 All ER 93.
37. *Heaton* v. *Bell* (1970) 46 TC 211, (1969) 2 All ER 70.
38. *Wilkins* v. *Rogerson* (1960) 39 TC 344, (1961) 1 All ER 358.
39. *Hartland* v. *Diggines* (1926) 10 TC 247, AC 289.
40. *Bent* v. *Roberts* (1877) 1 TC 199, *Tennant* v. *Smith* (1892) 3 TC 158, AC 150.
41. S.33, Finance Act 1977.
42. See ss.60–72, 7th and 8th Schedules, Finance Act 1976, as amended.
43. An adjustment is made too in calculating the employer's VAT liability – see Chapter 10.
44. The Chancellor of the Exchequer (Mr Nigel Lawson) made the point in his budget speech on 19 March 1985.
45. Ss.33–34, Finance Act 1977. S.34 inserts a s.63A into Finance Act 1976.
46. Ss.36–37, Finance (No.2) Act 1975, and s.71, Finance Act 1981.
47. S.62, Finance Act 1976, as amended by s.72, Finance Act 1981.
48. S.66, Finance Act 1976.
49. 10th Schedule, Finance Act 1984.
50. See, for instance, Kay, J.A. and King, M.A., *The British Tax System*, Oxford University Press, Oxford (1983), in Chapter 3 (page 50).
51. S.60, Finance Act 1976.
52. For a discussion of this topic see Royal Commission on the Taxation of Profits and Income, *Final Report*, Cmd. 9474, HMSO, London (1955), Chapter 28.
53. Strictly the cost of borrowing should be the real cost, not a nominal rate of interest which may include inflationary expectations.
54. In *Mason* v. *Ines* (1967) 44 TC 326, 2 All ER 926. See the judgement of Lord Denning in the Court of Appeal.
55. For a brief discussion see Muten, L., 'Leading issues of tax policy in developing countries', in Peacock, A. and Forte, F., *The Political Economy of Taxation*, Basil Blackwell, Oxford (1981).
56. For a fuller discussion see Chapter 16 of the Meade Committee's report (referenced at note 31 above), and the Green Paper, *Wealth Tax*, Cmnd.5704, HMSO, London (1974).
57. A good idea of the many possibilities for minimizing tax liability can be derived from a study of *Tolley's Tax Planning*, Tolley Publishing, Croydon (published annually).
58. See *Report No.1* of the Royal Commission on the Distribution of Income and Wealth, Cmnd.6171, HMSO, London (1975).

EXERCISES AND DISCUSSION TOPICS

1. (a) Calculate the assessable capital gains arising on the following sales.
   (i) Mr F has been in business as a retail grocer for 8 years. In June 1986 when he was aged 63½ he sold one of his two shops at a gain, after indexation, of £72 000

(ii)   Mr G bought a holiday home for £22 500 in June 1982 and gave it to his wife in January 1985. Mrs G sold it in October 1986 for £35 000.

(iii) Mr H purchased 2 000 shares in Redro plc in June 1981 for £3 460. On 31 March 1982 these were quoted at £1.70 per share. Further purchases were made as follows:

July 1982   1 000 shares costing   £1 850
August 1984   1 200 shares costing   £1 540

He sold all his shares in Redro plc, with the exception of 500, in September 1986 for £6 950.

(b) Mr J bought an oil painting in December 1985 and sold it in November 1984 for £2 825. Calculate the allowable loss.

(c) In April 1986 Mr K sold part of his collection of fourteenth century Chinese jade for £22 500. He had inherited the collection from his uncle, who died in January 1973, when it was valued for probate purposes at £20 000. The value of the part retained was agreed at £13 500, and that of the whole at 31 March 1982 at £30 000. Calculate the gain arising on the sale and the cost, for future capital gains purposes, of the part retained.

ICSA, December 1985 (Question updated.)

2. (a) Giles bought 150 acres of land for £187 500 on 1 May 1983. On 1 July 1984 he sold, for £9 250, a five-acre field, which had been included in the original purchase. On 1 July 1984 the 150 acres were valued at £215 000. The remaining 145 acres were sold on 1 October 1986 for £230 000.

You are required to calculate Giles' capital gain for 1986/87 (before annual exemption) on the assumption that he elected to defer any gain on the disposal on 1 July 1984 until the subsequent disposal. Ignore costs of acquisition and disposal.

(b) Freda sold a house to her daughter Susan for £10 000 on 1 November 1983. The market value of the house at the time of sale was £30 000 and the house had been purchased by Freda in 1973 for £8 000. It had never been Freda's main residence. Susan sold the house through an estate agent on 1 September 1985 for £35 000.

You are required to calculate:

(i)   the capital gain, if any, chargeable on Freda in 1983/84 (before annual exemption), assuming that any relevant relief is claimed by both Freda and Susan;

(ii)   the capital gain then assessable on Susan in 1985/86 (before annual exemption).

Ignore costs of acquisition and disposal.

(c) Alan acquired a 55 year lease of a retail shop for £32 000 on 1 October 1970. On 20 August 1982 he extended the premises at a cost of £20 000. On 1 October 1985 he sold the lease for £75 000. The value of the lease on 31 March 1982 was £50 000.

You are required to calculate the capital gain assessable on Alan for 1985/86 (before annual exemption).

Note: The sale proceeds of land can be deducted from the cost carried forward where they amount to less than 5% of the total value and £20000.

ACCA, *Level 2, June 1986* (Part of question updated.)

3.
Wendy House
Ascot

B I Gears
A Lyons & Co
London SW5 7XQ

25 April 1987

Dear Mr Gears

I recently inherited £100000 on the death of my father. I intend to retain £5000 in a building society for immediate needs and the balance of £95000 will be invested as follows:

	£
Unit trusts	10000
National Savings Certificates	10000
Single premium life assurance policies (known as investment bonds)	15000
Antiques	20000
Government stocks	15000
Ordinary shares in public companies quoted on the Stock Market	20000
Hire-A-Gnome Ltd. – qualifying for income tax relief under the business expansion scheme	5000
	£95000

You will no doubt have gathered that my purpose in arranging matters thus is to achieve capital growth. I am somewhat concerned though that I may have a capital gains tax liability on that growth. I should be grateful for a brief explanation of the position if I realize any of the above assets at a profit. You will be aware that neither myself nor my wife has any other assets of a material nature.

Yours sincerely
Peter Pannett

You are required to write a letter to Mr Pannett explaining the capital gains tax treatment of the above assets if sold.

IoT, *Associateship Intermediate Examination, May 1986*

4. You are required to state what you understand by the expression 'wasting assets' in the context of capital gains tax and explain the consequences of an asset being classified as such.

IoT, Associateship Intermediate Examination, May 1986

5. Discuss the effect on family taxation (as discussed in Chapter 4) of the introduction of an income tax on the assumed value of a wife's household duties.

6. Compare and contrast a comprehensive income tax with an expenditure tax (as described in Chapter 3).

6   Capital taxes

In Chapter 5 we looked at the tax on capital gains in the UK, and considered it as an extension of the tax on income rather than as a tax on capital. We looked also at the proposals for an annual tax on wealth, again as an extension of the income tax, although it could be used to tax capital if the rates of tax were high enough. In this chapter we will look at taxes imposed directly on capital (wealth) but they will be taxes on the transfer of wealth only. First we will consider the UK tax and then look at the wider issues and arguments.

INHERITANCE TAX (IHT)

The UK system for taxing transfers of wealth has been revised substantially on two occasions in recent years. From 1894 until 1974 the tax was called estate duty and was imposed mainly on transfers on death. From 1974 until 1986 lifetime gifts were included in the scope of the tax and it was called capital transfer tax (CTT). From 1986 it reverted to being a tax on transfers on or shortly before death and acquired a third name, inheritance tax (IHT). The following brief account relates to the last of these taxes. However, the reader should be warned that this is a very complicated tax and it is impossible to cover more than a fraction of the detail, which may be very important in a particular case.

    IHT applies to all of the property of a person domiciled or deemed to be domiciled in the UK.[1] If not so domiciled it applies only to property in the UK. Most, but not all, gifts made before death are potentially exempt transfers (PETs) with IHT becoming payable on them only if death occurs within seven years of the gift. If death occurs between three and seven years after the gift the IHT liability is reduced by a tapering formula.[2] When a gift becomes chargeable as a result of death within seven years the value of the gift is taken as of the time when it was made (e.g. shares are valued at their price when given, not as of the date of death) but the rates of tax to be used are those in operation at the date of death.

    The rates of tax follow a familiar pattern with a substantial threshold followed by rising rates of tax imposed band by band. At the time of writing the tax rates rise from 30% in the first band to 60% at the maximum (see Appendix). The threshold and rate bands are indexed to follow any price rises so that the real impact of the tax is not changed inadvertently, but the indexation changes can be varied if Parliament so decides.[3]

The design of the tax can best be illustrated by a simple example, but first we must look at some exemptions. The main ones are as follows:

1. *Small gifts* not exceeding £250 per year per recipient from any one donor. This exemption covers items such as birthday presents, but note that if the value is £250 or more the exemption is lost completely so far as gifts to that recipient are concerned.[4]
2. *Normal expenditure out of income.* This implies regularity, and would apply, for instance, to life assurance premiums paid to benefit some other person on the death of the donor.[5]
3. *Gifts in consideration of marriage.* These may amount to £5000 from each parent and parent in law, £2500 from each grandparent, and £1000 each from other donors.[6]
4. *Other transfers* each year up to a total of £3000 per donor. If the exemption is unused, or only partly used, in any year the unused element can be carried forward one year only and added to the exemption for the next year.[7]
5. *Transfers between spouses* (who are taxed separately). This exemption applies both to lifetime gifts and to transfers on death, unlike the previous items in this list which apply only to lifetime gifts. The exemption is restricted if the recipient spouse is not domiciled in the UK.[8]
6. *Gifts to charities,* either lifetime or on death.[9]
7. *Gifts to political parties,* unlimited if more than one year before death, otherwise limited to £100000.[10]
8. *Gifts for national purposes* or for public benefit, as defined. As with item (5) the exemption applies both to lifetime gifts and to transfers on death.[11]

Let us now see how some of these exemptions can affect the calculation of liability to IHT. The rates of tax used are those for 1986/87.

Facts

Mr Wiseman had been in good health until March 1986 and had made only small gifts such as birthday and Christmas presents. He had been paying regular premiums on a life assurance policy taken out for the benefit of his daughter who had still to complete professional training. Thus he was covered by exemptions (1) and (2) above and had made no use of exemption (4). In April 1986 he learned that he had a potentially fatal illness and thereafter made the following gifts.

> 1.5.86 £5000 each to his daughter and son-in-law on
> the occasion of their marriage.
> 10.5.86 £20000 to his wife.
> £10000 to his daughter.
> £10000 to his son.
> 1.6.86 £5000 to Oxfam.
> £1000 to the Liberal Party.

He died on 10.7.86 and his estate was valued at £145000, including his house which was worth £55000. The house, plus £30000, was left to his widow and the residue was divided equally between his son and daughter. The daughter received £5000 under the terms of the insurance policy.

Commentary

The gifts on 1.5.86 are exempt (item (3)) as is the gift to his wife on 10.5.86, the value of the house and the £30 000 left in the will (item (5)). The gifts on 1.6.86 are both exempt (items (6) and (7)). The proceeds of the insurance policy belong to the daughter outright and do not form part of the estate. The calculation of IHT liability is as follows:

	£	£
Gifts to son and daughter	20 000	
less: Annual exemptions, 1985/86 (unused) and 1986/87	6 000	14 000
Estate at death	145 000	
less: Transfer to spouse	85 000	60 000
Taxable amount		74 000
less: Threshold		71 000
		£3 000

Tax due: £3 000 at 30% = £900

This tax will be borne by the residue of the estate, i.e. by the son and daughter. It may be noted that if Mr Wiseman had taken no action, or had died suddenly, more tax would have been due as he would have lost the benefit of the marriage exemptions (£10 000) and the two annual exemptions (£6 000). The extra tax (at 30%) would have been £4 800.

This example illustrates the need to plan well in advance if the tax burden is to be minimized. In particular it pays to divide wealth between spouses so that both can take advantage of the limited exemptions (items (1), (3) and (4)) and so that if both die full advantage is taken of the doubling of the threshold and of the lower rate bands. It is clear that, apart from some exceptions still to be explained, no IHT is due if all wealth is given away more than seven years before death, but this idea raises non-tax problems such as loss of control of the family wealth and the donor's need for personal wealth to provide him with an income and to cover unexpected events.

It was suggested above that some lifetime transfers are taxable. One important example of this is transfers to a discretionary trust.[12] Such trusts can be created on terms which may make it impossible to relate the assets to any specific beneficiaries. A transfer of capital into such a trust is treated as a taxable event, and in the case of a series of such transfers the total is accumulated over seven years and tax calculated accordingly. Thus, if the first transfer uses up the tax threshold, subsequent transfers are chargeable in full. After seven years the first transfer falls out of the account and the tax on later transfers takes into account only those previous transfers which fall within seven years of their occurrence. Note that the rate of IHT is half the normal rate (i.e. it starts at 15% instead of 30%), but that this may be increased to the full rate (subject to tapering) if the settlor (donor) dies within a defined period after the transfer. Somewhat similar rules can be applied to transfers of value out of a close company.[13]

Because gifts are potentially exempt if the death of the donor does not occur within seven years special provisions have been made for gifts with benefits reserved.[14] If, for instance, an elderly person transfers ownership of his house to his son but continues to live in it rent free he is continuing to enjoy the benefit of it. In those circumstances the time span for the 'death within seven years' charge applicable to these PETs does not begin to operate until that benefit is given up. Thus the donor's estate may have to pay IHT on the house even though formal ownership was relinquished ten years prior to his death. Clearly this provision can apply to any income producing asset where the benefit of the income is retained by the donor, and assets may still be caught if the benefit is enjoyed indirectly because there is legislation directed at so called 'associated operations'.[15] There are some relieving provisions where the benefit arises from a need to make reasonable provision after circumstances have changed. It is recognized too that gifts may have to be made to support impoverished members of a family and these gifts may be treated as exempt gifts no matter how soon the donor's death occurs.[16]

One problem that can arise with taxes on the transfer of assets is that cash may not be available to enable the tax to be paid promptly. A partial answer to the problem is to arrange for the tax to be paid in instalments. In the UK system payment by annual instalments spread over ten years is allowed, free of interest, in the case of the transfer on death of business assets, controlling shareholdings and certain other unquoted shares. It applies also to some agricultural property.[17] For non-business assets consisting of land and buildings payment by instalments is allowed but interest is charged on the unpaid balance. Interest is charged in all these cases if an instalment payment is late.

The instalment basis can also be claimed for tax due following a lifetime transfer of these assets provided that it was arranged that the donee would bear the tax. If the property was the object of a potentially exempt transfer (PET) this instalment basis also depends on it being still owned by the donee.[18] If he has sold it before the death of the donor the IHT is payable immediately.

However, the UK system goes a stage further in dealing with this potential liquidity problem by making relief available in the form of a reduced valuation of the kinds of property which may not be realizable without causing damage to a business activity. Where 'relevant business property' enters into the calculation of a taxable estate its true value is reduced by 50% if it consists of a business, or part thereof, or is a controlling shareholding. Assets owned personally but used by a trading company controlled by their owner, or by a partnership in which their owner is a partner, are reduced in value by 30%. This lesser reduction also applies to a minority shareholding in an unquoted trading company.[19] Various definitions must be satisfied before the relief is due.

The effect of giving relief in this way can be more advantageous than may appear at first sight. It may reduce the value of an estate to the point where it escapes completely from one of the higher rate bands, in which case the tax due may be reduced by proportionately more than the nominal reduction. Suppose that an estate is valued at £120 000, then the IHT due, with no such relief and using the 1986/87, rates would be:

£			£
71 000	at	0%	—
24 000	at	30%	7 200
25 000	at	35%	8 750
£120 000			£15 950

If however, the estate included relevant business assets valued at £50 000 before the relief, the total taxable value would be reduced by £25 000 to £95 000 and the tax on that would be £7 200 (the tax at 35% being eliminated). The reduction in tax liability is nearly 55% rather than 50%.

This reduction in value is also available if the busines or business asset was transferred as a PET and has become liable to IHT through the death of the donor within seven years. It must, however, have been retained by the donee until the date of death or been replaced by other qualifying assets.

If part of the estate passes to a surviving spouse that part is, as we have seen, excluded from the IHT calculation. However, the existence of the business asset relief adds a complication to the calculation. Three issues may be identified.

1. If some or all of the business assets are left to the surviving spouse the valuation relief is irrelevant to those assets. It may, however, be available against any remaining business assets if they are left to other beneficiaries or are realized by the executors so that the cash proceeds can be passed to those other beneficiaries.
2. If business assets are left to a surviving spouse the valuation relief may not be available when that spouse dies. The conditions for relief must be met when the second death occurs.
3. If the business assets are not left specifically to the surviving spouse but are realized for her/his benefit along with other beneficiaries then, in calculating the chargeable part of the estate (i.e. that part which does not pass to the surviving spouse), the valuation relief must be apportioned between the chargeable and non-chargeable elements.

These points are demonstrated in Examples 6.1 and 6.2 at the end of the chapter.

Valuation relief is also given in respect of agricultural property. The 50% relief is available to owner occupiers and to long-term owners who have a right to vacant possession within 12 months. Otherwise the rate of relief is 30%. Relief is due also against the value of woodlands, and indeed the value of growing trees may be excluded entirely from the value of the estate, although IHT may become due later on the full value of those trees when they are sold.

Before we move on to a general discussion of capital taxes it should be noted that, as is the case with other types of tax relief, the effect of the business, agricultural and woodland reliefs may be to increase the attraction of such assets to the wealthy investor. Thus the tax benefit becomes capitalized in the price of the asset at a value which reflects the high tax advantage to such people. This may mean that the 'ordinary' farmer finds it impossible to buy agricultural land at a price which would enable him to make an economic return. Not only may the tax relief have failed to solve the problem envisaged, it may have made things worse.

TAX ON CAPITAL TRANSFERS – THE ISSUES

What is the nature of the case for a tax on capital transfers? We have already reviewed the arguments for levying taxes based on capital, as a reflection of ability to pay, in the discussion of an annual wealth tax in Chapter 5. Capital transfer taxes are levied directly on wealth but at irregular intervals and with uncertain impact. A tax on lifetime gifts is, to some extent, under the control of the taxpayer, while one arising on death alone can be mitigated by lifetime gifts.

Let us consider a tax levied on the death of the owner of wealth. Levying it at this point has a number of advantages.

1. The event is not controllable but it occurs for the great majority in a fairly narrow age range.
2. In many cases the assets owned by the deceased have to be identified and valued anyway because of the need to distribute them fairly under the terms of a will or under intestacy.
3. The tax is levied on the estate of the deceased but occurs at a time when he is not aware of his 'loss'. His inheritors receive net of tax sums but they may be content to receive their 'windfall' without being too concerned that it is less than it might have been.
4. There seems to be little or no evidence that the existence of such a tax affects willingness to work and to save, indeed in the case of the inheritors the tax may reduce the incentive to join the idle rich!

However, such a tax is not without some disadvantages. They include the following.

1. It can cause hardship where death occurs earlier than expected, especially if the same wealth is, as a result, taxed twice in quick succession.[20]
2. It may also create hardship where wealth is retained within the family and is not easily realizable. Thus family businesses, farmers, and the impecunious owners of stately homes may be placed in financial difficulty, especially if the rates of tax are high.
3. Unless it is backed up by a tax on lifetime gifts it is easily avoided, but once the tax is so extended the simplicity of the one event trigger is lost.

The rationale of such a tax is not just ability to pay. It is seen by some as a means of reducing inequalities of wealth, although the need for this must depend on personal value judgements. Some might suggest that the distribution of wealth depends more on the fundamental nature of the society and of the economy than on the tax system. A socialist might argue that the main wealth of the community should not be held by individuals anyway. A capitalist might argue that the incentive to create and own wealth is vital to the development of a healthy economy and that a healthy economy is to the benefit of everyone (or nearly everyone). What does seem clear is that such taxes have done very little so far to reduce inequalities of wealth.[21]

It is reasonable to argue that all taxation possibilities should be considered in designing a balanced system unless the cost of collection is excessive, or unless they cause distortions which are damaging to the economy as a whole. We have seen in Chapter 1 that the yield of IHT and its predecessor CTT in the UK is quite small, amounting in 1986/87 to only 0.7% of all central government taxes.[22] The administrative cost of collection runs at about 3% of its yield, which compares with an average of 1.7% for all direct taxes.[23] These figures do not include compliance costs. The figures seem to support the proposition that the tax in its present form is not worth the trouble of collecting it.[24]

When the UK introduced CTT in 1971 an alternative approach was suggested. This took the form of an accessions tax (sometimes called, at that time, an inheritance tax, just to confuse things). The idea that lay behind it was that it would be levied on the recipients of gifts and inheritances by reference to their lifetime totals of such receipts.[25] It will be seen that this may be linked to the idea of a comprehensive income tax (CIT) discussed in Chapter 5.

The main argument in favour of an accessions tax is that it would be fairer than CTT or IHT. Under IHT the tax is the same whether the assets all pass to someone already wealthy or are distributed to a number of less wealthy people. As the tax is effectively borne by those who inherit the wealth this implies that IHT does not tax according to ability to pay. Furthermore, an accessions tax might encourage a wider distribution of wealth by gift or by will.

Unfortunately the transition from IHT to an accessions tax would be difficult. When IHT's predecessor, CTT, was introduced it absorbed many of the characteristics of *its* predecessor so that transitional problems could be minimized. Similarly IHT now uses most of the CTT legislation. An accessions tax would mean designing a completely new, indeed revolutionary, system in what is in legal terms a very complex area because of the many ways in which rights to wealth can be designated under trust law and otherwise. Not all of the tax avoidance possibilities would be foreseen and resources would be consumed by all concerned in devising and understanding the new tax and in developing appropriate practices and policies to respond to it. Nevertheless, such taxes do exist (and did exist in the UK at one time) and a country which was seeking to introduce a tax on transfers of wealth without all the clutter of the existing system might well consider that an accessions tax is the more desirable model.

EXAMPLES

Example 6.1 Business asset reliefs

Mr N. G. Neer died on 17 October 1986 leaving the following assets after deduction of allowable expenses.

	£
Controlling shareholding (50% reduction due)	120 000
Assets let to the company (30% reduction due)	65 000
Other assets	75 000
Total estate	£260 000

He leaves the controlling shareholding and £20 000 of 'other assets' to his wife. The remainder of the estate is divided between his children and other beneficiaries.

	£	£
IHT is due as follows:		
Controlling shareholding – left to wife		Nil
Assets let to company	65 000	
less: 30%	19 500	45 500
Other assets	75 000	
less: Left to wife	20 000	55 000

Taxable estate		100 500
less: Threshold		71 000
		£29 500

Tax due:		
24 000 at 30%		7 200
5 500 at 35%		1 925
Total tax due		£9 125

Example 6.2 Apportionment of business asset relief

The facts are the same as in Example 6.1 except that the widow's entitlement is expressed as £140 000 with the residue then being divided between the children and other beneficiaries. The calculation now becomes:

	£	£
Controlling shareholding	120 000	
less: Widow's share 140/260	64 615	
	55 385	
less: 50%	27 693	27 692
Assets let to company	65 000	
less: Widow's share 140/260	35 000	
	30 000	
less: 30%	9 000	21 000
Other assets	75 000	
less: Widow's share 140/260	40 385	34 615
Taxable estate		83 307
less: Threshold		71 000
		£12 307
Tax due (12 307 at 30%)		3 692.10

NOTES AND REFERENCES

1. S. 6, Inheritance Tax Act (IHT Act) 1984, previously called the Capital Transfer Tax Act – see s. 100, Finance Act 1986.
2. S. 101 and paras. 1–5, 19th Schedule, Finance Act 1986, and 1st Schedule, IHT Act 1984.
3. Ss. 7–8, IHT Act 1984, and para. 36, 19th Schedule, Finance Act 1986.
4. S. 20, IHT Act 1984.
5. S. 21, IHT Act 1984.
6. S. 22, IHT Act 1984.
7. S. 19, IHT Act 1984.
8. S. 18, IHT Act 1984.
9. S. 23, IHT Act 1984.
10. S. 24, IHT Act 1984.

11. Ss. 24–27, IHT Act 1984.
12. Para. 1, 19th Schedule, Finance Act 1986, and Part III, IHT Act 1984. Note that transfers into certain kinds of settlement are PETs.
13. Ss. 94–102, IHT Act 1984, and para. 20, 19th Schedule, Finance Act 1986.
14. 20th Schedule, Finance Act 1986.
15. S. 268, IHT Act 1984. Note also the possible impact of the decision in *Furness* v. *Dawson* (1984) 1 All ER 530, where a pre-ordained series of transactions is devised with tax reduction in mind.
16. Para. 6, 20th Schedule, Finance Act 1986
17. Ss. 227–229 and 233–234, IHT Act 1984.
18. Para. 31, 19th Schedule, Finance Act 1986.
19. Part V, IHT Act 1984, and s. 105, Finance Act 1986.
20. The UK system allows relief if a second death occurs within five years – s. 141, IHT Act 1984.
21. See, for instance, Harrison, A., 'Recent changes in the distribution of personal wealth in Britain', in Field, F. (ed.), *The Wealth Report*, Routledge & Kegan Paul, London (1979).
22. HM Treasury, *Financial Statement and Budget Report 1986–87*, HMSO, London (March 1986).
23. Board of Inland Revenue, *Report for the Year Ended 31st December 1985*, Cmnd. 9831, HMSO, London (1986), at page 47.
24. See Sutherland, A., 'Capital Transfer Tax: adieu', in *Fiscal Studies*, Volume 5, Number 3, pp. 68–83 Basil Blackwell, Oxford (1984).
25. Also discussed in the Meade Committee, *The Structure and Reform of Direct Taxes*, Institute for Fiscal Studies, London (1978), Chapter 15.

EXERCISES AND DISCUSSION TOPICS

1. Eliot died on 15 August 1986, domiciled in England. His first wife died many years ago and his second wife, who survives him, is domiciled in West Germany.

   Eliot had three children by his first marriage and gave them £20 000 each in May 1986. The remaining assets at the date of death, as valued for probate, were as follows:

	£
Freehold house in England	124 000
Quoted investments	235 600
Personal chattels	5 600
Bank balances	18 400
House in West Germany	57 500

   His debts due at the date of death totalled £6 460 and his funeral expenses were £970.

   Eliot was also the life tenant of a family trust which was set up on the death of his aunt on 30 October 1984. The initial value of the trust fund was £48 750 less capital transfer tax paid out of it amounting to £6 850. When Eliot died it was valued at £68 700.

   Under the terms of his will Eliot made charitable bequests totalling £117 000 and gave his wife the right to occupy the house in England rent-free for life. The residue of the estate was divided equally between his children.

Since obtaining probate the executors have made the following sales of quoted investments:

	Probate value £	Sales proceeds £	Selling expenses £
1 February 1987	67 600	58 600	943
30 March 1987	34 600	37 900	654

Required:
  (a) Calculate the value of the estate for purposes of inheritance tax and the total tax due thereon.
  (b) Calculate the tax refund that is due (if any) as a result of the sales of quoted investments.
2. 'It will be seen that [the idea of an accessions tax] may be linked to the idea of a comprehensive income tax discussed in Chapter 5' (see page 106). Explain the meaning of this sentence and discuss the implications of the relationship between the two taxes.
3. The valuation reliefs (business assets, agricultural property) add considerably to the complexity of inheritance tax. Are they a necessary and effective form of relief? Discuss.

7 The UK system of corporation tax

THE GENERAL SCHEME

The underlying concept of the system is that profits are charged to tax at a flat rate and that part of that tax is credited (imputed) to the shareholders when they receive their dividends. It is known as an imputation system.

The nature of this system can be illustrated quite simply before we go on to look at some of the complications. Suppose that a UK company earns a taxable profit of £1 million in its accounting period (AP) for 12 months ending on 31 March 1987. All of its profits arise in the UK and are therefore subject only to UK tax. This profit will be charged to corporation tax (CT) at 35%, so the total tax due will be £350000.

Now suppose that it pays a dividend of £284000 to its shareholders on 1 December 1986 (i.e. within the same AP). That dividend will be treated in the hands of the shareholders as if it had already borne IT at the basic rate for the IT year 1986/87, i.e. 29%. Thus it is as if the dividend was:

	£
Gross dividend	400000
less: IT at 29%	116000
Dividend as paid	£284000

However, this basic rate of IT is not payable by the company in addition to the tax on its profits. In effect the CT (£350000) can be divided into two components:

Tax borne by the company	£234000
Tax imputed to the shareholders	£116000

Now suppose that two of the shareholders each own 1% of the share capital and so each receives a cash dividend of £2840. Shareholder A is a charity and so exempt from IT. It will receive a refund of the tax credit of £1160, thus giving it a total cash benefit of £4000.

Shareholder B, on the other hand, is a wealthy widow whose other income brings her into the 50% IT rate band. She will have to pay more tax on the dividend and this is calculated as follows:

	£
Cash dividend	2840
add: Tax credit	1160
Income for tax purposes	£4000
Tax thereon at 50%	2000
less: Tax credit	1160
Tax still to be paid	840

Her net cash benefit will then be:

Cash dividend received	2840
less: Tax still to be paid	840
Cash remaining	£2000

It should be noted that the tax credit enters twice into the calculation of tax due, once as an addition to the income, and then as a deduction from the tax on that income.

This system of taxation is imposed on corporate bodies (most of which are limited liability companies) and on unincorporated bodies such as clubs and societies. It is not imposed on partnerships except in so far as a company is a partner. The normal professional partnership is subject to income tax only.[1]

Like people, companies are taxed according to where they are resident. In many countries this is determined by the country of registration, and there is a certain logic in this approach as all companies are created under the laws of a particular nation state (or of a state therein). The UK approach is different. It looks for the place where control is exercised, this being in most cases the place where the board of directors meets.[2] Once a company is resident in the UK it cannot change its place of residence without the permission of the UK Treasury.[3]

A company which is found to be resident in the UK is liable to CT on the whole of its income and capital gains, worldwide. This requirement need not be quite so formidable as it may sound as relief is given for the tax already paid in other countries. The other side of the coin is that the UK profits of companies resident elsewhere are also liable to CT in the UK.

Companies are required by the Companies Act to prepare accounts annually[4] and liability to tax is based on these accounts. Thus no matter what accounting date is chosen tax is calculated for the accounting period (AP). There are a few exceptions to this treatment. If, for instance the company's accounts cover a period of more than twelve months they are divided into two APs and the profits apportioned between them.[5]

However, although the APs for different companies end on many different dates, depending on the companies' choices, any change in the rate of CT takes effect from the same date for all companies. The common date is 1 April and CT is imposed for a so-called financial year (FY) starting on that date. The year starting on 1 April 1986 (and ending on 31 March 1987) is known as the financial year 1986, and so on. This means that taxable profits may have to be apportioned, as the following example will show.

Suppose a company had taxable profits of £1 million for an AP which consists of the calendar year 1986. The rate of tax for FY 1985 was 40% and for FY 1986 was 35%. Thus we get:

		£
1.1.86 to 31.3.86 (part of FY 1985) 3/12 of £1 million at 40%		100000
31.3.86 to 31.12.86 (part of FY 1986) 9/12 of £1 million at 35%		262500
Total CT payable		£362500

PROFITS AND CHARGES

Corporation tax is charged on both income and gains and these two elements will be considered in turn.

Income is calculated in much the same way as it is for IT purposes. Trading income is discussed in Chapter 9. Other income is calculated in accordance with the rules set out in the Schedules and Cases as described in Chapter 2. There are two important differences as compared with IT. All income is calculated for the AP and not for the IT year, and the preceding year basis discussed in Chapter 2 is not used at all.

One particular item of income is excluded from the scope of taxable income for UK companies. Dividends they receive from other UK companies will have been paid out of profits which have already been charged to CT and so they are not taxed again. These dividends are called franked investment income (FII).

Capital gains are calculated in the same way as they are for individuals,[6] with relief for capital losses of the same or earlier years, but an adjustment is then made before they are added to income to produce the profit figure on which CT is payable. The underlying idea is that gains should only be taxed at a rate of 30% (the same rate as for individuals) whatever the rate of CT. This is achieved by reducing the gain by an appropriate fraction.

Thus in FY 1986 when the rate of CT was 35% a gain of £700 would be taxed as follows:

	£
Chargeable gain	700
less: Fraction (1/7)	100
Taxable	600
Tax at 35%	210

It will be observed that the tax of £210 is 30% of £700 but it is necessary to do the calculation as shown. It may also be observed that the appropriate fraction is that which reduces 35% to 30%, i.e. 1/7 of 35% is 5%. (See Appendix for a list of fractions for other years.)

Once the taxable income and the reduced gains have been aggregated to produce a profit figure a deduction can be made for the 'charges' actually paid in the AP. These consist of yearly interest, annuities and other annual payments. Thus loan interest, bank interest and covenanted payments to charities may be deducted. Charges are deductible from the (reduced) capital gains as well as from the income. This is the main reason why capital gains (as reduced) are brought into the main calculation instead of being taxed separately at 30%.

The relief for charges usually depends on the company deducting IT at the basic rate when paying them. This IT is accounted for quite separately from the tax on profits as the company is acting merely as a tax collector. For instance, if it had a profit of £800000 before charges and the charges were £60000 the tax payable assuming a basic rate of IT of 29% would be

	£
Corporation tax (on 800000 – 60000) at (say) 35%	259000
Income tax (60000 at 29%)	17400

The charges actually paid would amount to £42600 (i.e. 60000 – 174000) but the recipients would then be credited with the IT as if they had paid it at 29% on a gross income of £60000. If appropriate, repayment of all or part of the £17400 could be claimed, or additional IT might be due if the recipient's marginal rate exceeded 29%.

DISTRIBUTIONS AND ACT

Although dividends carry the tax credit which has been explained above (see p. 110) companies may still prefer to make payments to their investors in other ways. For instance, interest is fully deductible as a charge in calculating taxable profits, which dividends are not. However, the distinction between interest and dividends, while clear in principle, is not always clear in practice and there is a body of legislation which seeks to tax some payments as if they were dividends even when they are not. All of these payments are given the name 'distributions'.

The definition of distributions is lengthy and will not be covered in detail,[7] but we will illustrate it by two examples. If a company issues bonus debentures out of reserves pro rata to equity shareholders (i.e. no money passes) then any interest paid on these debentures will be treated as a distribution. Likewise, if a company issues bonus shares, and then redeems those shares, it has, in effect, paid cash to its shareholders out of its reserves and this too is treated as a distribution. These, however, are exceptional cases.

A more important aspect of the system for most companies is the concept of advance corporation tax (ACT). The problem that this is intended to solve can be seen if reference is made to the numerical example at the beginning of this chapter. In that example the total tax due from the company was £350000, but it was shown that part of it was credited to shareholders and could be refunded (i.e. to the charity). The problem that this raises for the tax administration is that the tax may have to be refunded before it has been received from the company, and, as we shall see, it may not be received at all.

The solution that has been adopted works as follows.

1. The amount of the tax credit on dividends has to be paid quarterly at the end of the quarter (January – March and so on) in which dividends were paid. This is the payment that is called ACT.
2. The balance (or mainstream) tax is then paid 9 months after the end of the AP to which it relates. This is referred to as MCT. In the case of companies in existence before April 1965 the delay may be longer because of transitional provisions made when the system was changed.[8]

It is important to note that, as shown in the early example, it is the ACT on dividends paid *in* the AP which is set off against the CT for the AP, not the ACT on dividends expressed to be paid (later) out of the profits of that AP.

We have already seen that dividends received by a UK company from another UK company, the so-called franked investment income (FII), will not be taxed as profits of the recipient. The paying company will have paid ACT on these dividends and this can be used to reduce the ACT liability of the receiving company in respect of its own dividends. (See Example 7.1 at the end of the chapter.)

This special treatment of ACT already paid on the FII does not apply to the IT which has been deducted from interest received (which was explained on p. 113 above). As this interest, not being 'franked', will be part of the company's taxable profits the IT already deducted from it can be used in one of two ways.

1. It can be set off against the company's obligation to account for tax deducted from the interest it pays. Or:
2. The tax can be deducted from the CT due on the interest received.

(See Example 7.2.)

Returning now to ACT, so far it has been assumed implicitly that the ACT is fully deductible in calculating the MCT. Unfortunately for the company this may not be the case and it leads to complications. The two crucial factors are:

1. The ACT set off is restricted to 29% of the income chargeable to CT. In other words CT in excess of 29% on income plus all CT on the gains (less charges) must always be paid.[9]
2. If ACT has been paid but cannot be fully set off because of these restrictions the excess can be used up as if it belonged either to one of the previous six APs (taking the latest first) or to future APs, taking the first opportunity. The restriction described in (1) above must be applied in each of those periods. If this does not resolve the problem the ACT becomes an extra tax which means that the marginal cost of a dividend is effectively increased by 29/71 or 40.85%.

These points are illustrated in Example 7.3.

LOSSES

Companies, like individuals, may fail to produce profits and where there are losses it is important for them to be relieved against tax liability. The relief takes several forms, is guided by detailed rules, and gives some opportunity for planning to obtain maximum benefits.[10]

The main reliefs are for trading losses. For a single company (excluding groups) they can be relieved in four ways which may overlap.

1. They can be used against non-trading income and gains (the latter as reduced by the fraction) of the same AP.
2. Any excess can then be used against the income, including trading income, of the immediately preceding AP provided its length is no greater than that of the loss

period; if it is longer the relief is restricted to the income etc. for a similar duration, calculated by apportionment.

3. If any trading loss still remains unrelieved after these two reliefs have been given it can be carried forward and used against future trading income, but not against other income or gains, taking the earliest period first.

4. When a trade ceases any trading loss incurred in the final twelve months, calculated by apportionment if two APs are involved, can be set against trading income of the preceding three years.

In the case of carry forward relief (item (3) above) the loss can include excess charges in any year, but only in so far as they are incurred for trading purposes. Thus interest on money borrowed to provide trade assets qualifies but payments under deed to an unrelated charity do not.

The only other loss relief available is for capital losses, as calculated under the capital gains tax rules. The relief follows that for individuals, being available against gains of the same period or against future gains.

See Example 7.4 for the interaction between intems (1) to (3) above.

SMALL COMPANIES

A common feature of company taxation around the world is a lower rate of tax on the profits of small companies. This may, as in Portugal, be a lower rate on the first slice of profits of all companies or it may, as in the UK and many other countries, be withdrawn once the profits exceed the stated limit.

The features of the UK system will be explained using the tax rates specified for the FY 1986. A small company is defined quite simply as one with profits not exceeding £100000 for one year. If the AP is less than a year the limit is reduced pro rata. Up to the limit the rate of tax is 29% instead of 35%. The full rate of 35% is still applied to any capital gains (as reduced by the fraction).

Should the profits lie between £100000 and £500000 and consist wholly of income (no gains) the calculation goes as follows:

	£
Profit (say) £250000 at 35%	87500
less: Abatement (£500000 – £250000) × 3/200	3750
CT payable	£83750

In effect income in the abatement band is charged at a marginal rate of $36\frac{1}{2}$% until, at £500000, the average rate of tax has been pulled up to the regular rate of 35%.[11] The calculation is more complicated if the profits include FII or gains. (See Example 7.5.)

Taxing small companies in this way gives rise to two problems. The first is the effect of the higher marginal rate of tax in the abatement band. This increases the impact of taxation on small company decisions at the margin and could therefore accentuate any economic distortions. The marginal rate for FY 1986 at $36\frac{1}{2}$% is only $1\frac{1}{2}$ percentage points above the regular rate of CT, but there have been times when that marginal rate was as high as 67%, thus leaving only one-third of the marginal profits at the disposal of the company. The Portugese system avoids this problem but to change would involve a loss of revenue.[12]

The other problem arises out of the obvious temptation to use multiple small companies instead of one large one. This has been countered in the legislation by requiring one small company limit (i.e. the £100000 and £500000 explained above) to be shared equally between any number of companies which are under common control. But this can have a disadvantageous effect in the genuine case. Thus if two connected companies have taxable profits of £75000 and £10000 respectively, a total of £85000, the first will find that it is not a small company at all as its limit is £50000 (i.e. ½ of £100000) so it will fall into the abatement band. If the two companies were combined as one the profits would be less than £100000 and they would be taxable at the lower rate of 29%

CLOSELY CONTROLLED COMPANIES

The 'small' companies dealt with in the previous section were defined solely by their level of profits in the year. Thus a company which, by other definitions, such as capital employed, number of employees or turnover, was a large company might be taxed as a small company in a particular year if it suffered a temporary decline in its fortunes. There is, however, another kind of company which also attracts special tax treatment and which will often be small, although not necessarily so. This is the so-called 'close company'.

The characteristic of this company is that it is closely controlled by a small number of shareholders and therefore lacks the market discipline which exists for a company which relies on its supply of capital through the financial markets. Close companies are perceived as companies whose main shareholders and directors are likely to be the same people. As such they may arrange the company's affairs to suit their own interests, possibly to the detriment of the tax revenue.

Before looking at such arrangements we will consider briefly the definition of a close company in the tax legislation.[13] It should be noted that certain words in it are interpreted in special ways. The core of the definition is that it is a company which is controlled by five or fewer 'participators' or by participators who are 'directors'. Thus it is apparent that for any five not to control the company there must be at least eleven altogether.

There are two important (and some lesser) exceptions to this definition. The first is the company which is controlled by another company which is not itself a close company. The second is the company whose shares are quoted on a stock exchange and 35% or more of whose shares are held by the public. In both cases it is assumed, by implication, that there will be 'independent' shareholders whose needs must be satisfied.

The main definition of a close company has a rather wider meaning than the words used above might be taken to imply. The use of the word 'participator' rather than 'shareholder' extends the meaning considerably. A participator is assumed by legislation to have the power of his 'associates', a word which includes close relatives, partners and fellow trustees. Thus the shares held by a husband, his wife and their children (of whatever age) are treated as if held by one participator. It is easy to see that a family business, even at the second or third generation stage, may find it difficult to escape this definition.

Another extension of the definition arises from the meaning given to the word 'control'. In a narrow sense this means voting control, the ability to determine the decisions of a general meeting of the shareholders. However, the close company definition of control is widened to include people who have a right to acquire or exercise control. People who are entitled to the greater part of the company's profits, or are entitled to the greater part of the assets in a winding up are also included. Thus if a company has £1000 of share capital and £10000 of non-voting loan capital, the owner of the latter would be deemed to have control of the company. This attitude may be intepreted as a case of realism overcoming legal niceties.

The main feature of the close company legislation lies in its concern for the level of distributions by the company. The rationale lying behind this is that there may be no market pressure to maintain a normal dividend level and there may be tax advantages in retaining profits, so that they are taxed at a rate of 35% or less, rather than distributing them to shareholders whose personal tax rates are, perhaps, 60%.

However, tax reduction is not the only motive for keeping profits within the company. Many small family companies engaged in trade have an urgent need for more capital and will keep dividends at the lowest possible level for that reason alone. The close company legislation does not expect such companies to make any distributions.

At the other end of the spectrum is the company which invests in shares and securities. Here the close company legislation levies tax as if the entire income had been distributed, whether or not that is the case. Given the fact that companies have no annual exemption for capital gains there can be few cases when such a company has any advantage over personal direct ownership of the investments. The position is different for the large investment trust companies which are not close companies.

In between these extremes stands the property investment company. For them the normal rule is that they should distribute one half of their after tax income unless it can be shown that its retention is required for purposes other than the acquisition of more land and buildings. The distribution rules become more complex when a company has a mixture of different types of income. Thus a company with both property and trading income need distribute nothing if the two sources together fall short of £25000 in the year. Between £25000 and £75000 there is an abatement formula. Example 7.6 shows the effect of these rules.[14]

When a close company's expected distribution level for an AP has been established it is compared with the dividends paid in respect of the AP within a reasonable time. No extra distribution is actually enforced. All that happens is that extra tax is levied as if the required distribution had actually been made. Most companies, faced with this requirement, do make the distribution. If the extra tax is paid by the company but a further qualifying distribution is made subsequently the tax on that distribution can be adjusted.

The remaining legislation affecting close companies is much less important and will not be covered in detail. It deals with benefits such as living accommodation provided for participators (and not already caught under the Schedule E rules described in Chapter 5) and loans made by the company to shareholders (instead of transferring the cash to them in the form of a taxable dividend).

Special treatment of companies operating on a small scale and owned by few people is not confined to the United Kingdom. The nature of the problem depends on several factors. It depends on the way companies are taxed (discussed in Chapter 8) and on the forms of business ownership which are provided in the country's laws. Laws requiring a minimum capital contribution for companies may inhibit company formation in the small business sector anyway. The special tax treatments tend to fall under two main headings.

(1) Companies may be taxed as partnerships and vice versa. In the United States either the tax authority or the taxpayer may seek to argue for the alternative treatment. A similar option used to be available to closely controlled French companies, and there is still an option for partnerships to be taxed as if they were companies.

(2) More widespread is the concern of tax authorities about the possibility of reducing or deferring tax liability by retaining income in companies where the rate of tax is below the top personal rate. The United States has passed legislation directed against both personal holding companies and against the unreasonable retention of earnings. In another part of the world, Australia, New Zealand and Singapore have all taken steps to counteract the benefits of retaining profits within companies, especially where closely held. Australia has also sought to tax loans to shareholders as if they were distributions of profits and New Zealand has been concerned about 'excessive' remuneration paid to members of the family which owns the company.

These examples show the widespread and universal nature of tax problems around the world. Countries learn from each other, just as taxpayers do, and differences in the detail of company law, social and economic background and of tax systems cannot hide this element of universality. In Chapter 8 we shall go on to look at the company tax systems found in other countries and to consider their effects.

GROUPS OF COMPANIES

We have seen that special rules apply where one company pays a dividend to another so that as long as profits remain within the company sector of the UK economy no further tax is payable. Thus it follows that when a dividend is paid by a subsidiary company to its holding company the existence of a group organization is not prejudicial to tax liability compared with running the business under the umbrella of a single company. The question now is whether groups should be entitled to special treatment in other ways.

The development of the group form has been an important feature of business in this century, both nationally and internationally. Gradually in the UK, the USA and elsewhere it became clear that group (consolidated) accounts were necessary if a full picture was to be shown to holding company shareholders and other interested parties. However, in many ways the various companies in a group retain their own legal status and individuality and this remain the overriding principle so far as tax is concerned.

Nevertheless, the UK tax system has come to recognize that for some purposes groups operate as entities and reliefs have been provided accordingly. The legislation is complex in detail but its effects can be outlined without too much difficulty. It features four main reliefs, two concerned with ACT, the others with losses and capital gains. Each relief has its own definition of what constitutes a group. The reliefs apply to consortia.[15] They are available only to companies resident in the UK, but these may comprise the UK elements in a multinational group if they are controlled via a UK holding company.

The first relief relates to the payment of dividends by a 51% subsidiary to its parent company.[16] The two companies can elect to pay a dividend without accounting for ACT on it, the dividend then becoming 'group income' instead of FII to the recipient. The relief applies only to dividends paid intra-group, not to those paid to the minority shareholders of the subsidiary.

The effects of the relief are threefold.

(1) The subsidiary may be able to avoid paying ACT which would be unrelieved because there is insufficient CT to cover it (as illustrated in Example 7.3).

(2) The parent company will pay more ACT when it pays its own dividends as it will have lost the ACT credit on the dividend received as group income.

(3) There will be a delay, possibly for many months, in the payment of some of the group's ACT in so far as it becomes due only when the holding company pays a dividend rather than becoming due as soon as intra-group dividends are paid. The election for the relief can be applied to any part of a dividend.

A similar sort of relief is available when charges (interest etc.) are paid between members of such a group. The charges are paid gross, instead of IT being deducted at source. The CT due on the charges is accounted for by the recipient. The scope of this relief is wider than for group income as it covers intra-group payments by the parent company and between co-subsidiaries, but this time there is no provision for a partial election.

The second relief also relates to ACT. A parent company may find itself with unrelieved ACT (as in Example 7.3) while its subsidiaries have CT payable and FII received which more than cover their own ACT liabilities. In these circumstances the parent company is allowed to surrender ACT to one or more of its 51% subsidiaries.[17] The relief applies only to ACT paid on dividends, not on other distributions, and it must be used by the subsidiary in the same year. These two reliefs are illustrated in Example 7.7.

Turning now to the third relief, this is called group relief.[18] It allows one company in the group to use the trading losses of another in order to reduce the tax on its profits of all kinds. The profits and losses of the two companies must be for the same period and, except for consortia, the two companies must have a 75% relationship (as defined in s.258 of the Taxes Act 1970.) One company's loss may be split between two or more profitable companies in the same group.

The legislation deals with a number of complication and avoidance possibilities. One complication concerns the rights of minority shareholders. The whole of a company's trading loss may be used notwithstanding the fact that the loss making company has some minority shareholders (up to 25%). However, that company will then have to pay tax on the full amount of any future profits, the loss normally available having been used. The minority shareholders will have received no benefit from the use of the trading loss by the majority and will, to that extent, be disadvantaged. Any group company which has benefitted should therefore pay the subsidiary for the value of the loss relief it has used and so it is provided in Taxes Act 1970 s.258 (4) that any such payment will be ignored in calculating the tax liability of both companies. The payment must be made for the full value of the loss relief, not just the minority's share, as it is made to the company as such, not just to the shareholders who have been disadvantaged. (See Example 7.8.)

Finally there is a relief directed at the consequences of selling chargeable assets between companies within a group.[19] Again there must be 75% control. The basis of the relief is that such sales shall be deemed to be made at a price which produces neither gain nor loss. When the asset is sold outside the group at some later date the selling company is liable not on its own gain but on a gain calculated on the basis of the no loss, no gain transfer price when it acquired it. It is provided that the tax due can be recovered, if necessary, from other members of the group.

This relief is taken a stage further by extending the roll-over relief provision (see Chapter 5, p. 78) so that it applies to the group as a whole. Thus if one company sells an asset outside the group and is liable to tax on a gain, that gain can be set off against the cost incurred by another company in acquiring a qualifying asset. In effect the group is treated as if it had a single fund into which the proceeds of assets sales are paid and from which new assets are financed.

No relief is provided on a group basis for capital losses. Thus the group may find itself in a position where one of its companies, X, has a chargeable gain which accrued partly when the asset was owned by another of its companies, Y, while Y has a realized capital loss on another asset for which no immediate relief is available. One solution to this would have been to transfer one of the assets to the other company under the group provisions before the outside sale was made, thus ensuring that both gain and loss were made by the same company. This example illustrates how important it is for groups to plan their transactions and their groups elections in good time and on a group-wide basis. They must ensure too that the detailed conditions for relief have been satisfied. It is no good trying to argue that some result is morally or equitably due if the letter of the law has not been satisfied.

EXAMPLES

Example 7.1 ACT and FII

A company received and paid the following dividends during its AP ended 31 March 1987. All dividends received were from UK companies. The CT liability on the profits for the AP is subsequently agreed as £260000 (payable 1.1.88).

	£
Dividends paid:	
1.11.86 Final for previous AP	80000
20.3.87 Interim for this AP	20000
Dividends received:	
1.6.86 From A Ltd.	4000
1.3.87 From B Ltd.	6000

ACT calculations are as follows:

£

1st quarter (April – June):
Dividends from A. ACT credit £4000 × 29/71   1633.80
No refunds available yet.

2nd quarter (July – Sept.):
No dividends paid or received.

3rd quarter (Oct. – Dec.):

Final dividend paid. ACT due £80000 × 29/71	32676.05
less: Credit on A's dividend (above)	1633.80
ACT payable	£31042.25

4th quarter (Jan. – Mar.):

Interim dividend. ACT due £20000 × 29/71	8169.01
less: ACT credit on B's dividend (£6,000 × 29/71)	2450.70
ACT payable	£5718.31

MCT due on 1.1.88   260000

CT as stated above	31042.25	
less: ACT paid in AP	5718.31	36760.56
		£233239.44

Note that the the credit for ACT on dividends received does not alter the total tax (ACT + MCT) payable by the company, only the division between the two items.

Example 7.2 Interest received and paid

The company in Example 7.1 also received and paid interest as follows. The gross interest has been taken into account as income and charges in calculating the CT on profits for the AP.

		£
31.7.86	Interest received (net)	1420
1.12.86	Interest paid (net)	10650
1. 2.87	Interest received (net)	1420

£   £

1st quarter (April – June):
No interest received or paid.

2nd quarter (July – Sept.):
31.7.86

Interest receivable – gross	2000
IT thereon at 29%	580
Net interest received	£1420

The IT suffered remains available for set-off.

3rd quarter (Oct. – Dec.):

1.12.86 Interest payable – gross	15000	
IT thereon at 29%	4350	4350
Net interest paid	£10650	
IT suffered on interest received (above)		580
IT still payable		£3770

4th quarter (Jan. – Mar.):

1.2.87 Interest receivable – gross	2000
IT Interest receivable at 29%	580
Net interest received	£1420

As the company has already paid £3777 on interest payable it can now claim a refund of the IT suffered in the 4th quarter.

Example 7.3 ACT set-off

The following figures relate to a company for successive APs. It will be assumed that the CT rate is 35% and the IT rate 29% for both periods.

	AP 1 £000	AP 2 £000
Taxable income	900	700
Capital gains (less the 1/7 fraction)	100	50
	1000	750
Charges	40	40
Net amount taxable	960	710
Dividends paid in the AP	600	900
ACT thereon at 29/71	245.07	367.60

Taking each period in turn and looking at the tax due we get:

AP 1:	£000
CT due, 960 at 35%	336.00
less: ACT	245.07
MCT	£90.93

The maximum ACT set-off in AP 1 is 29% of £900000 (£261000), the capital gains absorbing the charges of £40000.

AP 2:	£000
CT due, 710 at 35%	248.50
less: ACT (limited to 29% of £700 000)	203.00
MCT	£45.50

The maximum ACT set-off is calculated in the same way as in AP 1. The position in respect of ACT is as follows:

	£000
ACT paid in AP 2	367.60
less Used in AP 2	203.00
Unused	164.60
less: Usable now in AP 1*	15.93
Carry forward to AP 3	£148.67

* ACT of AP 2 usable in AP 1 is limited to the difference between the ACT for AP 1 (£245070) and the maximum set-off for the AP (£261000).

Example 7.4 Trading losses

A company has the following results for 3 APs, each of which is a calendar year.

	1984 £	1985 £	1986 £
Trading income (losses)	24000	(42000)	10000
Rental income (Schedule A)	2000	2500	2700
Capital gains (*less* the fraction)	600	–	1200
	26600	(39500)	13900
less: Charges	2000	2000	2000
	£24600	(£41500)	£11900

The charges consist each year of £1500 of loan interest and a £500 covenanted donation to a non-trade charity.

Loss reliefs	£:	
1985	Trading loss	42000
	less: Rental income	2500
	Loss still available	£39500
1984	Income and gains as shown	26600
	less: Loss relief	26600
	Profits chargeable	Nil
	Loss available as above	39500
	less: Used in 1984	26600

	Carried forward to 1986	12900
	add: Unused trade charges for 1984 and 1985	3000
	Total to carry forward	£15900
1986	Trading income	10000
	less: Loss brought forward	10000
	Rental income	2700
	Gains	1200
		3900
	less: 1986 charges	2000
	Profit chargeable to CT	£1900
	Unused loss to carry forward to 1987 (15900 − 10000)	5900

Note how the loss is used against profits in 1984 and 1985 before deducting charges and how the relief in 1986 is confined to trading income.

Example 7.5 Small companies

In its AP ended 31 March 1987 a company had a trading income of £250000, capital gains of £50000 and received UK company dividends of £25000 net. Its total profits, including FII, will be:

	£	£
Income		250000
Capital gains	50000	
less: 1/7	7143	42857
FII (grossed up) 25000 × 100/71		35211
Total		£328068

So the company is not 'small' but is in the abatement band.

	£
CT due:	
35% of profits excluding FII:	
(250000 + 42857) at 35%	102499.95
less: Abatement:	
$(500000 - 328068)\ \dfrac{250000}{317857} \times \dfrac{3}{20}$	2148.88
CT due	£100351.07

Note that in calculating the abatement the full profit including FII is used in the comparison with the upper limit of £500000 but the resulting abatement figure (after multiplying by 3/20) is then scaled down so that only the taxable income, not the gains or FII, is abated.

Example 7.6 Close company distributions

Assume a company which is 'small' but which has three kinds of income: investment, estate (property income) and trading. Its tax rate is 29% on income and 35% on gains (after deducting the fraction). The position for the AP can be summarized as follows:

	£ Gross	£ Tax	£ After Tax
Investment income	2000	580	1420
Estate income (E)	20000	5800	14200
Trading income (T)	70000	20300	49700
Gains	1000	350	650
Totals	£93000	£27030	65970
(Deduct the gains as they are deemed to be irrelevant)			650

Revised total	65320
(The investment income can be deducted as it is less than the smaller of £3000 or 10% of the estate and trading income)	1420
Further revised total	£63900
Estate income is now abated (using the formula* below):	
Estate income as above	14200
less: Abatement*	1233
Estate income as reduced	12967
50% thereof is deducted	6484
Distributable income	6483

None of the trading income is distributable

*The abatement formula is one half of $(\frac{E}{E + T} \times 75000) - E.$

Thus in the figures in the example this gives:

$$\tfrac{1}{2} \text{ of } [(\frac{14200 \times 75000}{63900}) - 14200] = 1233$$

Example 7.7 Group income

The group consists of a holding company, H, and two subsidiaries, S (60% owned) and T (80% owned). Income and dividends for the AP ending 31 March 1987, all of the companies using the same accounting date, were as follows:

	H £000	S £000	T £000
Income	1000	200	700
FII (net) (S & T only)		300	–
Dividends paid (net)	1200	600	240

The rate of CT is 35% and the basic rate of IT 29%.

Company S:

Dividend to minority (40% of £600000)]	240000
FII	300000
FII available to cover dividend to H	60000
Dividend to H (60% of £600000)]	360000
Payable as group income (no ACT)	£30000

S has no ACT liability as its own FII covers the dividends paid other than the group income.

Company T:

Dividend to minority (20% of £240000)]	48000
ACT due thereon at 29/71	19605.63
Dividend to H (80% of £240000)]	192000

The dividend to H may be paid as group income.

Company H

Dividend paid	1200000
ACT thereon at 29/71	490140.84
Covered by FII from S (60000 × 29/71)	24507.04
ACT payable	465633.80
ACT deducted from CT, maximum*	290000.00
Unrelieved ACT	£175633.80

This unrelieved ACT can be surrendered to T as follows:

	£	
CT on T's income (£700000 at 35%)		245000
less: ACT already paid (see above)	19605.63	
ACT surrendered by H	175633.80	195239.43
MCT payable		£49760.57

The maximum ACT set-off for T is 29% of £700000	20300

*on £1000000.

Example 7.8 Group relief

Major Ltd. owns 80% of the ordinary share capital of Minor Ltd. In the AP ending 31 March 1987 Major made a taxable trading profit of £60000 but Minor suffered an agreed loss of £40000. Major made a taxable profit in the previous AP but Minor did not (so it cannot use its loss against the previous APs profit as in Example 7.4) and they have no other income or charges.

	£
Major: Trading income	600000
less: Group relief (Minor's loss)	40000
Taxable profit	£560000
Tax thereon at 35%	196000
Minor: Trading income	Nil

Notes
1. Clearly the immediate value of the loss relief to Major is 40000 at 35% = £14000.
2. If Minor makes a profit in the AP to 31 March 1988 or later it will lose the benefit of the loss relief that would have been brought forward. Minor is not a small company because it is linked with Major so it pays CT at the full rate.
3. Major should pay a sum not exceeding £14000 to Minor to preserve the position of the minority shareholders. This sum may be less than £14000 in so far as the value of the loss to Minor may be reduced (discounted) by reason of the delay that Minor would have experienced in getting effective relief for the loss.

NOTES AND REFERENCES

1. S.526, Taxes Act 1970. Note that there are special arrangements for certain kinds of company such as insurance companies and savings banks – see Part XII, Taxes Act 1970.
2. The leading case on this subject is *De Beers Consolidated Mines Ltd.* v. *Howe* (1906) AC 455, 5 TC 198.
3. S.482, Taxes Act 1970.
4. S.241, Companies Act 1985.
5. The full provision is in s.247, Taxes Act 1970.
6. But note that there is no annual threshold for companies as there is for individuals.
7. The main details are in ss.233–237, Taxes Act 1970, and s.60, Finance Act 1982.
8. In the case of pre-1965 companies the due date will normally be 1 January not less than 9 months after the end of the AP. Thus a company making up accounts to 30 April 1986 may be able to wait until 1 January 1988 before it pays its mainstream tax – see s.244, Taxes Act 1970.
9. 29% is the basic rate of IT for 1986/87. For other years the appropriate basic rate of IT is the figure to be used. See Appendix for a list of basic rates.
10. The detailed provisions can be found in Part VII, Taxes Act 1970.
11.

	£	
Tax due on £100000 is	29000	(29%)
Tax due on £500000 is	175000	(35%)
Difference £400000	146000	

Marginal rate is $\dfrac{146,000}{400,000} \times 100 = 36.5\%$

The marginal rate will change if either the small comapny rate or the main rate of CT change, or if the abatement band is changed. The abatement fraction depends on all three elements – see Appendix for the fractions for other years.
12. In the Green Paper, *Corporation Tax*, Cmnd. 8456, HMSO, London (1982), the revenue loss at that time was estimated as £120 million.
13. The main definitions are in ss.282, 283, 302 and 303, Taxes Act 1970.
14. These rather complex calculations are governed by the legislation in the 16th Schedule, Finance Act 1972 (as amended).

15. A consortium is joint ownership of a company by two or more independent companies, usually to achieve a specific purpose which requires that they pool their resources.
16. Ss.256–257, Taxes Act 1970.
17. S.92, Finance Act 1972.
18. Ss.258–264, Taxes Act 1970.
19. Ss.272–281, Taxes Act 1970.

EXERCISES AND DISCUSSION TOPICS

1. Hide Ltd. and Seek Ltd. are associated companies and for the twelve month accounting period to 31 March 1986 they have the following results:

	Hide Ltd. £	Seek Ltd. £
Trading profit	80000	260000
Chargeable gains	900	–
Dividends from UK companies (excluding tax credits)	–	420
Debenture paid (gross)	600	–

April 1985 Hide Ltd. had an unrelieved trading loss of £20000. During the accounting period ended 31 March 1986 dividends were paid by the companies as follows: Hide Ltd. £14000; Seek Ltd. £63000.

Required:
Calculate the mainstream corporation tax payable by each company based on the information given.   *ICSA, June 1985* (Question updated.)

2. (a) In relation to corporation tax, what is meant by group income?
   (b) Minor Ltd is the 80% subsidiary company of Major Ltd. and both companies have been trading in the UK since 1975. Their recent results have been as follows:

Years ended 31 March	1984 £	1985 £	1986 £
Major Ltd.:			
Trading profit/(loss)	48000	36000	(10000)
Dividends paid	54000	30000	Nil
Minor Ltd.:			
Trading profit	34000	18000	12000
Dividends paid	2000	4000	3000

Assumptions to be made:
   (i) Major Ltd. will surrender any surplus ACT, but not losses, to its subsidiary.
   (ii) A group income election under s.256 is in operation.
   (iii) Loss relief will be claimed as early as possible.

Required:
Prepare computations showing the mainstream corporation tax payable, if any, by each company in respect of each of the three years.
ICSA December 1985, (Question updated.)

3. Galbraith Ltd. is a company resident in the United Kingdom making garments for sale to the tourist industry at its factory in Callander. It has always made its accounts up to 30 September. It was incorporated in 1956 and commenced its present trade in the same year. It has no associated companies. The company's results for the last four years are as follows:

Year ended 30 September	1982	1983	1984	1985
Trading profit (as adjusted for taxation)	83000	12500	48000	199000
Bank interest received	14100	26300	18500	12400
Chargeable gains	–	9300	–	3400
Dividends received from UK companies (net)	7100	6510	2650	8250
Dividends paid	10300	4700	7850	24850
Loan interest paid (gross)	–	–	5700	5700
Capital allowances:				
Writing down allowances	14710	12250	16280	19290
First year allowances	57230	16800	68500	15250

[*Note*: The trading profits shown are before deduction of capital allowances.]

You are required to:

(a) calculate the corporation tax liability for the four years after claiming maximum advance corporation tax and loss relief at the earliest possible times, and
(b) in respect of the corporation tax assessed on the company for the accounting period ended 30th September 1985, state when this will be due for payment and how this date is ascertained.

ACCA, *Level 2, December 1984* (Question updated and guidance added in square brackets.)

4. Impact Ltd., a company resident in the United Kingdom for taxation purposes, is an investment holding company and owns 100% of the share capital in five other companies. Impact has the following results for the year ended 31 December 1986:

	£
Schedule D, Case III	15217
Schedule A	12006
Taxed interest (gross)	5000
Franked investment income from a subsidiary	10000
Group income from another subsidiary	18000
Deed of covenant (net)	750
Chargeable gains (before FA 1972, s.93 relief)	8054

During the year ended 31 December 1986 Impact Ltd. paid a dividend of £16000.

You are required to calculate the corporation tax payable by Impact Ltd. for the year ended 31 December 1986.

IoT, Associateship Final Examination, Paper II, November 1985
(Question updated and part deleted.)

8 Alternative forms of company taxation

VARIATIONS ON THE IMPUTATION SYSTEM

We have seen in Chapter 7 how the UK system of corporation tax (CT), an imputation type, actually works. Similar systems are used in other countries and these illustrate the ways in which the same model can be used flexibly in adapting it to differing circumstances and requirements.

The UK system in general allows only partial imputation, the tax credit on the dividend being less than the tax levied on the underlying profits. This is not true of small companies as their profits are taxed at the same rate as the imputed tax credit. The effect can be seen in Illustration 8.1 which uses a basic IT rate of 29%[1] and assumes shareholder rates of A – 25% and B – 50%. The illustration looks at the slice of profit (£100) required to cover the dividends shown so the effect is to treat that slice as fully distributed.

Illustration 8.1

		Small company		Large company	
		A	B	A	B
		£	£	£	£
(a)	Profit to cover dividend	100	100	100	100
(b)	Tax	29	29	35	35
(c)	Dividend (a) – (b)	71	71	65	65
(d)	Tax credit, 29/71 of (c)	29	29	26.55	26.55
(e)	Gross dividend (c) + (d)	100	100	91.55	91.55
(f)	Income tax (on (e))	29	50	26.55	45.77
(g)	Net benefit to shareholder (e) – (f)	71	50	65	45.78
(h)	Tax borne by company (b) – (d)	Nil	Nil	8.45	8.45
(i)	Total tax burden (f) + (h)	29	50	35.00	54.22

In the case of the small company the total tax due is the shareholder rate on the underlying profit. The larger company has a residue of tax which is fixed (at £8.45 in the illustration) whatever the shareholder's personal rate. This residue is the part of the company tax which is not imputed. It will be noted that one result of this is that the total tax burden in B is less than twice that in A. Of course on profits that are not distributed both the shareholder tax rate and the degree of imputation are irrelevant.

Some countries take the view that the tax rate on all distributed profits should be taxed only at the shareholder's personal rate, whatever the size of the company. Thus in Singapore company profits are taxed at a rate of 40%, but all dividends are then deemed to have been taxed at that rate when they reach the shareholder.[2] The only reservation is that the company must have paid sufficient tax on its profits to cover the tax credit. Failing this it will have to pay additional tax but this has no effect on the shareholder's position.

A similar result can be achieved in a different way. In Norway corporations pay national income tax only on their retained profits, dividends being treated as a deductible expense but then taxed in the hands of the shareholders. As the figures in Illustration 8.2 show, this has the same effect as a system which imposes a dual rate of tax on corporate income when it levies a nil rate on the distributed element.

Illustration 8.2

£		Full imputation £	Dividends deductible £	Dual rate 40/0%
(a)	Profit	100	100	100
(b)	Dividend paid	30	50	50
(c)	CT on (a) at 40%	40		
	CT on (a) – (b) at 40%		20	20
	CT on (b) at 0%			0
(d)	Profit retained			
	(a) – (b) – (c)	£30	£30	£30
(e)	Shareholder income (b)	30	50	50
(f)	Tax thereon at 40%	0*	20	20
(g)	Net income (e) – (f)	£30	£30	£30

* Covered by the imputed tax credit of £20000 on a cash dividend of £30000, i.e. 40% of the grossed-up dividend.

Thus the formal structure of a tax may differ and this may have some technical consequences but these need not produce any real difference in the impact of the tax. A further variation can be found in Hong Kong. All corporate income is fully taxed there, but dividends do not enter into the calculation of taxable income of the shareholders. This is disadvantageous for the low rate shareholder who cannot claim a refund of all or part of the company tax, but it is advantageous for the higher rate shareholder. Much depends on the range of personal tax rates in the country concerned.

The arrangements in West Germany exhibit an unusual combination of systems. Company income is taxed at two rates, 56% if retained and 36% if distributed, the latter being levied on the profit needed to cover the distributions, not on the distributions themselves. Dividends are then subject to a further 25% withholding tax (unless a lower rate is agreed for payments to foreign shareholders). The results can be seen by referring to Illustration 8.3.

Illustration 8.3.

		£	£
(a)	Profit		1000
(b)	Dividend (say)		320
(c)	Company tax: 500000 at 56%	280	
	500000 at 36%	180*	460
(d)	Profit retained (a) – (b) – (c)		£120

* The distributed profit is deemed to be 500000 as, after charging tax on 500000 at 36%, 320000, the amount of the dividend, remains. Note in the next line how the profit retained is 44% of 500000, i.e. the undistributed profit less tax at 56%.

Now consider the dividend:

		£	£
(e)	Dividend declared (as (b))		320
(f)	Less extra tax withheld at 25%		80
(g)	Cash paid to shareholders (e) – (f)		240
(h)	Tax credits available:		
	Company tax, 36% of 500000 (line (c) above)	180	
	Extra tax withheld (f)	80	260
(i)	Effective gross dividend		£500

It will be seen that the dividend is treated as if tax of £260000 (52%) had already been paid on income of £500000. This may cause many individual shareholders to claim a refund but the high rate of tax already levied is a powerful weapon against tax evasion on undeclared dividend income. The highest rate of personal tax in West Germany is 56%.

The various systems discussed so far have all tried to reflect an identity between the company and its shareholders by ensuring that they were not both fully taxed on the same profits. We turn now to a very different approach.

THE CLASSICAL SYSTEM

From a legalistic point of view it can be argued that a company's existence is totally separate from that of its owners/shareholders.[3] This argument has been developed to the stage of treating them as separate subjects of taxation as well. Several countries in Europe, including Belgium, Denmark and the Netherlands, approach company taxation from this angle. However, the example we will take by way of illustration is the United States.[4]

The effect of the system, usually known as the 'classical system', is to tax distributed profits twice, once when earned and then when distributed. A dividend received by a shareholder from a large US company will have been taxed as follows:

		£
(a)	Underlying profit	100
(b)	Company tax at 46%	46
(c)	Dividend ((a) − (b), full distribution)	54
(d)	Shareholder tax at 40% (say) on (c)	21.60
(e)	Cash remaining (c) − (d)	£32.40

Thus the combined rate of tax is 67.6% ((b) +(d)).

This high rate of tax is mitigated in many cases because there are lower rates of tax on smaller companies. At the time of writing the tax due on an annual profit of $100 000 would be $25 750 at which point any addition to profit would be taxed at the full rate of 46%.

This so called 'economic double taxation' is modified if the dividends are paid to other companies in the United States. If it were not so the tax could be treble, quadruple or more according to the number of companies through which the dividend passed on its way to the ultimate shareholder. Just as in the UK inter-company dividends are 'franked', so in the United States 85% of dividends received by companies are deducted from their taxable profits.[5]

It should be apparent by now that the element of double taxation in the classical system may have important consequences for economic and financial decisions.

ECONOMIC DISTORTIONS CAUSED BY COMPANY TAXATION

It is never easy to show what effect taxation has had on an economic equilibrium. So many factors are operating simultaneously that any single one can seldom be isolated. Nevertheless it is necessary that we make some attempt to show what happens, even if only by a process of deductive reasoning.

Let us consider first the effect of taxation on a decision to form, or not to form, a company. In other words does the taxation system discriminate between companies and unincorporated businesses? We noted at the end of Chapter 7 that in some countries companies may be taxed as partnerships and vice versa, thus demonstrating that one form of taxation may be preferable to the other.

One tax advantage obtained by forming a company can lie in the ability to regulate the flow of personal incomes to shareholders and directors. Under a progressive income tax system with a company tax rate below the higher personal rates there can be significant benefits, especially when a business is growing and most of its profits are being ploughed back. In this respect, contrast the company with the partnership whose income may be taxed at the higher personal rates whether drawn out of the business or not.

Conversely, a company may be at a relative disadvantage, especially under the classical system, if its level of distributions is high and subjected to double taxation as shown in the previous section. Double taxation does not apply to 'small' companies in the UK, although partial imputation still leaves two layers of taxation. However, double taxation does not happen even under a classical system if profits can be drawn out in a tax deductible form, such as directors' remuneration or loan interest. If, for instance, a company has a profit of £10000 and pays out all of it as additional remuneration then there will be not tax on the company. Despite these reservations there will be cases in some countries where forming a company results in tax disadvantages relative to a partnership.

Companies are formed for good commercial reasons. That is, after all, the reason why the idea of incorporation was developed in the first place. If the tax system distorts the decision to form a company, that implies that there is a move away from an economic optimum. Furthermore, there could be discrimination in respect of whole sectors of the economy where incorporation is necessary for other reasons or, alternatively, sectors where it is not usual or possible (perhaps because of the regulation of the learned professions).

Once a company has been formed the tax system may then distort the many decisions it must make. For instance, within the bounds of commercial possibility companies may be financed by different proportions of equity and loan capital and may use asset leasing to various degrees. The choice between equity and loans is likely to be distorted if interest is tax deductible and dividends are not. On the other hand, equity investors may be looking for capital growth as well as dividends and their capital gains may be taxed more favourably or not at all. Many possibilities exist but we will confine the discussion which follows to the choice between equity and loans and will assume that there is a classical system which taxes dividends twice but allows loan interest to be deducted in calculating taxable profits.

The immediate response of companies to the introduction of a classical system was seen in the UK in 1965–66. (The present imputation system dates only from 1973.) Many companies, reacting to the apparent tax advantages, resorted to loan finance when they went to the capital markets for new capital. Indeed, some people argued at the time that this was a desirable effect in view of the relatively low gearing of UK companies compared with other countries.[6] However, market forces will tend to respond to such a move as follows:

(1) Higher gearing increases the risk factor because interest, unlike dividends, is payable whether or not there are profits, and this increased risk is likely to be reflected in the 'price' paid for loan finance.
(2) A generally increased demand for loans will also tend to increase the 'price' in order to induce lenders who would have preferred equity to transfer their funds into loans.
(3) A restricted supply of equity investment opportunities in the market will tend to increase share prices.

Thus the market balance between equity and loans is altered (distorted) and companies find that the relative tax advantage of loans has been capitalized in relative prices. It follows that despite the tax distortion an individual company may not be able to afford to indulge in loan capital beyond its normal level.

The level of distributions is another decision which may be influenced by the tax system. It has been argued that the classical system tends to favour the retention of profit because of the additional tax payable by most shareholders when they receive a dividend. Illustration 8.4 helps to make the point clear.

Illustration 8.4

		Nil distribution £	Full distribution £
(a)	Profit	1000	1000
(b)	Tax thereon (say)	350	350
(c)	Profit after tax (a) – (b)	£650	£650
(d)	Dividend	Nil	650
(e)	Tax thereon (say) 40%	—	260
(f)	Available for re-investment	650(c)	£390(d) – (e)

There is, of course, another difference between the two cases. In the Nil distribution case the £650 can only be invested by the same company, whereas the £390 can be invested by the shareholder in another company or in a different kind of investment. Thus it is argued that the classical system tends to guide re-investment into whatever opportunities are available to the company which earned the profits. This is not an efficient process as compared with giving the shareholder complete freedom to invest where better opportunities may exist or where management is more efficient.

What effect does the imputation system have in removing these distortions? Clearly it can remove, or at least reduce, the element of economic double taxation but its effect still depends on the differences between the shareholder tax rates and the dividend credit rate and on the existence of a capital gains tax. In Illustration 8.5 UK rates of tax are used. The tax on profit is at 35% and there is an imputation credit of 29% (i.e. 29/71 of the net dividend). Three different shareholder IT rates are considered, (1) 0%, (2) 29%, and (3) 50%.

Comparing the Nil distribution column with the others we see that in case (3) there is still a bias against distribution, but (2) is neutral and (1) favours distributions. However, these calculations ignore any potential capital gains tax on the enhanced value of the shares resulting from the profit retention. If we assume that the rise in share value is the same as the profit retained, and that after discounting for the effect of the delayed realization the present value of the CGT rate is 15%, we find that the benefit of the rise in share values following non-distribution is reduced from £650 to £552.[7]

It can be seen from this example that the direction of the distortion depends on the circumstances of the shareholder. It seems to follow from this fact that some shareholders (e.g. tax exempt charities) will be attracted to high distribution companies, while others (e.g. rich individuals) will be looking for high retention leading to capital growth. If so, it also follows that there will tend to be a concentration of particular types of shareholder in particular types of company. This form of market segmentation is another kind of distortion and may increase the risk of a portfolio because it is not spread fully over the range of opportunities available.

Another kind of distortion arising from the tax system stems from the rules about the calculation of taxable profit. One example will suffice. Reliefs for capital expenditure may, as in the UK, vary according to the nature of that expenditure. Until 1984 there was a spectrum of reliefs ranging from immediate write off to no relief at all. It is clear that investment in the former type of asset was being favoured, as were those industries which used such assets.

Illustration 8.5

		Nil distribution	Full distribution		
			(1)	(2)	(3)
		£	£	£	£
(a)	Profit	1000	1000	1000	1000
(b)	CT thereon	350	350	350	350
(c)	Profit after tax: (a) − (b)	£650	£650	£650	£650
(d)	Dividend	Nil	650	650	650
(e)	Tax credit (29/71 of (d))	Nil	265.49	265.49	265.49
(f)	Total IT due: 0/29/50% of (d) + (e)	Nil	Nil	265.49	457.74
(g)	Tax still due (refund): (f) − (e)	Nil	(265.49)	Nil	192.25
(h)	Shareholder cash: (d) −(g)	Nil	915.49	650	457.75
(i)	Available to re-invest	£650	£915.49	£650	£457.75

Another aspect of the distortion produced by these reliefs lies in the choice between capital intensive and labour intensive activity. Whether one is more efficient than the other depends on the costs involved and tax relief is one element in the net cost of the assets to be used.

Let us take a proposal for a four year project with annual revenues of £10000. The labour intensive approach requires an annual labour cost of £5000 and other costs of £3000 together with the purchase of an asset costing £5000 with no residual value. The capital intensive approach reduces the annual labour cost to £2000 but other costs rise to £4000. The asset cost is now £11000. In both cases the tax rate is 35%, tax is paid one year after the revenue is received and the discount rate is 10%. If we assume that relief for the cost of the asset is given in full in the year of acquisition the resulting calculations will appear as in Illustration 8.6.

It will be seen that the capital intensive scheme produces a net present value (NPV) of £806 compared with £769 for the labour intensive scheme. This result is close but the former scheme has the advantage. A lower discount rate would increase the relative advantage as can be seen from the non-discounted totals of £1950 and £3250, but a higher discount rate could produce negative returns for both schemes.

Now consider a change in the tax system so that relief for the cost of the fixed assets is spread evenly over the four years. The revised calculations are shown in Illustration 8.7 which shows only the lower lines of the calculations.

The labour intensive scheme has become the more desirable with a present value of £584 against £400. It seems reasonable to assume that if this change in relief is applied to all companies there will be an impact on the demand for labour. If there is no surplus of this type of labour this may result in higher wages, thereby affecting the outcome of the project itself as the labour cost figures will be affected.

It may be noted too that the present value of both projects has fallen because even the

Illustration 8.6

Year		0	1	2	3	4	5	Total
		£	£	£	£	£	£	£
1.	***Labour intensive*:**							
(a)	Revenue	—	10000	10000	10000	10000	—	40000
(b)	Labour cost	—	(5000)	(5000)	(5000)	(5000)	—	(20000)
(c)	Other costs	—	(3000)	(3000)	(3000)	(3000)	—	(12000)
(d)	Surplus before depreciation (a) – (b)– (c)	—	2000	2000	2000	2000	—	8000
(e)	Asset cost	(5000)	—	—	—	—	—	(5000)
(f)	Tax at 35% (on (d) –(e)	—	—	1050*	(700)	(700)	(700)	(1050)
(g)	Net flows (d) – (e) –(f)	£(5000)	£2000	£3050	£1300	£1300	£(700)	£1950
(h)	Discount factor	1	0.9091	0.8264	0.7513	0. 6830	0.6209	
(i)	Present value (g) × (h)	£(5000)	£1818	£2521	£977	£888	£(435)	£769
2.	***Capital intensive*:**							
(a)	Revenue	—	10000	10000	10000	—	40000	
(b)	Labour cost	—	(2000)	(2000)	(2000)	(2000)	—	(8000)
(c)	Other costs	—	(4000)	(4000)	(4000)	(4000)	—	(16000)
(d)	Surplus before depreciation (a) – (b) – (c)	—	4000	4000	4000	4000	—	16000
(e)	Asset cost	(11000)	—	—	—	—	—	(11000)
(f)	Tax at 35% (on (d) – (e))	—	—	2450*	(1400)	(1400)	(1400)	(1750)
(g)	Net flows (d) – (e) – (f)	£(11000)	£4000	£6450	£2600		£(1400)	£3250
(i)	Present value (g) × (h)	£(11000)	£3616	£5350	£1953	£1776	£(869)	£806

*Assumes that the excess over project income of the tax relief on the asset can be deducted from the tax on other profits of the same year. In 1(f) the relief on £5,000 exceeds the income of £2,000 by £3,000 and 35% of that is £1,050.

labour intensive one involves some capital outlays. It may be deduced that some very marginal projects will now not start at all, with consequences for the economy as a whole.

SOME CONSEQUENTIAL PROBLEMS OF MULTINATIONAL BUSINESS

We are not concerned in this book with the taxation of multinational business but we will look briefly at its impact on national tax systems. Consider first the case of a

Illustration 8.7

Year	0	1	2	3	4	5	Total
1. *Labour intensive*:	£	£	£	£	£	£	£
(d) Surplus before depreciation	—	2000	2000	2000	2000	—	8000
(e) Asset cost	(5000)	—	—	—	—	—	(5000)
(f) Tax at 35%*	—	—	(262)	(262)	(262)	(262)	(1048)
(g) Net flows	£(5000)	£2000	£1738	£1738	£(262)	£1952	
(h) Present value	£(5000)	£1818	£1436	£1306	£1187	£(163)	£584
2. *Capital intensive*:							
(d) Surplus before depreciation	—	4000	4000	4000	4000	—	16000
(e) Asset cost	(11000)	—	—	—	—	—	(11000)
(f) Tax at 35%*	—	—	(437)	(437)	(437)	(437)	(1748)
(g) Net flows	£(11000)	£4000	£3563	£3563	£3563	£(437)	£3252
(h) Present value	£(11000)	£3616	£2944	£2677	£2434	£(271)	£400

*35% of (surplus less 25% of asset cost).

company resident and taxable in one country but having shareholders resident in another country. These shareholders may be individuals or they may consist of a holding company and/or other companies.

In some ways the classical system works well in this kind of situation. The company is taxed in the country where it makes its profits and the shareholder tax can be levied quite separately in the country where they reside. There may be a problem if the country from which the dividends are paid requires the company to deduct tax from the dividends in addition to the tax on the profits. The shareholder is then dependent on his home country giving credit for the extra tax withheld in calculating his home liability, and on that tax being at a lower rate than his actual rate (unless arrangements are made for all or part of it to be repaid). This sort of problem is usually dealt with through bilateral treaties between the countries concerned.

However, there may still be a problem for a holding company. As we have seen, dividends paid between companies within one country usually add little or nothing to the recipient's tax bill but when such dividends cross a national frontier it becomes vital that:

(1) the recipient country either exempts them from further tax, or allows credit to be given for any extra dividend tax deducted and for the profits tax underlying the dividend, and

(2) any dividend tax be levied at a low rate in the country of origin so that the combined rate (on profit and on dividend) shall not be excessive in relation to the recipient country tax rate on profits.[8]

Unless these conditions are satisfied the higher rate of tax on foreign earnings will discriminate against foreign investment of this type. This fact may be used by countries which wish to discourage either inward or outward investment for economic or political reasons.

The problems are increased if either country, or both, have an imputation system. The difficulty arises from the use of part (or all) of the tax on profits to give shareholders a tax credit. Countries which themselves have a classical system may not recognize the imputed tax as being equivalent to the direct dividend tax imposed on their own residents. Where bilateral agreements (tax treaties) have been signed between countries in this position they have often required the 'imputation' country to repay the tax credit to the foreign shareholder directly and replace it by a separate dividend tax levied by deduction at source.

Another kind of problem arises where a company subject to an imputation system (as in the UK) receives foreign income which has already been taxed. Although credit can be given for that foreign tax the offset of advance corporation tax (ACT) may then be restricted. Illustration 8.8 shows how this may happen.

Illustration 8.8

	£000
UK company:	
Foreign income (tax paid thereon £400000)	1000
UK income	500
Total income	£1500
Dividend paid in AP	600
ACT paid on dividend (29/71 of £600 000)	245.07
Tax calculation:	
CT on total income (35% of £1.5 million)	525
less: Credit for foreign tax	350
CT still due	175
less: ACT set off (restricted to 29% of £500 000)	145
MCT still payable	£30

The credit for foreign tax is restricted to the UK tax rate of 35% so the foreign tax balance of £50000 (5% of £1 million) goes unrelieved. ACT can only be set off to the extent of 29% of the UK income,[9] leaving £100070 unrelieved but available for use against the CT of other APs.

These complications would still exist even if all countries decided to adopt the imputation system. The scheme which was devised (but not yet adopted) to harmonize company taxation in the European Communities proposed an imputation system but envisaged some rather complicated arrangements whereby one member state would recover from another state those tax credits repaid to a shareholder which related to company taxes which had been paid in the first place to that other state. This process could pass through several countries if a multinational holding company paid dividends out of the profits earned by its subsidiaries in several member states.[10]

The conclusion seems to be that in an increasingly multinational business world a country cannot afford to adopt a system of company taxation without taking into account the international effects. Thus the sort of revolutionary system to be described at the end of Chapter 9 might be excluded from serious consideration because it would leave that country out of line with its trading partners.

NOTES AND REFERENCES

1. This is the rate for 1986/87. Rates for other years are given in the Appendix.
2. The details here and in the following discussion are taken from *Tax Digests 39 and 40*. Institute of Chartered Accountants in England & Wales, London (1985).
3. See *Salomon v. Salomon & Co.* (1897) AC 22, and the discussion, for instance, in Chapter 5 of Gower L.C.B., *Principles of Modern Company Law*, Stevens, London (1979).
4. See note 2 above.
5. This statement is true in general but depends on certain requirements being satisfied.
6. Gearing is the ratio between loan and equity capital. It is sometimes called 'leverage'.
7. 552 = 85% of 650. If the nominal rate of CGT is 30% a delay of 10 years discounted at just over 7% per annum gives an equivalent current rate of 15%.
8. For instance, a rate of 50% on profits and 25% on dividends gives a combined rate of 62½% which is likely to be well above the rate levied on domestic profits.
9. See Chapter 7.
10. See Chown, J.F., 'The Harmonisation of Corporation Tax in the EEC', in *British Tax Review*. Sweet & Maxwell, London (1976), at page 39.

EXERCISES AND DISCUSSION TOPICS

1. You are considering emigration to set up a manufacturing enterprise in one of three countries, A, B or C. Commercial prospects, living conditions and personal tax rates are similar in each case but your company would be taxed differently, viz.

Country	A	B	C
Company tax system	Imputation	Imputation	Classical
Tax rate on profits (%)	45	40	30
Imputation rate (% of net dividend)	50	66.67	Nil
Capital gains tax rate (%) on companies and individuals	30	30	Nil

You anticipate that if all goes well you will distribute only a small proportion of your profits in the early years but when the business prospers you hope to draw out a larger part of your profits in order to diversify your investment and reduce the risk of loss.

Required:
Discuss the effect of these tax systems on your choice of country.

2. Mr and Mrs Nightingale, who have recently become your clients, own 96% of the shares of Tinsmiths Ltd. and are the only directors of the company, which is engaged

in metalwork; the remaining shares are owned by by Bechmesser, who is manager of the business. They have asked you for your advice in connection with the taxation aspects of the following matter.

The company has never paid a dividend, but the Nightingales have been told by a friend that it is now better to pay dividends rather than directors' remuneration. They are taxed separately on their earnings and for the last three years their marginal tax rates have been 50% for Mr Nightingale and 40% for his wife; the company's taxable profits after remuneration have been in the range £30000 to £50000.

Requirement:
Draft a memorandum in preparation for a meeting with Mr and Mrs Nightingale to discuss the taxation aspects of the matter.

3. The following information was reported on one day in *The Financial Times* and relates to three UK companies.

	X	Y	Y
Dividend cover – times	3.8	2.2	2.0
Dividend yield (%)	1.6	3.5	9.4
Price/earnings ratio	23.8	14.9	7.5

Bearing in mind the nature of the United Kingdom tax system discuss the implications of these figures for the kinds of shareholder these companies are likely to attract.

4. The following information has been extracted from the records of Nerston Ltd, a UK resident company, for its trading year to 31 March 1987.

	£
Trade profits	80000
Overseas income (gross)	200000
Debenture interest paid (before deduction of income tax)	40000
Capital gains (before abatement)	24000
Dividends paid in the year, final dividend	
for the year to 31 March 1986	126000

Debenture interest was paid on 7 July 1986 and dividends were paid on 1 December 1986; overseas tax due on the income of £200000 arising in an oversease country was £500000 paid on 30 November 1986.

Required:
Compute mainstream corporation tax payable for the accounting period to 31 March 1987, giving effect to all reliefs available and showing any advance corporation tax not utilized.

ACCA, Level 3, December 1985 (Question updated.)

9   What is business income?

Once it is accepted that business profits, whether earned by companies, partnerships, sole traders or other bodies, are to be taxed it becomes desirable to use a definition of profit that is administratively feasible and at the same time fair to those who are to be taxed. The first four sections of this chapter will describe the way in which profit is defined for UK tax purposes. The last two sections will discuss possible variants.

THE HISTORIC COST ACCOUNTING BASE

It is likely that a tax system will operate more cheaply and smoothly if it uses information that is needed for other purposes and concepts that are already familiar. Such is the case in the UK. The calculation of taxable income arising from trades, professions and vocations starts with the accounts (already required by law in the case of companies) prepared in accordance with the accepted conventions.

These conventions are described in any good introductory accounting text. What follows is only a brief description of those which are important for tax purposes.

The accounts of a business consist of a series of balance sheets, usually drawn up at one year intervals, linked by income statements showing the profit made during each of those intervals. In most cases assets appear in the balance sheets at their original cost figure less, where necessary, the accumulated depreciation which has been charged against income year by year to reflect the use made of a wasting asset over its useful life. The income is calculated on an accruals basis, the incoming earned during the period and the related outgoings being matched to produce a final net income figure. Thus sales are recorded when made and interest receivable is credited to the period to which it relates, in both cases without regard to the timing of receipt of the cash (unless there is an expectation that no cash will be received at all). Costs are recorded for the period to which they relate, irrespective of the timing of the actual cash payment. Goods purchased for resale are not charged against profit until they are resold or lost.

An important distinction has been made between fixed and circulating capital. Fixed capital consists of those assets which are purchased for use in the business, for instance the factory in which production is to take place. Circulating capital consists of assets which are purchased for resale, either in their existing form or as part of a processed product. This distinction can be important for tax purposes as the sale of fixed assets will normally give rise to a capital gain, if anything, whereas the sale of current assets (circulating capital) will produce income.

While the distinction can easily be stated it is not so easily defined in particular cases. Thus small tools are often written off as current assets even though they may have a useful life lasting several years and so display the characteristics of a fixed asset.

One of the overriding accounting conventions is that of prudence. This means that profit should not be anticipated and that future benefits arising from costs incurred should not be assumed unless there is firm and reliable evidence that they will arise. Thus goods for resale are valued at their cost, not at their expected selling price (unless the latter is below cost) and advertising and product development costs are usually written off when incurred rather than being held over to be charged against the future income which they are expected to produce.

Part of the rationale for prudence is that owners and creditors should not be given too rosy a picture of the business's prospects. However, if tax liability is the main consideration prudence can be used to reduce the tax bill, or defer part of it until a later year. The degree of prudence adopted may have a significant effect on the tax burden.

The exploitation of accounting conventions to reduce tax liability is, however, limited by the attitude of the courts. The courts act as the final arbiters in the resolution of disputes about tax liability and have been required to make many decisions without the benefit of statutory guidance. Two topics are offered as examples of such decisions.

The first concerns the valuation principles to be adopted for trading stock (inventory). The standard basis is cost, or market value, whichever is lower. Three strands can be identified in the decisions that have been made. The first is the definition or identification of cost. Thus it was established by court decision, not by statute, that the FIFO principle (first in first out) was to be used, not LIFO (last in first out), although the latter is common in the USA. LIFO is more favourable for tax purposes when prices are rising. Another aspect of cost is the extent to which overhead or indirect costs are to be included in the value of completed or partially completed items. In the Duple Motor Bodies case the courst did not give a general decision but did decide in that case that only direct costs need be included.[1]

The second strand concerns the comparison between cost and market value: should they be compared item by item or by taking all items in aggregate? The latter method is unlikely to produce a market value below cost unless the stock is largely of one type. The decision in the Cock, Russell case followed the normal accounting practice of comparing it item by item.[2]

The third strand is the meaning of the term 'market value'. Does it mean replacement cost, or selling price, or something else? In a case involving BSC Footwear the court concluded that it meant expected selling price, possibly reduced by any expenses directly incurred to make the sale.[3]

The second topic is the distinction that has to be made between business and personal income and expenditure and is important mainly for unincorporated businesses. It is one of the basic tenets of accountancy that business activity must be distinguished from activity which is personal to the owner of the business. When Lady Zia Wernher transferred thoroughbred horses from her stud farm (a business activity) to her racing stables (a personal activity, a hobby) it was held that the income of the stud farm must bring in the market value of the horses at the time of transfer.[4] This may seem to be an exotic example but the same principle can be applied to every trader who takes business goods for his own use. Nevertheless the principle does have some limitations. In a later case an attempt was made to tax the novelist Hammond Innes on the value of the copyright in *The Doomed Oasis* which he gave to his father. The courts decided in his favour, arguing that to do otherwise would mean that no-one could give professional services freely without having to pay tax on the value thereof.[5]

The role of the courts is only part of the story and the legislative constraints on the calculation of income have become increasingly important. Even so, the courts still have a vital interpretive role.

THE LEGISLATIVE CONSTRAINTS

Guidance on the calculation of business income falls into two broad categories, the rather general terms of the nineteenth century legislation, most of which is now contained in s.130, Taxes Act 1970, and the more precise and detailed legislation on particular issues which has been enacted more recently. Examples will be given of each type but these can be only a small selection of the many aspects which have been discussed by the courts.[6]

S.130(a) contains the most general guidance in that it prohibits the deduction of any expenditure unless it is 'laid out or expended wholly and exclusively for the purposes of the trade, profession or vocation'. This may sound to be no more than common sense but the courts have interpreted it restrictively in two respects. The first of these lies in the use of the words 'wholly and exclusively'. These have been taken to mean that there must be no other purpose even where the expenditure would not have been incurred but for the existence of the business. A self-employed carpenter found that he was not allowed to deduct the 'extra' cost of lunches which arose because he was working too far away from home to return there for the mid-day break. Lunches were held to be a personal necessity and could not be divided into two parts, one to be treated as a business expense.[7] Similarly Ann Mallallieu, a barrister, was not allowed to deduct the cost of clothing which she bought only to wear in court and which was not of type which she would wear otherwise.[8] Again clothing is a personal expense and the fact that the costs incurred partly reflect business or professional needs does not bring it within the term 'wholly and exclusively'.

The second leg of s.130(a) is the phrase 'for the purposes of the trade'. This has been used to justify a distinction between trading expenditure as such and expenditure incurred by particular owners. The leading case concerns a company which incurred fines and legal costs when it was found to be in breach of wartime trading regulations (during the 1914–18 war). Clearly there would have been a public policy incentive for the court not to allow mitigation of a fine imposed by another court by using it to reduce a tax liability. The court decided that the breach of regulation was not in itself a trading activity but an activity of those who directed the trade.[9] The fact that tax still had to be paid on the illegally acquired profits no doubt added to the sense of grievance felt by those concerned.

The second example seems to be more straightforward. Bassett Enterprise Ltd. was the subject of a take-over and the new owners arranged for it to pay off the service contracts of the former owners as part of the deal. The court held that the cost to Bassett arose out of the change of ownership and not out of the trade as such.[10] It may be noted that in more normal circumstances the cost of hiring and firing employees and directors is tax deductible as a cost incurred 'for the purposes of the trade'.

The next sub-section, s.130(b), refers to unincorporated businesses and prohibits any deduction for the maintenance of the proprietor or his family. This reinforces s.130(a) but it can also provide justification for apportioned deductions in respect of costs such as those of combined living and working accommodation and vehicle running expenses when it is partly used for private or dual-purpose journeys (the latter being non-deductible under the 'wholly and exclusively' phrase discussed above). The approach is different where companies are concerned. Then the costs are likely to be deductible as being incurred in connection with the employment of the person who benefits. However that person may be liable to tax under the terms of the Schedule E rules.[11]

S.130(i) is also of interest as it deals with the valuation of debtors, which can be a highly subjective process. The main valuation problem is that there may be a long list of debts some of which will, as usual, turn out to be irrecoverable, but which ones and to what extent is not yet known. Where tax is at stake it is in the trader's interest to exaggerate the risk and so s.130(i) prohibits any provision for bad debts unless it is related to specific debts about which there is information leading to an expectation of loss. One consequence of this is that, if a company decides to reduce an existing general provision and so re-credits part of it to the income account, that credit is not taxable because the original debt was not itself deductible for tax purposes.

No problem arises with debts that are actually written off as irrecoverable except that if they are recovered subsequently they will then be taxable. Later legislation ensures that bad debts recovered after the trade itself has ceased will be taxed as income of the former trader (under Case VI, Schedule D).[12]

An example of more modern legislation is contained in s.411, Taxes Act 1970, which deals with business entertaining in a very detailed and somewhat arbitrary fashion. The section was introduced in 1965 as a response to evidence that so-called 'business entertaining' was being used as a cover for private enjoyment without any very clear intention that a business process would be involved. The legislation envisages a wide range of possible activities such as meals, theatre visits, the provision of accommodation and sporting activity (even grouse shooting) and embraces the families and servants of the business people concerned. It also applies to gifts. The courts held that it applied even to the activities of journalists when they 'entertain' potential informants.[13]

Much of the detail in S.411 specifies what is not to be a prohibited deduction. Foreign customers, as carefully defined, and the company's own employees are excluded from the prohibition, although there can be problems if the entertainment in question benefits a mixture of categories. Gifts carrying a prominent advertisement are allowed provided they do not consist of food or drink and are not worth more than £10 per recipient per year. Thus the cost of a bottle of whisky or a turkey given to a customer at Christmas is disallowed but the 'pin-up' calendar is not.

Before we can say that we have established the ground rules for calculating taxable income there is one more topic to be explored.

THE DISTINCTION BETWEEN CAPITAL AND REVENUE

Reference was made earlier in this chapter to the distinction between fixed and circulating capital. If a fixed asset is sold any gain that results is not income but it may be chargeable to tax as a capital gain, usually at a lower rate of tax or with the benefit of roll-over relief.[14] Following the same logic the purchase of such an asset cannot be charged directly as an expense of earning income, unlike the cost of an asset purchased for resale. (Even then there may be a question about the period to which the cost should be allocated.) However, the distinction between the two kinds of asset is stated much more easily than it can be applied in practice as the two categories merge in a rather grey area. In illustrating this hazy borderline we will first consider asset disposals and then go on to look at acquisitions.

One difficulty that arises is when compensation is received for the loss of an asset. This is not a normal business transaction but some degree of equivalence may be detected. Thus in the Gliksten case it was held that compensation for the loss by fire of a stock of timber was taxable, being in one sense equivalent to the sale thereof.[15] Similarly compensation received by Short Bros. for the cancellation of a contract to build a ship when it was already partly built was treated as being equivalent to their income from the sales of completed ships.[16] For all we know they completed the ship and sold it to some other buyer.

More difficulty arises with the loss of what are clearly fixed assets because their value to the business cannot be divorced from their use to make profits. The complete loss of such an asset may be treated like a sale thereof, but the loss of use of it for a limited period may give rise to compensation which is intended merely to plug the hole in the profits. Two cases illustrate the point. In the first The Caledonian Railway Company (yes, this is a very old decision!) paid compensation, calculated by reference to the profits foregone, to a quarry company in return for an undertaking by the latter not to dig the land adjacent to the railway tracks. The court accepted the argument that part of the quarry company's fixed asset, the land, had been sterilized permanently and that the position was equivalent to the sale of part of that fixed asset. In the second case the owners of a jetty received compensation for damage and loss of profits following a collision by a ship which resulted in the jetty being unusable for just over one year. This time the court decided that the 'loss of profits' compensation was merely filling the hole in the profits and was therefore taxable as part of the income of the period concerned.[17]

In the cases described so far the fixed and current assets were tangible but the classification problem can be even more difficult when the asset consist of rights. The leading case involved a cartel arrangement between Van Den Berghs (now Unilever) and its Dutch counterpart by which they shared the market for margarine. The arrangement became inoperable because of the 1914–18 war in Europe and eventually the British company received compensation related to the loss of profits and in the context of a re-negotiated agreement. The court held that the agreement was fundamental to the structure of the company's business and was therefore a fixed asset. Thus the compensation received was capital.[18] This decision can be applied to quite modest sums provided they satisfy the description given above.[19] In contrast to these cases are those of commission agents working for several principals, usually on short-term contracts whose mix changes often. Loss of such a contract is not treated as the loss of a fixed asset and any compensation therefore falls into the 'hole in the profits' category and is taxable as income.[20]

Turning now to the expenditure side of the account, the difference between fixed and current assets can be crucial to tax liability because relief for the cost of fixed assets, if available at all, will be spread over many years and so will be much less valuable than immediate relief. A clear statement of principle was made by Lord Cave in the Court of Appeal in 1926 and this has provided the foundation for later decisions. His statement was to the effect that expenditure will normally be capital if 'made, not only once and for all, but with a view to bringing into existence an asset or advantage for the enduring benefit of the trade'.[21]

It is clear that this statement applies to tangible assets acquired for long-term use but again the main difficulties have arisen with intangibles such as legal rights. Three fairly recent cases will be taken to illustrate the principle involved. Granada Motorway Services negotiated a change in the terms one of their leases so as to remove from the sales-related part of the rent calculation the effect of the tax component in the price of goods sold. The effect was significant in the sales figures for tobacco and cigarettes. The company paid £122220 in return for the revision of the lease and the court held that this was a capital sum as it produced an enduring advantage.[22] Thus the outlay was not deductible in calculating income for CT purposes.

In the second case Watney Combe Reid, a brewery company, had made payments to the tied tenants of some of its outlets as part of an expansion and improvement programme which involved installing managers instead of tenants. Again it was held that there was an enduring advantage as a result of these payments and so they were capital.[23] It may be noted in passing that there is no need for the Inland Revenue to show an actual quantifiable advantage, all that is needed is a hope or expectation. Thus abortive expenditure remains capital.

The third case concerned a payment by a credit card company (Access) to a rival organization in return for the latter giving up its participation in the Mastercharge scheme, and thereby ceasing to be a rival in that line of business. There was a clear advantage to Access and it endured.[24]

In the many other 'capital versus revenue' cases which have gone to the courts the arguments about repairs can be picked out as illustrating the pitfalls lying in wait for the ignorant and unwary. In normal circumstances the cost of repairing fixed assets is just a part of the running expenses of a business. Suppose, however, that an asset is in poor condition and is sold as such, leaving the new owner to undertake necessary repairs. In the Law Shipping case a ship was purchased in such a state of disrepair that the cost to the new owner of the necessary repairs totalled more than the cost of the ship itself. The court held that this repair cost was to be treated as if it was part of the cost of the ship (which it was agreed was a fixed asset).[25] The obvious way round this decision seems to be for the seller to undertake any necessary repairs before selling the asset, but this does not make commercial sense, especially if the seller is tempted to take short-cuts in doing the work.

A similar sort of problem arises when repairs are combined with or subsumed under desirable improvements. There can be no doubt that improvements to fixed assets constitute capital expenditure but the courts have decided that if they are mixed inextricably with or remove the need for repairs no apportionment can be made and the whole outlay is capital.[26]

There has also been considerable discussion about the distinction between repairs and replacements. A repair will involve replacement of a part (a roof tile, for instance) but replacement of the entirety is not a repair. What, then is the 'entirety'? For the free standing industrial chimney owned by Bullcroft Main Collieries it was the chimney itself, not the business complex as a whole.[27] In different circumstances where a chimney was part of a factory structure and did not stand by itself it was not treated as an entirety.[28] More recently the same issue arose when the Burnley Football Club replaced its Brunton Road Stand. It was decided that the stand had a separate existence within the stadium so the cost of the new structure amounted to the replacement of an entirety.[29] It may be deduced that a substantial repair to a more modern stadium, itself designed and built as an entity, would lead to a more favourable result from the owner's viewpoint, but in the Burnley case the stadium had been developed piecemeal and the structures differed widely in their age and style.

If an expenditure is capital, is that the end of any hope for tax relief? The answer to this question is our next topic.

CAPITAL EXPENDITURE RELIEF

The first approach to capital expenditure relief is contained in s.130(f). Taxes Act 1970, which implies that no relief at all can be claimed, and this piece of legislation still stands. However, it is a well established accounting practice that in calculating income a deduction should be made to recognize the fact that fixed assets such as machinery and buildings are being used up. This does not apply to freehold land as that does not wear out. The deduction depends on estimates of the expected useful life of the asset, on any residual value and on the pattern of depreciation over that life. All of these estimates are highly subjective. In some countries the accounting deduction is allowed for tax purposes provided it falls within defined parameters. The British approach is quite different.

In the UK tax computation the accounting figures for depreciation are ignored but quite separate deductions, known as capital allowances, replace them. This approach has two consequences. Accountants are free to pursue their own ideas about depreciation and to change them in the light of new circumstances and in response to new theories. The government in its turn is free to change the deduction system for economic and other reasons without having to concern itself with the effect on the income figures reported to shareholders, creditors and others. What follows from this is that the accounting profit may be quite different from the taxable profit and so an actual tax burden shown in accounts may reveal a rate of tax on accounting profit which is far removed from the nominal rates of tax specified for the years concerned.

Having a statutory system of capital allowances means that it specifies those groups of assets which qualify for relief. If an asset does not fall within a defined group no relief for its cost is available. This is an important feature in the UK as no relief is provided for commercial buildings such as shops and offices. The two principal qualifying groups are (1) industrial buildings, and (2) machinery and plant, and these will now be outlined.

Industrial buildings

The relief for industrial buildings applies to structures as well as buildings and includes addition to existing assets. There is a detailed and comprehensive list of qualifying activities which include manufacturing, processing, warehousing, transport, mining, quarrying and fishing.[30] Small proportions of non-qualifying expenditure are treated as if they qualify, e.g. an office within a factory.

The basis of relief is that the cost when new (excluding land) is written off evenly over 25 years at a rate of 4% per year. Before 1 April 1986 an initial allowance was given in the first year so the building was written off in less than 25 years but the 25 year 'life' was still important if the building was sold within that period. When such a sale occurs the allowances already given are withdrawn but only to the extent that the sale price (for the building, not the land) exceeds the unrelieved expenditure. If the selling price exceeds the cost price a chargeable gain may arise as well. The new owner can claim relief on his outlay, but not in excess of the original cost of the building, over the balance of the 25 year period. This relief is available even if the unrelieved residue had been reduced to zero as a result of the pre-1986 allowances. However, if the building has passed the 25 year point no reliefs are withdrawn and the new owner can claim nothing. These points are demonstrated in Example 9.1 at the end of this chapter.

Clearly such an arbitrary system leads to problems in practice. The purchaser of a new building will need to know exactly what reliefs are available as they affect the net cost to him, and any necessary apportionments (e.g. between building and land) will have to be agreed between the parties. Further complications arise if the original building has been added to or improved as it will then consist, for tax purposes, of two or more 'buildings' of different ages.

Machinery and plant

Unlike industrial buildings the scope of the words 'machinery and plant' is not defined in the statute and so their common meaning has been relied on by the courts in deciding disputed cases. The result has been to produce quite a wide-ranging working definition as the courts have looked at the functional characteristics of disputed items. Thus they have included furniture, fittings and curtains in a hotel,[31] a dry dock,[32] and a swimming pool built for the use of the customers of a holiday camp.[33] On the other hand they have sought to define a careful line so as to exclude buildings, even a temporary hutment,[34] and things such as lighting which go with buildings.[35] At one time they drew back from allowing relief for reference books owned by a professional man[36] but this view has since been modified.[37]

The system of relief for machinery and plant is quite different from that given for industrial buildings. Relief is given on all purchases, new or used, at a rate of 25% per year, calculated on the reducing balance basis. Thus after 5 years nearly a quarter of any expenditure remains unrelieved.[38] There were additional first year reliefs before 1986 which resulted in a more rapid write-off.

When plant is sold the reliefs already given need not be withdrawn directly. Most plant is dealt with in one combined calculation, the 'pool', and any sale proceeds merely reduce the pool for purposes of future calculation. This pool system does not apply for so-called 'short life' assets which can be held separately and may lead to balancing relief if sold within 5 years.[39] (See Example 9.2.)

Three other types of asset are excluded from the main pool. Motor cars in general are dealt with as a separate pool. Expensive motor cars (i.e. cost exceeding £8000) are subject to a £2000 annual relief restriction and each is dealt with individually. In the case of unincorporated businesses any assets, such as the proprietor's car, which are partly used for private purposes have to be dealt with individually. This would be unavoidable anyway if the proportion of private use varies from year to year.

Capital allowances can be claimed on a variety of other assets, each according to rules applicable to the category. Such assets include hotels, patent rights, scientific research, know-how, and agricultural buildings. These items will not be covered in this book.

THE EFFECT OF PRICE CHANGES

It will be realized by now that the calculation of taxable trading income described in the previous sections of this chapter is firmly based on the historic cost accounting conventions and that the statutory modifications serve only to limit choices which could otherwise be used to limit or delay tax liability. However, it has been argued that such a tax system is unfair when prices are rising and a part of the historic cost based profits has to be retained in the business to provide the funds needed to maintain the capital invested in real, as opposed to money, terms. This is not the place to enter into the arguments about systems of accounting designed to deal with changes in either specific prices or prices generally. We will content ourselves with looking at adjustments that have actually been made for tax purposes and we will consider whether any general adjustment is possible.

It is instructive to look at the response to a crisis that occurred in the UK late in 1974 when rates of general price inflation had risen sharply and many business had severe liquidity problems because of their need to finance current assets at those higher prices. As an emergency measure businesses were allowed to reduce their tax bills by deducting from taxable profits the amount of any increase in investment in inventory during their accounting year. Stock relief, as it was called, continued for some years but had to be modified frequently to deal with problems of implementation which had not been foreseen. It was abolished in 1984 when the rate of inflation had fallen substantially and was expected to fall further. In its later form the relief sought to achieve objectivity by the use of a general index adjustment but this meant that it gave little help to those companies which had to face sharply rising prices in particular commodities. It is perhaps unfortunate that the UK tax law never followed the US example and adopted the LIFO basis of cost identification as that mitigates the problem of rising prices. However, a change to LIFO could only be introduced after due notice as it would require modifications to the existing accounting systems. There would, too, be problems in the transition.

The other big issue in accounting for rising prices is the depreciation calculation. With general inflation running at the sort of rate seen in the UK in the 1970s the price of a fixed asset could easily double before it had been in use for 5 years. Accounts would then show sales at current prices while one element in the costs deducted appeared in the same accounts at a money figure which represents a quite different currency level. The problem for taxation purposes was eased by the existence in past years of substantial capital allowances given in the first year of use before the price level had time to alter significantly. In fact most plant and machinery was being written off in the year of acquisition.

However, these were no more than piecemeal arrangements for relief and nothing was done to adjust other items that were affected by inflation. Thus when interest rates rose to high levels, partly as a response to the effect of inflation in eroding the purchasing power of fixed capital values expressed in nominal terms, no attempt was made to define income in terms of some concept of a 'real' rate of interest. In many countries with persistently high levels of inflation the financial system itself has adjusted so that money is lent on an index-linked basis and a 'true' rate of interest is charged on the adjusted capital. It may well be that a tax adjustment is only feasible when the financial system itself has been modified.

Nevertheless a problem of discrimination remains. It has been argued, for instance, that the favourable reliefs for plant and machinery and for the rising prices of inventory were discriminatory against those businesses which were also affected by inflation but which traded in other ways. The reverse case may now be said to exist in so far as businesses which depend on the use of long-life depreciable assets and heavy investment in inventory are relatively worse off than others so long as inflation continues. The absence of special reliefs does not mean that the tax system is neutral.[40]

The two accounting systems that have been considered for use in computing taxable income are current cost accounting (CCA) and current purchasing power accounting (CPP). It seems likely that the possibility of using some such system for taxation purposes contributed to the original attempts to develop them for regular use. In fact the use of CCA as finally recommended was confined to a small minority of mainly large companies, yet it is apparent that it could only be used for taxation if it was applied to all businesses.

Unfortunately the CCA system that was developed was not really suitable for tax purposes, and indeed this objection may be inherent in any such system.[41] Many of the adjustments to be made depended on subjective judgements, for instance the estimated current cost of an asset purchased some years ago and no longer available in the same form because of technological change. Nor is it possible in the real world to match the current cost of each sale against the revenue from that sale and various approximation methods were suggested. Likewise the monetary working capital and gearing adjustments depended on the classification of financial assets and liabilities. Even if the doubts about the ability and willingness of small firms to adopt it could be overcome it seems that the subjectivity of CCA made it unacceptable for tax purposes.[42] Perhaps some development of a CPP system, while theoretically less justifiable, might have had a better chance of success.[43]

The final section of this chapter deals with a much more revolutionary proposal but this has the incidental effect of overcoming the inflation problem.

CASH FLOW BASES

When it reported on its fundamental examination of the system of direct taxation in the UK the Meade Committee[44] argued that if companies were to be taxed at all they should not be taxed on income because of the economic distortion produced thereby. In considering the proposals which are about to be described it should be borne in mind that they are related to the personal expenditure tax applicable to individuals which was described in Chapter 3. Such a tax would also apply to unincorporated businesses.

The Meade Committee proposed a cash flow tax and set out two variants, one based on cash flows arising from real assets only (R), the other on flows arising from both real and financial assets (R + F). In the first case all cash coming from the sale of goods and services and from the sale of non-financial assets would be taxed after deduction of corresponding outflows. Thus the accrual basis of conventional accounting would be abandoned and the distinction between capital and revenue would be irrelevant.

At the time of the Meade proposal the almost immediate relief for many capital outlays made it appear that transition to the R base would not be difficult. However, it would have meant that there would be no tax liability on investment income and no relief for interest paid, unlike the existing system, so there would be problems, for instance, for companies which had borrowed heavily on the basis that interest payments were tax deductible.

This problem leads us to the alternative, the R + F base. This would add to the R base all transactions in financial assets, with the exception of UK equity. Thus the receipt of a loan would be a cash inflow (taxable) but would be offset by resulting cash outflows such as the purchase of property or the repayment of an existing loan. However, this R + F base can be taken one stage further.

Using Meade's terminology all cash flows fall into four categories, real (R), financial (F), tax (T), and equity (S). It can be shown that these flows must balance and so we get (using $\overline{R}$ etc. to indicate outflows):

$$R + F + T + S = \overline{R} + \overline{F} + \overline{T} + \overline{S}$$

This can be re-arranged to give:

$$R - \overline{R} + F - \overline{F} = \overline{T} - T + \overline{S} - S$$

The left-hand side of the equation is the R + F base and $\overline{T} - T$ must be a function thereof. It follows that $\overline{S} - S$, which is the net amount of equity outflows, can be used to provide the calculation of $\overline{T} - T$. For the most part $\overline{S} - S$ will consist of dividends paid less received, but it embraces new capital subscribed, capital repaid, and investment or disinvestment in other UK companies.

The interesting point that arises from expressing tax liability in terms of $\overline{S} - S$ is that it is no longer necessary to use annual accounts as the relevant transactions will be few in number. This in turn means that all companies can be taxed on the basis of a common financial year. It should be noted that the tax rate will appear to be very high. If the tax rate for the R + F base is 50% then the same tax will amount to 100% of the S base! It is of course the same tax.

It is reasonable to argue that this system of company taxation could not be introduced by itself and that there would be some difficult transitional problems. If it does nothing else, and it may not, the exercise helps to widen perspectives in looking at the basis of business taxation.

EXAMPLES

Example 9.1 Industrial buildings allowances

Facts:
Engineers Ltd. bought a plot of land for £50 000 in 1980 and had a factory built on it at a cost of £40 000. The building was completed and brought into use in January 1981. In January 1987 Engineers Ltd. sold the factory to Processors Ltd. for £95 000, of which it is agreed £60 000 should be apportioned to the land. Both companies prepare their accounts for calendar years.

Reliefs–Engineers Ltd.

			£	£
AP	1981	Cost of factory (excluding land)		£40 000
		Initial allowance (50%)*	£20 000	
		Writing-down allowance (WDA) (4%)	1 600	£21 600
		Residue		£18 400
AP	1982	–1986 (5 years):		
		WDA (1 600 × 5)		£8 000

Residue		£10400
AP 1987 Sale proceeds (excluding land)		£35000
Balancing charge		£24600

The balancing charge is added to the taxable income for 1987.
*The rate for that time, since abolished.

Reliefs – Processors Ltd.

Cost of factory:	
Residue at 31.12.86	10400
Balancing charge as above	24600
Qualifying expenditure	£35000

Balance of the asset's 25 year life:
January 1987 to January 2006 = 19 years

$$\therefore \text{ Annual WDA } \frac{35000}{19} \qquad\qquad £1842$$

Note how the WDA for Processors Ltd. is greater than it was for Engineers Ltd.

Example 9.2 Machinery and plant

Facts:
Distribution Ltd. started to trade in April 1985 when it purchased 3 vans at a total cost of £30 000 and a car for the manager at a cost of £5 000. In June 1987 it sold one of the vans for £2500 as it was surplus to requirements. The company makes up its accounts to 31 March each year.

Reliefs:		Pool £	Car £
AP to 31.3.86:			
Cost incurred		30000	5000
Initial allowance (50%)*	15000		
Writing down allowance (WDA) (25%)	7500	22500	1250
		7500	3750
AP to 31.3.87:			
WDA (25%)		1875	938
		5625	2812
AP to 31.3.88:			
Van sold		2500	
		3125	
		781	703
Unrelieved balance		2344	2109

* As it then was, now abolished.

Note how the sale of the van produces no immediate liability (contrast Example 9.1) but reduces future reliefs on the remaining vans.

NOTES AND REFERENCES

1. FIFO versus LIFO and related points were discussed in *Patrick* v. *Broadstone Mills* (1953) 35 TC 44, (1954) 1 All ER 163, and in *Minister of National Revenue* v. *Anaconda America Brass Co. Ltd.* (1956) 1 All ER 20, and the oncost point in *Duple Motor Bodies* v. *Ostime* (1961) 39 TC 537, 2 All ER 167.
2. *CIR* v *Cock, Russell & Co. Ltd.* (1949) 229 TC 387, 2 All ER 889.
3. *BSC Footwear v. Ridgeway* (1971) 47 TC 495, 2 All ER 534.
4. *Sharkey* v. *Wernher* (1955) 36 TC 275, 2 All ER 493.
5. *Mason* v. *Innes* (1967) 44 TC 326, 2 All ER 926.
6. A useful indication of the wide range of matters considered by the courts over the years can be found in Grout, V., *Tolley's Tax Cases*, Tolley Publishing Co., Croydon (annually).
7. *Caillebotte* v. *Quinn* (1975) 50 TC 222, 1 All ER 412.
8. *Mallalieu* v. *Drummond* (1983) 2 All ER 1095.
9. *CIR* v. *Alexander von Glehn & Co. Ltd.* (1920) 12 TC 232, 2 KB 553.
10. *Bassett Enterprise Ltd.* v. *Petty* (1938) 21 TC 730.
11. Under the benefits in kind legislation, see Chapter 5.
12. Chapter V of Part VI, Taxes Act 1970.
13. *Fleming* v. *Associated Newspapers Ltd.* (1972) 48 TC 382, 2 All ER 574.
14. Roll-over relief (ss. 115–123, Capital Gains Tax Act 1979) discussed in Chapter 5 is an important feature for continuing businesses as they are likely to use the proceeds of asset sales to buy new ones. With a minimum of planning a trading company is unlikely to pay CGT. Things may be different for an investment company.
15. *Green* v. *J. Gliksten & Son Ltd.* (1929) 14 TC 364.
16. *Short Bros. Ltd.* v. *CIR* (1927) 12 TC 955.
17. *Glenboig Union Fireclay Co. Ltd.* v. *CIR* (1922) 12 TC 427; *London & Thames Haven Oil Wharves Ltd.* v. *Attwooll* (1966) 43 TC 491, (1967) 2 All ER 124.
18. *Van den Berghs Ltd.* v. *Clark* (1935) 19 TC 390. It will be noticed that the fixed asset in question would not have appeared in the balance sheet of either company.
19. *Sabine* v. *Lookers Ltd.* (1958) 38 TC 120. The sum involved was only £3000.
20. *Kelsall, Parsons & Co.* v *CIR* (1938) 21 TC 608 is the leading case but there are many others which have depended on particular facts.
21. *Atherton* v. *British Insulated & Helsby Cables Ltd.* (1925) 10 TC 155. The actual decision is now irrelevant as the creation of a pension scheme, which was the purpose of the expenditure in question, is covered by later legislation.
22. *Tucker* v. *Granada Motorway Services Ltd.* (1979) 53 TC 92, 2 All ER 801.
23. *Watney Combe Reid & Co. Ltd.* v. *Pike* (1982) STC 733.
24. *Walker* v. *The Joint Credit Card Co. Ltd.* (1982) STC 427.
25. *Law Shipping Co. Ltd.* v. *CIR* (1923) 12 TC 621.
26. *Thomas Wilson (Keighley) Ltd.* v. *Emmerson* (1960) 39 TC 360.
27. *O'Grady* v. *Bullcroft Main Collieries Ltd.* (1932) 17 TC 93. The judgement is recommended for both its brevity and its humour.
28. *Samuel Jones & Co. (Devondale Ltd).* v. *CIR* (1951) 32 TC 513.
29. *Brown* v. *Burnley Football & Athletic Co. Ltd.* (1980) 53 TC 357, 3 All ER 244. The court noted the alleged responsibility of the building work for the team's lack of success on the field! At the time of writing they have descended to the 4th Division despite the new stand.
30. The full definition is in ss. 7–11, Capital Allowances Act 1968 (as revised by Finance Act 1982).

31. *CIR* v. *Scottish & Newcastle Breweries* (1982) 55 TC 252, 2 All ER 230.
32. *CIR.* v. *Barclay Curle & Co. Ltd.* (1969) 45 TC 221, 1 All ER 732.
33. *Cooke* v. *Beach Station Caravans Ltd.* (1974) 49 TC 514, 3 All ER 159.
34. *St. John's School* v. *Ward* (1974) 49 TC 524.
35. *Cole Bros. Ltd.* v. *Phillips* (1982) 55 TC 188, 2 All ER 247. A detailed study of this case illustrates the problem of knowing where to draw the line in practice. Compare it with the Scottish & Newcastle case referred to in note 31 above.
36. *Daphne* v. *Shaw* (1926) 11 TC 256.
37. *Mumby* v. *Furlong* (1976) 50 TC 491, 1 All ER 753.
38. $(1 - 0.25)^5 = 0.24$.
39. This applies from 1 April 1986 – see s.57 Finance Act 1985.
40. For a fuller discussion of this point see Devereux, M.P. and Mayer, C.P., *Corporation Tax: The Impact of the 1984 Budget*, Institute for Fiscal Studies, London (1984), and Confederation of British Industry, *Tax – time for change*, CBI, London (1985).
41. See the Green Paper, *Corporation Tax*, Cmnd. 8456, HMSO, London (1984), especially the discussion in Part III.
42. The details of the system adopted for a short period are contained in SSAP 16 (Accounting Standards Committee, London). This was developed from the report of the Sandilands Committee.
43. This was the original proposal of the accounting profession in 1973 before the appointment of the Sandilands Committee.
44. Institute for Fiscal Studies, *The Structure and Reform of Direct Taxation*, Allen & Unwin, London (1978).

EXERCISES AND DISCUSSION TOPICS

1. Mr Potter (who is 65 years of age and single) has been in business for many years. His profit and loss account for the year ended 30 June 1985 is as follows:

	[£]	[£]
Sales		45000
Less:		
Stock 1.7.84	2500	
Purchases	34000	
	36500	
less: Stock 30.6.84	3500	33000
		12000
Depreciation	250	
Light and heat	350	
Rent and rates	625	
Cleaning	225	
Accountancy	400	
Sundry	500	2350
Net profit		£9650

It has been agreed with the Inspector of Taxes that 20% of light and heat, rent and rates, and cleaning expenses are private. Mr Potter paid mortgage interest under MIRAS of £426 during 1986/87.

You are required to compute the Schedule D, Case I, profit and show the net tax payable by Mr Potter.

IoT, Associateship Intermediate Examination, May 1986
(Question updated.)

2. Discuss the taxation implications of the following transactions for all of the parties concerned:
   (a) A Ltd. supplied goods to B Ltd. which was one of its most important customers. B Ltd. ran into financial difficulty and A Ltd. made it a loan "to preserve an important part of its market'. B Ltd. subsequently went into liquidation and A Ltd. had to write off both the loan and the amount due for goods supplied.
   (b) C Ltd. sold its apple orchard to D Ltd. in August. A good crop was expected and the price agreed reflected this expectation.
   (c) E Ltd., a shipping company, placed an order for a ship. When the ship had been partly built it cancelled the order and paid a sum as compensation to the shipbuilder.
   (d) F Ltd. sought skilled labour from the Job Centre and was told that there was none available. A director of F Ltd. discovered two weeks later that the Job Centre had offered such labour to a rival company, G Ltd., and he accused the Job Centre manager of accepting bribes from that company. Subsequently F Ltd. agreed to bear the legal costs and damages awarded by the court in the case brought against the director by the Job Centre manager as a result of this unfounded (unprovable?) accusation.
3. Stoneyhurst Ltd. is a trading company, resident in the United Kingdom, which makes up its annual accounts to 31 March. It has no associated companies. The company's profit and loss account for the year ended 31 March 1986 was as follows:

Notes		£	£
	Gross trading profit		372100
1.	*Add*: Surplus on sale of house	17150	
	Debenture interest (gross)	3250	
	Dividends received from UK companies (gross)		
		4600	
	Building society interest received (net)	700	
2.	Bank deposit interest	360	26060
			398160
	Deduct:		
	Lighting and heating	1290	
	Repairs and renewals	1600	
3.	Depreciation	34650	
	Wages and salaries	24450	
	Directors' remuneration	35480	
4.	Subscriptions and donations	1350	
	Postage, stationery and telephone	525	
5.	Loan interest payable	17500	
6.	Professional expenses	6820	
7.	Miscellaneous expenses	1815	125480
	Net Profit		£272680

Notes

1. The asset disposal account of the house sold during the year was:

	£		£
Cost (April 1979)	17850	Accumulated depreciation	4000
Profit and loss	17150	Sale proceeds (September 1985)	31000
	£35000		£35000

[The house was worth £24,000 on 31 March 1982.]

2. The bank deposit account was opened 17 August 1985 and interest of £300 was credited to the account on 31 December 1985. £60 interest had accrued on the account at 31 March 1986.

3. *Depreciation*. Profits/losses on the disposals of plant and equipment/cars have been included in arriving at this figure.

4. *Subscriptions and donations*:

	£
Golf club subscription for sales director	150
National Trust	50
Political party	300
Local charities	75
Works social club	750
Trade association	25
	£1350

5. *Loan interest*. There was an accrued liability at 31 March 1986 for loan interest of £1500. There was no opening accrual.

6. *Professional expenses*:

	£
Audit and accountancy	3000
Costs of successful tax appeal	500
Legal fees re collection of bad debts	180
Costs of defending action by former director for wrongful dismissal	300
Legal costs on acquisition of a new seven-year lease on a warehouse	500
Architect's fees for designing a new warehouse which was not proceeded with	2340
	£6820

7. *Miscellaneous expenses*:

	£
Entertaining – foreign suppliers	70
– UK suppliers	340
– UK customers	180

Round-sum expense allowances to
company salesmen   1225
                                        ────────
                                         £1815

You are also given the following information.

1. The company paid a dividend of £18900 to its shareholders on 13 March 1986.
2. The written down values of capital assets at 1 April 1985 were:

	£
Plant and machinery (main pool)	72125
1980 Pool	10438
Expensive car (cost over £8000) No. 1	8598
Expensive car (cost over £8000) No. 2	10520

3. The following items were purchased and sold during the year ended 31 March 1986:

Purchases:

		£
11 August 1985	Car for salesman	6500
23 October 1985	Moveable office partitioning	3518
7 March 1985	Plant and machinery	42500
28 March 1985	Plant and machinery	17192

Notes:
  (i) The private usage of the salesman's car is one-quarter
 (ii) The company's offices do not qualify for Industrial Buildings Allowance
(iii) The plant and machinery purchased for £42,500 was contracted for on
       2 February 1985.

Sales:

		£
19 April 1985	Plant and machinery	150
29 July 1985	Expensive car No. 2	7500
11 August 1985	Car (purchased on 13 August 1982 for £4500)	2150

4. The Industrial Buildings Allowance for the year ended 31 March 1986 is £4106.

You are required to compute the mainstream corporation tax payable for the year
ended 31 March 1985.

[Calculate the trading profit under Schedule D, Case I, first and then add other
income.]
   ACCA, Level 2, December 1985 (Question updated and guidance given in
                                                          square brackets.)

4. You are required to explain the distinction between revenue and capital expenditure

for the purposes of obtaining a deduction in computing Schedule D, Cases I and II profits.

IoT, Associateship Intermediate Examination, Paper I, May 1986

5. (a) Metalcraft plc is a light engineering company formed in 1975. During its twelve month period ended 31 March 1987 an expansion of its production facilities resulted in the sale of its original factory and the purchase of two industrial buildings as follows:

(i) The old factory was sold in September 1986 for £46000, including land £4000. It had been purchased in January 1975 for £48000, including the cost of land £8000, from Steelrite Ltd., who originally bought it new from a builder in July 1970, for £35000, including the cost of land, £5000.

(ii) A new factory was purchased in October 1986 at a cost of £150000, made up as follows:

	£
Land	25000
Production area	105000
Offices	14000
Canteen	6000
	£150000

(iii) A second-hand finished goods warehouse costing £42000 was acquired in December 1986 from Garden Productions Ltd.; the latter company had purchased it new in January 1980 for £40000. Both figures exclude the cost of the land.

Required:
Calculate the industrial buildings allowance/charges which may be claimed by Metalcraft plc for its accounting period to 31 March 1987.

(b) Approved expenditure on certain buildings, plant, machinery and mining works in development and special areas is eligible for Regional Development Grants.

Required:
· Outline how such grants are dealt with in calculating capital allowances.

Capital allowances (industrial buildings)

First cost incurred on or after 13 November 1974 – initial allowance	50%
First cost incurred on or after 11 March 1981 – initial allowance	75%
First cost incurred on or after 14 March 1984 – initial allowance	50%
First cost incurred on or after 1 April 1985 – initial allowance	25%
First cost incurred on or after 1 April 1986 – initial allowance	Nil

ICSA, December 1985
(Question updated.)

10 The main indirect taxes

In this chapter we will look at the main UK indirect taxes as they now exist, before going on in Chapter 11 to look at the general policy issues underlying them. The yields of these taxes are shown in Chapter 1 and it will be seen that the most important is value added tax (VAT). As this also has more direct impact on business operations generally we will examine it in some detail.

VALUE ADDED TAX (VAT)

VAT was introduced in the UK from 1 April 1973 as a tax on goods and services consumed. It replaced purchase tax, which was a tax on goods alone, and selective employment tax (SET), which was intended to be a tax on the labour employed in services industries. VAT was the indirect tax recommended for the tax harmonization process in the countries of the European Communities (EC) and had already been adopted by France and Germany.

The name VAT can be misleading as it might be applied to a tax on business calculated by reference to 'value added' rather than, say, profits.[1] However, the tax we now have is intended to be a straightforward tax on the consumer, and it is only the manner of collection which gives the appearance of a tax on 'value added'. The position is demonstrated in Illustration 10.1 which assumes a VAT rate of 15%.

Illustration 10.1

	Net £000	VAT £000	Gross £000
Sales ('outputs')	1000	150	1150
Purchases	600	90	690
Wages	100	–	100
Other costs	100	15	115
Cost of new machinery	120	18	138
Total 'inputs'	920	123	1043
Value added	80	27	107

The total transactions of a business during a quarter are summarized in the example. The turnover at normal tax free selling prices is £1 000 000 but £150 000 must be added to this in respect of the VAT due and the business must account for that tax. Thus the customer finds himself paying a price which is inflated by tax.

On the other side of the account the cost of goods purchased, other costs and the new machine (but not the firm's own labour) are all acquired at an inflated price, the VAT thereon having been paid by the supplier. However, the VAT paid on these inputs can be used as a credit against this firm's liability on its sales. Thus the tax actually payable in the example is £27 000, not £150 000.

Now consider the position of the firm's customers whose buying prices have been increased by 15%. If they are themselves in business they can in turn claim credit for the VAT so their net outlay is reduced to the price excluding VAT. If, however, they are final customers they pay the full price, there is no credit for the VAT and so the tax falls fully upon them.

Readers familiar with the usual accounting conventions may have been surprised to find that the inputs include the purchases figure, rather than cost of goods sold, and the entire cost of the new machinery. VAT does not attempt to observe the accounting convention of matching costs against the corresponding output, as it looks solely at the transactions of the period when they occur. This removes most of the problems created by the matching convention, but the sales, purchases and other transactions are included in the VAT calculation whether they are paid for in cash immediately or are subject to a credit period. One consequence of this is that relief has to be given to the seller for tax accounted for on credit sales if the debt is found subsequently to be bad.

There is no need to allocate costs to a particular sale in order to find the net VAT due. The tax is calculated globally and all costs incurred automatically give rise to a VAT credit if they have borne VAT. The only thing that really matters is that VAT has been charged at the correct rate on sales. In so far as the tax on a particular sale has been paid, in part, at earlier stages in the chain of supply it is taken into account automatically in the global account each quarter and there is no need to try to trace the VAT suffered on the matching costs, a virtually impossible task anyway.

Illustration 10.1 is a rather simplified version of the real world. There are many other features of VAT which can have important effects on business and on the economy and the more important of these will now be considered.

In theory VAT is at its best if it is charged at the same rate on all goods and services. In fact, several countries have multiple rates, usually imposing higher rates on goods and services which are perceived as luxury products. In the UK there are at the time of writing two rates, a standard rate (15%) and a zero rate (0%).[2] The latter is reserved for products which may be seen as necessities of life. Thus an attempt is made to reduce the burden of the tax on the poor, most of whose spending has to be devoted to these necessities.

Zero rated items include food (but not restaurant meals, pet food, chocolate, ice cream, etc.), water and sewerage services, books, building construction, childrens' clothing, fuel and power (but not petrol), public transport and prescription medicines.[3] Suppliers of these items can still claim credit, by refund if necessary, for the VAT suffered on their inputs. Thus a farmer selling zero-rated potatoes can claim for VAT suffered on purchases of vehicles and machinery which were acquired to enable him to grow and distribute them.

Exported goods and services are also zero rated. The idea is that exports can be sold free of VAT which would otherwise increase selling prices and reduce competitiveness in world markets. The VAT credit given on all inputs (by full or partial repayment where necessary) has the effect of removing the burden of VAT on all costs incurred, whether they relate to exports or not and irrespective of the point in the chain of production and distribution where the tax was actually paid.

The other side of the coin is the case of imports. VAT is imposed on these, unless they are zero-rated items, when they arrive in the UK. This makes it irrelevant whether UK traders acquire their inputs in the UK or from abroad. The effect of zero-rating exports and charging imports is that where goods pass between two countries, both of which have a VAT system, the tax rate is determined by the country of final consumption. Production in the supplying country will attract VAT at that country's rate until such time as the product crosses the frontier, at which point the VAT already paid will become refundable and the importer's rate will be imposed on the full transfer price by the importing country.

As well as the zero rate there is a category called 'exemption' which has a quite different effect. The need for it arises from one of the main conceptual difficulties of VAT. A simple example will demonstrate the problem. If we pay an insurance premium in respect of a house or car we are doing two things. First we are paying into a fund from which we can draw if we are unlucky enough to suffer loss of or damage to the asset. Secondly we are paying a sum to the insurance company for their services in organizing that fund and dealing with the claims on it. Strictly only the latter represents a taxable service but the premium cannot easily be apportioned. A similar problem arises with banking if the bank makes no direct charge for its services to us because it can set off its costs against the benefits it receives from profitable investment of our money. What, in that case, is the value of the service supplied to us on which VAT should be charged?.

The solution adopted is to exempt these services from VAT, which means that no VAT is charged but, unlike zero rating, no credit or refund of the input tax is allowed. Thus the cost of running the bank or insurance company is increased by the VAT suffered on inputs such as stationery and machinery. Exemption is applied to several other categories, not always for the reasons outlined above. These categories include the supply of land, postal services, education, betting, health services, burial and cremation. In the case of education, for instance, the activity is predominantly publicly financed and the main input is labour. Zero rating education would involve claiming comparatively small refunds from public funds, which financed the activity in the first place!

Let us now return to the figures used in Illustration 10.1 but introduce some of the complications that we have discussed since studying that example. The revised figures are shown in Illustration 10.2. Suppose that the sales of £1 000 000 now include £200 000 of exports and £100 000 of banking and insurance services, and that 20% of the wages and 'other' costs (but not purchases or machinery) relate to the banking and insurance. Let us suppose too that the 'other' costs include exempt supplies charged at £20 000.

In the illustration it has been assumed implicitly that the net price of exempt supplies remains unchanged. However, as exemption implies additional costs (the unrelieved VAT on inputs) these are likely to be reflected in the prices actually charged. The result is that exempt supplies may be more expensive for the business purchaser because 'VATable' supplies, although nominally more expensive, carry the right to a VAT credit,

Illustration 10.2

	Net £'000	VAT £'000	Gross £'000
Sales[4]: UK (Standard Rate VAT)	700	105	805
Exports	200	–	200
Exempt	100	–	100
	1000	105	1105
Inputs: Purchases	600	90	690
Wages	100*	–	100
Other costs –			
Standard			
Rated	80*	12*	92
Exempt	20*	–	20
New machinery	120	18	138
	920	120	1040

* Of which 20% relates to the exempt sales.

At the end of the quarter the VAT due will be calculated as follows:

	£000	£000
VAT on UK, non-exempt, sales		105
less: VAT on inputs: Purchases (all)	90	
Other costs (80% of 12)	9.6	
Machinery (all)	18	127.6
Refund due		(22.6)

Note that the full VAT credit is available for those inputs which relate to exports but there is not credit in so far as taxed inputs relate to exempt sales.[5]

whereas there can be no relief for the hidden VAT in exempt supplies. The position is reversed for the private consumer who gets no credit for VAT suffered anyway and who is likely then to suffer VAT on exempt purchases at an effective rate less than 15%.[6]

VAT can produce practical problems for retailers who sell mainly for cash and would find it too expensive to keep records of individual sales. Most of their customers will not require the formal invoice which is necessary if VAT credit is to be obtained.[7] Special arrangements have been devised for them and these are described in detail in the official booklet.[8] One obvious solution is to calculate the VAT due on sales on the gross amounts received or receivable. For this purpose the rate is not 15% but 15/115, or 13.04%. In those cases where the retailer sells goods or services in the exempt or zero-rated categories as well as standard rated it is necessary to apportion sales in order to establish the VAT liability thereon. This can be done by deducing sales revenue in each category from the record of purchases, making the appropriate adjustment for differing rates of gross profit. The result will be an approximation, but the cost of administering a tax (including compliance costs) must be taken into account and some degree of approximation may be desirable.

A conceptual problem, rather than a practical problem, arises in the case of second-hand goods such as antiques and motor cars. These are commonly traded between private owners either directly or through dealers. If VAT was charged in the usual way dealers would be forced out of business. If I sell my car to a dealer for £2000 I do not have to pay VAT on the sale because I am not in the car business. If, however, the dealer had to pay VAT on his normal selling price of, say, £2500 it would mean that he would be trying to sell the car for £2,875.[9] This increases his 'normal' mark-up of £500 (i.e. £2500 – £2000) by 75% and would make it inevitable that all used cars would be sold directly between private owners. The problem does not arise in the case of commercial vehicles if buyer and seller are both business enterprises within the VAT net.[10]

The solution to the problem is to charge the dealer with VAT only on his mark-up. In the example he would pay 15% of £500, and increase his mark-up by £75 or absorb the VAT in his mark-up and pay 13.04% of £500. The car is then sold as if exempt, which means that the amount of VAT, and therefore the dealer's mark-up, is not disclosed. One incidental result which can create problems in practice is that this system requires careful record keeping in the absence of the usual cross-check provided by the formal VAT invoicing procedure.[11]

As the two examples imply, VAT is accounted for quarterly. The quarters are staggered according to trade classification in order to avoid peaks of work load for the VAT office, but a business can still ask to use quarterly periods that fit in with its annual accounts. The VAT due for each quarter has to be paid one month after the end of the quarter and a penalty may be charged if payments are late (see Chapter 14). Where a net refund is due, as in Illustration 10.2, a claim may be made monthly instead of quarterly.

One consequence of the arrangements for payments of VAT quarterly in arrear is that the trade has the use of the VAT money for the period following the collection of the cash due on the sales which gave rise to the VAT liability. If cash sales of £10000 per month, net of VAT, take place with VAT thereon of £1500 per month then at the end of the quarter £4500 of VAT will be owing. This need not be paid for a further month by which time the 'loan' will have risen to £6000, but falling to £1500 as soon as the payment is made. Thus the average loan is ($\frac{1}{2}$ × 4500) + 1500 = £3750. This loan will be reduced to the extent that VAT suffered on inputs is set off against the VAT on sales.

Such 'loans' should be treated as a source of finance and may represent a significant benefit to the trader, especially if he is paying bank overdraft interest at a high rate. However, the VAT due is not the only factor in the calculation. VAT is added to the price when the sale is made, not when cash is received, so that when sales are made on credit accounts receivable (debtors) will also be increased by the amount of the VAT, thereby increasing the level of working capital.

On the other side of the account the suppliers' bills will be greater too and so the accounts payable (creditors) will be increased by the VAT, thereby reducing the level of working capital. The net position depends on the particular circumstances. A retailer selling for cash and buying on credit will be better off under a VAT regime than if the tax did not exist (assuming the tax does not affect his sales volume). A zero-rated supplier paying higher prices on taxable inputs and waiting for his VAT refund is likely to be worse off. It is not always clear that retailers are aware of these effects although they are very conscious of the direct costs to them of administering VAT, or 'acting as an unpaid tax collector' as many would prefer to describe it.[12]

THE SPECIFIC DUTIES

Rather like VAT the specific duties are intended to be a tax on the consumer but they are collected in a quite different way. They are imposed at high rates on a narrow product range. Thus their effect on business is confined to a few industries.

Substantial revenue is derived from the excise tax on hydrocarbon oils. The tax is imposed at a fixed rate per litre. Most of the revenue comes from the petrol and oil consumed by road vehicles, the tax on derv (diesel fuel) being imposed at a lower rate than on petrol. The tax is collected from the oil companies before delivery to the garages, hence the queues to buy petrol still taxed at the old rate when a sharp increase in the duty is announced.

In addition to this excise tax, VAT at the standard rate is charged on all hydrocarbon oils other than fuel oil, gas oil and kerosene, all of which are zero-rated. Thus the additional cost imposed on a business using transport vehicles includes the full excise duty on the petrol and derv but not the VAT thereon (at 13.04% of the price paid) as this will be credited against the VAT due on sales.[13] At the time of writing the excise duty on petrol amounted to about four times the VAT (the latter varying with the actual selling price) and the combined tax rate represented about 65% of the selling price.[14]

The next excise tax in order of yield is that imposed on tobacco products. The tax on cigars and tobacco is based on weight but VAT is then added to the tax inclusive price (i.e. as with petrol there is tax on tax). However, the yield from these products is trivial compared with that from cigarettes on which the tax is more complicated. The excise duty is imposed in two parts, an amount per 1 000 cigarettes and an amount related to the retail price. In addition VAT is charged at standard rate. The effect can be seen in the following example which is taken from the Report of the Commissioners of Her Majesty's Customs and Excise.[15] The tax on a packet of 20 king-sized cigarettes sold in April 1985 was as follows:

	[pence]
Selling price	133
Specific duty (£26.95 per 1 000)	53.9
Ad valorem duty (21% of 133)	27.9
VAT (13.04% of 133)	17.3
Total tax	99.2p

It may seem odd to charge VAT as well as an *ad valorem* duty but as VAT is accounted for by the retailer it is far easier for him to account for it on all goods sold rather than trying to segregate the sales of cigarettes from those of cigars, matches, sweets, chocolates and other standard rated items.

The excise tax on alcoholic drinks also varies according to the product. In the case of spirits, such as Scotch whisky, the duty is based on a litre of pure alcohol. The rate of tax is heavy and in 1986 it amounted to £4.73 on any 75 cl bottle of Scotch which contained 40% of alcohol by volume. If that bottle of whisky was sold for £8 there would be VAT of 61 pence as well so the total tax would have been just over two-thirds of the price paid.

The excise duty on beer is based on a hectolitre of worts, the liquid produced before fermentation has begun. The rate of duty is increased for each degree by which the original gravity exceeds 1030. In addition an adjustment of duty is allowed for normal wastage which is deemed to be 6%. The effect is that on a pint of beer sold in 1986 for 75 pence the duty would be about 18.1 pence and the VAT 9.8 pence. Thus about 37% of the price paid by the consumer consists of tax.

Wine is also taxed on the basis of an amount per hectolitre, being divided into three categories according to strength. There is a further tax on wine above the strongest category (above 22% of alcohol) but this is beyond the level used directly for human consumption. Table wine falls into the lowest category, the duty in 1986 being £98 per hectolitre, the equivalent of 73.5 pence per 75 cl bottle. Taking into account the VAT the total tax on a bottle of wine selling for £2.50 would be £1.06, or 42% of the price paid. Clearly the relative tax burden is lower on the more expensive wines, as only VAT increases with price. Fortified wines fall into the middle category for excise tax purposes.[17]

Betting and gaming produce in total about as much revenue as the excise duty on wine. The tax is imposed variously on general betting, on and off course, on football pools and on gaming premises and machines.

OTHER INDIRECT TAXES

Three other taxes will now be considered in outline. Each makes a substantial contribution to the public revenue.

Customs duties have long since lost their status as one of the most important taxes. They are now governed by international agreements, and especially by the European Communities' common tariff agreement. Most of the yield now comes from taxes imposed on imported manufactured articles.

Vehicle excise duty is the annual licence fee levied on motor vehicles and evidenced by the licence disc displayed on the vehicle itself. The tax on motor cars is a flat rate, but that on lorries is levied according to unladen weight. Thus the tax falls both on the consumer (the private motorist) and on industrial and commercial transport costs. In the latter respect it may be seen as an attempt to reflect the 'external' cost to the community of road maintenance resulting from the extra wear and tear caused by heavy vehicles.[18]

Finally there are local rates. The yield nationally is substantial but it still amounts to less than half the revenue required by local municipal government to meet its spending commitments. It is a tax imposed on the occupation of land and buildings. Thus in the case of residential property one person living alone in a large house will pay more tax than any number of people living together in a less palatial residence. The tax is related to income or wealth only in so far as that is reflected in the choice of residence. Many people feel that this is an unfair system but attempts to find better alternatives have been slow to succeed. Rates are imposed on business premises (but not on agricultural) and represent an addition to costs which may be passed on to the consumer in higher prices. It is not clear how such price increases fall upon the various social and economic categories in the community.

NOTES AND REFERENCES

1. This aspect was discussed in detail in NEDO, *Value Added Tax* (2nd edn.), HMSO, London (1971).
2. There is a separate tax on cars imposed at a rate of 10% of the wholesale value. VAT is imposed on top of this.
3. 5th Schedule, VAT Act 1983 – see also the General Guide, VAT Notice No. 700, Appendix A.
4. In published accounts the turnover figure consists of the net amount, i.e. £1 000 000 in the example – see SSAP 3, Accounting Standards Committee, London (1973).
5. If exempt supplies are small relative to total sales no restriction of VAT credit is made – see VAT notice No. 706.
6. Businesses with a very small turnover are not required to register for VAT and this has the effect of giving their sales the same characteristics as exempt supplies. Such businesses can elect to register and should do so if their sales are made mostly to other traders as they should then be able to reduce their net prices (or increase their profits at the same prices).
7. Invoices must contain specified information including a VAT registered number if they are to represent satisfactory evidence of entitlement to a VAT credit on the input. It is this which gives VAT its cross-checking feature as between traders.
8. VAT Notice No. 727, *Special Schemes for Retailers*.
9. i.e. £2500 plus 15% thereof.
10. A car used by a trader does not qualify for a VAT credit unless it is used for letting on hire.
11. See note 7 above.
12. For a detailed investigation of these points see Godwin, M.R., Sandford, C.T., Hardwick, P.J.W. and Butterworth, M.I., *Costs and Benefits of VAT*, Heinemann Educational Books, London (1981). See also the discussion on collection costs in Chapter 11.
13. No credit is allowed in so far as the petrol or derv is used for private journeys of the proprietor or of an employee of the business.
14. The excise duty on petrol was 17.94 pence per litre, which is equivalent to 81.6 pence per gallon. The calculation used to produce the tax figure in the text assumed a selling price at the pumps of about £1.60.
15. 76th Report, for the year ended 31 March 1985, Cmnd. 9655 HMSO, London (December 1985). This report provides the basis for most of the information in this section.
16. The excise duty assumes an original gravity of 1037 which is the average figure for beer sold in the UK.
17. Fortified wines such as sherry tend to fall into the middle band where the duty is greater by about 53 pence per bottle. Special rates apply to drinks such as cider, mead, perry, etc. – see the Report referred to in note 15.
18. See Chapter 1 for a discussion of externalities.

EXERCISES AND DISCUSSION TOPICS

1. Moser owns a health food shop making up accounts to 31 May. For value added tax purposes he has chosen to compute his output tax by using retail scheme D, which applies to traders who supply standard-rated and zero-rated goods and whose annual turnover does not exceed £200 000.

   Under scheme D gross takings (inclusive of VAT) for each tax period are split in proportion to the total amounts charged by suppliers for goods at each tax rate during the period; the VAT fraction is then applied to the gross standard-rate takings to produce the figure of output tax. An annual adjustment is made by applying the same basis to the total figures for the year.

The following figures are extracted from Moser's records for the year ended 31st May 1986:

| | Tax period ended | | | | Total for year |
	31.8.85 £	30.11.85 £	28.2.86 £	31.5.86 £	£
Gross takings	34776	43700	61594	50715	190785
Purchases for resale:					
Standard rated (net)	7200	14300	9800	11200	42500
VAT thereon	1080	2145	1470	1680	6375
Zero rated	11040	16445	18032	16100	61617
Business expenses:					
Standard rated (net)	1500	6200	1100	1260	10060
VAT thereon	225	930	165	189	1509
Zero rated	195	210	140	325	870
Exempt	85	55	60	120	320

Requirement:
Calculate the value added tax payable to or recoverable from Customs and Excise for each of the tax periods during the year ended 31 May 1986, together with the annual adjustment required for the year.

ICAEW, Professional Examination II, July 1986

2. International Limousines is a firm specializing in undertaking and car hire for weddings and funerals. It also has a number of 40-seat coaches which are used mainly for school transport contracts. The turnover (excluding VAT) for the latest VAT year was made up as follows:

	£
Limousine hire for weddings	6000
Limousine hire for funerals carried out by other undertakers	10000
Funeral services (including limousine hire totalling £12000	85000
Coach hire (including school contracts £48000	52000
Supply of coffins to undertakers	3000
	£156000

You are required to discuss the value added tax aspects of the above.

IoT, Associateship Final Examination, November 1985

3. Explain why it may be beneficial for an individual who is carrying on a business to register voluntarily [for value added tax] even though there is no legal requirement for him to do so.

ACCA, Level 2, December 1984 (Part question.)

11   The arguments about indirect taxes

Now that we have seen the shape of the main indirect taxes in the UK we can go on to consider the various arguments about their effects, looking both at national policy implications and at their impact on business activity.

SHIFTING

We saw in Chapter 8 that one of the uncertainties of company taxation lies in the question of who actually bears it in the end. Is it borne by the shareholders, or can the company pass it on wholly or partly to customers, employees and others? In the case of indirect taxation the implied assumption is that the tax will be passed on in the form of higher prices and that the trader is acting solely as an agent of the tax administration. The exposition of VAT in the last chapter was based on this assumption, and it seems clear that in the case of commodities such as whisky and cigarettes the tax burden is so high that the trader could absorb only a tiny fraction of it.

However, these taxes can impose burdens on traders, their suppliers and employees by their impact on the demand for the product. If tax forces up the price and demand is elastic then sales volume will fall, so reducing profits and employment in that industry, or else part of the tax will have to be absorbed by the trader, so reducing his profits and leading to the withdrawal of the marginal firms.

Has this been happening in the UK? It is always difficult, if not impossible, to be sure as many other economic and social factors will be operating at the same time. When SET was introduced an attempt was made to gauge its effect on the distribution trades. The evidence, although apparently pointing in the 'right' direction, could not be conclusive because the effect of the abolition of resale price maintenance was working its way through the system at the same time and that too could have been responsible for the greater economy observed in the use of labour.[1]

The apparent effect on sales of the tax on tobacco is obscured similarly by a non-tax factor. Over the seven year starting in 1978 the tax on cigarettes rose from about 55% of the selling price to over 60%. Over the same period the quantity consumed fell by about 17%.[2] Was this the effect of the high tax rate, or was it caused, in part at least, by the effect on people's behaviour of the published evidence of a link between smoking and various illnesses? Or was some other change in social habits at work at the same time? Perhaps dependence on cigarettes was being replaced by dependence on soft drugs, but we have no evidence for this because the supply of such drugs is both illegal and untaxed.

The evidence about the effect of the taxes on alcohol is more complex and in some ways more interesting. The consumption of spirits has fluctuated at a time when the relative impact of the excise tax has been falling.[3] No clear response to the pattern of taxation emerges. Consumption of beer, on the other hand, has fallen steadily over the 10 year period from 1975 whereas the relative burden of tax first of all fell and then recovered to a level very near to its starting point. Wine consumption rose steadily over the same period, apart from a hiccup in 1981 when the rate of duty was increased sharply. The considerable reduction in the rate of duty in 1984 in response to EC requirements may have accelerated the general upward trend in consumption, so much so that the tax yield soon overtook the pre-reduction figure.[4]

What do these trends tell us? It looks as if the change from beer to wine may be social trend which is affected only marginally by small tax changes. Consumption of the other main drinks seems to have reacted only slightly, if at all, to the small changes in tax rates from year to year. It may be the case that such relative changes are in any case masked by the larger changes needed to keep pace with general price inflation, but it does seem that the demand for alcoholic products is not elastic in its response to small tax changes. The industry operates in a very competitive environment and it looks as if any tax reductions, as in the case of wine in 1984, are passed on to the consumer rapidly and in full.

WELFARE AND EFFICIENCY

The effect of indirect taxes in distorting the 'natural' balance of the economy is thought to depend substantially on the design of those taxes. After looking at the main general issues we will consider the particular issues that arise in the context of the pattern of such taxes in the UK.

The first general issue concerns the distortion of relative prices. If an indirect tax is imposed at the same rate (relative to price) on all 'goods'[5] then it may seem that relative prices will not be distorted and that demand for all goods will fall in the same proportion. The tax will not itself alter the economic balance, although it should be borne in mind that its overall effect on the economy will depend on the use made of the tax revenues.

If, on the other hand, the taxes are imposed selectively, as are VAT and the excise taxes, then the relative price levels and the level of demand for each good will be distorted from the pre-existing pattern. If that pattern represented an optimum this implies that there will have been a loss of economic efficiency. For this reason it has been argued that the ideal form of indirect tax is one such as VAT imposed at the same percentage rate on all goods and services.

However, there are some reservations to be made about this proposition. Let us first consider the effect of variations in the elasticity of demand for a good. Suppose that a particular good is one which most people expect to buy in a more or less fixed quantity and for which there is no satisfactory substitute. An example might be toilet soap, or one of the addictive products such as cigarettes. A modest tax on such goods is unlikely to reduce the demand for them, although the 'income' effect (i.e. the loss of general purchasing power) may result in a slightly reduced demand for a wide spread of other goods.

Thus the previous proposition may be amended to state that the tax should not be imposed evenly, but more heavily on those goods with a low demand elasticity, and more lightly or not at all on those with high elasticity. In this way the volumes purchased would remain in the same proportions as before. Of course any such proposition needs only be stated to be seen to be impractical in the real world, but it does help to give us some guidance about the sources of those losses in welfare which result from the imposition of indirect taxes.

So far we have assumed implicitly that a tax-free pre-existing balance of demand is an ideal one and that we are therefore seeking to maintain it as closely as possible after the tax has been imposed. This may be true for many goods but it is not difficult to find goods for which it is manifestly not true. Quite apart from issues such as public goods and monopolies[6] some goods have production costs which are not borne by the individual producer but which ought to be reflected in the market price. A common example of such a cost is the damage done by atmospheric or other pollution. The cost of extracting oil from the earth is low but it can be argued that the use of this source of energy should be inhibited so that other energy sources are maintained against the day when the oil and gas may run out. Market prices unaffected by taxes may reflect only short-term factors and so fail to reflect the obligation that the present generation owes to future generations.

Another reason for increasing a price by imposing a tax is to reflect society's view that habits such as smoking and drinking should be discouraged. This view may be based on economic factors such as the consequential costs (hospitals, accidents) imposed on society if people smoke and drink to excess.[7] Or it may reflect concern about the loss of productive work caused by the effects of excess indulgence. Additionally the tax may be justified on paternalistic grounds, saving people from themselves when they fail to recognize the long-term consequences of their habits. On the other hand these taxes produce substantial revenues and so governments' attitudes may be ambivalent. What we have seen in recent years is that small changes in the level of taxation on such products have little or no effect on their consumption, although this fact does not inhibit governments from using the assumed deterrent effect to justify tax increases.

We may observe too the possible effects of the particular form of a tax, especially the excise duties. In the case of spirits it is the alcohol content that is being taxed. A high class whisky attracts the same rate of excise duty as a bargain basement variety provided that both have the same ability to produce a state of inebriation in the consumer. Similarly with wine. The excise duty on a bottle of 'plonk' costing £2 is the same as that on a fine claret costing £50 or more. The impact of VAT on the price of the claret will have left the excise duty far behind.

Cigarettes are a rather odd case, and present policy seems to be confused. One might expect the aim to be a reduction in consumption, particularly of those products which are believed to be the most harmful to health. Levying a tax per cigarette appears to encourage manufacturers to reduce the tax burden by producing the largest possible cigarettes and it lends no support to the use of filter tips despite evidence of their effect in reducing the health hazard. The second part of the tax, that imposed by price, may encourage the production of filter tips if the filter is cheaper than the equivalent volume of tobacco and the greater costs of manufacture do not upset the balance of advantage but it appears to do nothing to push consumption towards the low tar tobaccos.[8] In looking at these problems it should be borne in mind that while the demand for cigarettes as such may be inelastic, it does not follow that this is true of the demand for particular types of cigarette for which other types are close substitutes.

Another issue that is discussed frequently is the balance between petrol tax and vehicle excise duty. It was suggested in Chapter 10 that the latter reflected the effect of vehicle weight on road maintenance costs borne out of public funds. This argument can now be taken a stage further. The excise tax is payable irrespective of the distance travelled by the vehicle. In 1986 car owners paid £100 whether they covered 1000 miles or 50 000 miles. Of course the second group would pay more tax on their purchases of petrol or derv. For an average car owner covering 10 000 miles annually the excise duty (but not VAT) paid on petrol would have totalled about £275 in that year.[9]

The argument that arises from this situation is that the duty on petrol should be increased and the annual tax on the vehicle abolished. Such a change would have three main effects.

(1) It would relate the tax burden more closely to road usage and to the consumption rate, the latter reflecting broadly the size of the engine and the weight of the vehicle.
(2) It would reduce the burden on those who found a car necessary for occasional use only (e.g. pensioners?).
(3) It would reduce tax evasion in so far as there is ample evidence of vehicles being unlicensed whereas the duty on petrol is paid by a few, mainly large, oil companies.

As with all proposals to change the tax system such ideas are strongly opposed by those who would be worse off, in this case the high mileage motorist. Many of them will be using their car for business purposes so an increase in the rate of excise duty would add to business costs (unlike the VAT on petrol). Others may live in remote country areas with facilities such as schools, churches and shops a long way away. What must be clear is that there is nothing sacrosanct about the present balance between the two taxes and these conflicting issues have to be balanced in deciding what the pattern should be at any time.

The balance of tax between petrol and derv is another matter for discussion. It can be argued that derv is a more desirable fuel as it produces fewer harmful pollutants and is more economical than petrol. Thus there may be social reasons for favouring derv. However, a sharp reduction in the tax on derv would affect the relative costs of running the millions of vehicles already in use or awaiting sale and would present problems for a motor industry which has its production of derv-powered vehicles attuned to the present tax regime. In particular, car production within the UK could be disadvantaged as against imports of derv-powered vehicles from those countries which favour such vehicles already in their tax systems. There is, for instance, a noticeable contrast between German and British cars in this respect.

COLLECTION COSTS

The distortions in the economy caused by the factors discussed in the previous section may not be measurable in any precise way but can be seen to have great potential importance. Collection costs, on the other hand, are much more obvious. The time and money involved can be measured, and they are less likely to be overlooked in evaluating a tax proposal. The question that arises is whether they are reasonable as a proportion of the tax yield, because all such costs are a direct loss to the economy. In any such evaluation account must be taken of compliance costs, those imposed on the taxpayer and others, as well as costs incurred by the official administration.

The costs of administering most of the taxes discussed in this chapter are reported

annually by the Commissioners of Customs and Excise. The figures in Table 11.1 are
for 1984/85 and are taken from the report for that year.[10]

The first figure to note is that the overall cost was 1.11% of the revenue yield of
£35½ billion. This compares with a cost/yield percentage of about 1.7 for all the direct
taxes collected by the Board of Inland Revenue.[11] Within both of these totals there are
wide variations between individual taxes.

Are these collection costs, which exclude all compliance costs, reasonable? There can
be no absolute answer to this question. A tax that is very cheap to collect may be
economically damaging in other ways. A tax that is intended to be fair and equitable
may be more complex and therefore more expensive to administer. Yet again we see the
need to strike a balance between conflicting objectives. The shape of any tax must be
examined from an operating cost viewpoint. Let us look at these costs for some of the
taxes listed in the table.

At first sight the customs duties seem to be expensive to administer. However, closer
examination of the full report reveals that about half the cost is concerned with
necessary activities which produce no tax revenue. These include preventing the
importation of illegal drugs and registering the arrival of ships from abroad. It is clear
from common observation that many of the customs staff at airports and ports have a
deterrent, rather than a revenue collecting function. Customs duties are largely outside
the direct control of the UK government, except in so far as it can force its views upon
the EC. They are of considerable economic importance in so far as they help to secure
the balance of international competition.

Table 11.1 Costs of collection – Customs and Excise 1984/85

Tax	Staff	Cost £million	Yield £million	Cost as % of yield
VAT	12544	191.3	18535	1.0
Car tax	112	1.8	745	0.2
Hydrocarbon oil	529	8.8	6199	0.1
Alcoholic drink	2056	29.0	3761	0.8
Tobacco products	241	3.6	4140	0.1
Betting & gaming	411	6.4	661	1.0
Customs duties	9651	152.4	1475	10.3
Total	25577	£393.5	£35536	1.11

Reproduced by permission of the Controller, Her Majesty's Stationery Office. © Crown
copyright.

Tobacco products and hydrocarbon oils both stand out as excise taxes which are very
cheap to collect at 0.1%. Thus in any argument about these taxes the cost of collection
is of no consequence except in so far as it would provide an argument against more
expensive alternatives. The reasons for this cheapness are two in number.

(1) The rates of tax are very high in relation to the price of the product.
(2) There are very few collecting points for these taxes and the records of the companies concerned will be well maintained and reliable.

It will be seen that the ratio for alcoholic drinks is much less favourable. There are many collecting points and the rates of duty, apart from spirits, are lower. Thus the staff needed is over eight times that for tobacco products although the tax yield is lower.

In all these cases, and in the case of the car tax, compliance costs are likely to be very low. The taxes fall on well organized companies which need to impose their own internal checks anyway. However, these companies will suffer a financial burden in so far as they have to pay the tax before they collect the tax inclusive sales revenue on the products concerned.

Turning to VAT we can take a more detailed look at the effects of tax design on costs of administration and compliance, helped by an in-depth study produced in 1981.[12] Looking back over the years since 1978/79 the cost of administration has fallen from 1.9% to 1%. This may seem at first sight to be a commendable effort by the tax authority but the biggest single factor causing it is not a fall in costs but a rise in revenue.[13] In 1978/79 there was a standard tax rate of 8% plus a higher rate of 12½% on a limited range of outputs. From June 1979 the standard rate was increased to 15% and applied to all chargeable outputs. Thus the tax yield rose considerably without any necessary increase in the cost of administration. Indeed the change from two rates to one should have reduced costs by eliminating some of the problems and complexities of the tax.

The 1981 study suggested that the compliance costs incurred by chargeable businesses, even allowing for the financial benefit of receiving cash from the customer before the tax itself became payable, were of the order of 8% of the tax yield. It was clear that such a high figure means that great attention needs to be paid to any feature of the system which adds significantly to the operating costs. The study made a number of suggestions and some of them have been adopted. Multiple rates were seen as causing work in defining the boundaries between the categories but there were other problems of definition, of which one of the most difficult was the distinction between building repairs (standard rated in 1981) and alterations and improvements (zero rated, but now standard rated).[14]

An important finding of the study was that costs were relatively heavier for small businesses, and for traders dealing in a mixture of VAT categories. Indeed it was estimated that for many small traders the costs they incurred were greater than the tax yield. Thus it is important that the threshold for compulsory registration should not be allowed to fall in real terms and that the special schemes for retailers should be kept as simple as possible, even at the expense of some loss of accuracy.

One significant result of the study was to draw attention to the economic effects of these high compliance costs. In so far as relatively higher costs fall on small traders and on some particular kinds of trading activity, those traders are suffering adverse discrimination when they seek to compete with those not so disadvantaged. Thus compliance costs are not just a simple economic loss to the community, they can cause economic distortions of the same type as those which result from differential tax rates.

RISING PRICES

In the case of direct taxes we have seen that rising prices and wages can result in higher average tax yields unless thresholds and rate bands are index–linked in some way.[15] In the case of indirect taxes it is the nominal rate of tax which matters most.

As we have seen in Chapter 10 excise taxes are based on some physical property, the weight, volume or number of units of the products. As prices rise the relationship between the fixed tax and the rising selling price will alter, and the spending power implied by a given tax yield will decline. If prices are rising a government which takes no action to change rates of tax will be reducing the burden of that tax. Governments may face problems which are political rather than economic in so far as tax changes designed to do no more than keep pace with inflation will be misrepresented as tax increases, especially in the less subtle organs of the popular press (although television and radio are not immune from this practice). Contrast this with the apparent generosity of governments when direct tax thresholds are increased solely to prevent a rise in the real burden of those taxes.

However, not all indirect taxes give rise to this problem. VAT is based on selling prices and as those prices rise so does the money yield of the tax. Given that additional administrative costs are incurred if there is a change in the rate of VAT it is fortunate that it need not be changed unless there is a policy decision to change the real impact of the tax. On the other hand regular adjustments need to be made to the registration threshold so as to exclude from the tax charge those small businesses where costs of collection would be a high proportion of the tax collected.

The official presentation of tax changes in the UK is now designed to isolate the true policy changes from those changes which are no more than inflation adjustments. The information in Table 11.2 is taken from the Financial Statement and Budget Report, 1986/87.[16]

Table 11.2 The budget measures 1986

	1986/87 (£million)	
	Changes from an indexed base	Changes from a non-indexed base
Excise duties:		
Petrol/derv	+135	+465
Vehicle Excise	−135	+5
Tobacco	+175	+315
Alcohol	−175	—

Reproduced by permission of the Controller, Her Majesty's Stationery Office. © Crown copyright.

From this we see the effects of the 1986 budget proposals on the tax yields for 1986/87. The real burden of the tax on petrol and derv has increased, but £330 million (i.e. 465 – 135 in the table) of the increased yield serves only to keep pace with rising prices. The vehicle excise duty was not changed for most categories, and this is the equivalent of a tax cut of £135 million.[17] The real burden of the tax on alcohol was reduced by £175 million by leaving the nominal rates of duty unchanged. Tobacco taxes were increased in both real and nominal terms, the nominal increase being nearly twice that needed to keep pace with inflation.

NOTES AND REFERENCES

1. See Reddaway, W.B., The Effects of Selective Employment Tax, First Report. The Distributive Trades, HMSO, London (1970).
2. 76th Report of the Commissioners of Her Majesty's Customs and Excise, Cmnd. 9655, HMSO, London (1985).
3. Ibid. Tables 19 and 20.
4. Ibid. Tables 23, 24, 25 and 26.
5. The word 'goods' is used here in the economic sense and includes services.
6. See Chapter 1.
7. However, it should not be forgotten that if people live longer because of moderate habits the cost of caring for the elderly will rise.
8. For further discussion see Chapter 8, pages 128–129, of Kay, J.A. and King, M.A., The British Tax System (3rd ed.), OUP Oxford (1983).
9. The duty was 17.94 p per litre (about 81.63 p per gallon) until March 1986 when it was increased to 19.38 p per litre. Assuming 30 miles to the gallon, 333 gallons at 81.63 p gives a total of £272.
10. Chapter 2 of the Report which is referenced at note 2 above.
11. Board of Inland Revenue, Report for the Year Ended 31st December 1985, Cmnd. 9831, HMSO, London (1986), at Appendix I, Table 4. The average for the last four years is 1.71.
12. Sandford, C.T., Godwin, M.R., Hardwick, P.J.W. and Butterworth, M.I., Costs and Benefits of VAT, Heinemann Educational Books, London (1981).
13. The figures referenced in note 10 above show that the number of people involved in VAT work has fallen by only 2% over that period.
14. The standard rating of building improvements and certain related alterations and recon-structions was effective from 1 June 1984 – See s.10 and 6th Schedule, Finance Act 1984.
15. See Chapter 2.
16. HM Treasury, Financial Statement and Budget Report, 1986–87, HMSO, London (March 1986), at page 47 (Table 4.1).
17. It will be seen that these figures reflect a switch from vehicle excise duty to petrol taxation – a topic that was discussed in general terms on p. 172 of this chapter.

EXERCISES AND DISCUSSION TOPICS

1. Summarize the evidence for and against the proposition that higher indirect taxes on specific goods reduce the demand for those goods (i.e. that the demand for them is elastic).
2. To what extent do taxes in the United Kingdom reflect government's belief that it is wiser and more knowledgeable than the 'man in the street'?
3. (a) List the various taxes that are borne as a result of owning and using a motor car.
   (b) Discuss ways in which they might be re-arranged to produce the same total yield for the Exchequer but in different proportions.
   (c) What would be the purposes and virtues of the re-arrangements you have considered?
4. Do the very low costs of collecting the taxes on tobacco and oil products, compared with the somewhat higher costs for VAT, suggest that the former taxes should be increased and the latter reduced? Give reasons for your conclusions.

12 Making use of the system

Although an introductory text such as this one cannot go into the finer detail of the tax system it should be apparent by now that the system has its own peculiar rules and regulations. Thus it is not sensible for anyone to go ahead with financial transactions as if taxation did not exist. In this chapter we shall look at some of the ways in which taxation can be relevant to such transactions. None of the arrangements will amount to sophisticated tax avoidance, but that topic will be discussed in Chapter 13. We shall be concerned merely with the opportunities that exist to take advantage of the obvious, and often intended, effects of the tax system. Three subjects will be considered, personal savings, organizing a family business, and running a business.

TAX EFFICIENT SAVING

People may try to save out of income, or they may wish to invest inherited wealth. A wide range of investment opportunities is presented to them at home or abroad. First of all they have to decide which criteria are important to them in coming to investment decisions. Are they prepared to take risks? Do they want quick access to all or part of the invested wealth, or if the investments are long term, for how long? Do they wish to choose to invest in accordance with personal beliefs, perhaps avoiding South African investments or tobacco companies? Considerations such as these must come first, but having laid down their strategy in broad terms they must then look at the detailed decisions in the light of the taxation consequences.

Two overriding principles should be borne in mind in making the choices. The first is maximization of the net of tax return, an aim which must be clearly distinguished from minimizing tax liability. For instance, some forms of national savings produce a tax-free return which minimizes tax liability, but is this less beneficial than an alternative investment which produces a higher rate of return after tax has been paid on it? The second principle is that choice depends on the particular circumstances of the investor. An investor who is liable to IT at the top rate will not be making the same investment choices as one who is below the threshold. Anticipated changes in personal circumstances must be taken into account. A long-term investment by an otherwise impecunious student will not be chosen wisely if he fails to take into account his expectations that he will complete his studies and move on to a well-paid job, or perhaps expects a substantial inheritance.[1]

The return on an investment may take the form of income, or of capital gains (chargeable or not) or both. A capital gain will be taxed, if at all, when the investment is realized. Income is likely to be paid or credited at regular intervals and taxed then, although it may be withheld until the end of the period of the contract. Let us now look at actual cases.

One category of investment produces income but no gains. Bank deposits and building society shares fall into this category. As we have seen already in Chapter 2 on p. 21 the interest is taxed in a special way whereby the basic rate tax is covered by a so-called 'composite rate' tax paid by these institutions at a rate below the basic rate.[2] The investor then pays tax only to the extent that he is liable above the basic rate, this extra tax being calculated not on the interest receivable, but on the interest grossed up at the basic rate. Whether this small tax advantage makes such investments worthwhile will depend not on the rate of tax but on the net of tax rates of return available elsewhere. Note that in making such a comparison the interest rates should be compared on a similar basis which takes into account differences in the frequency of payment.[3] Such an investment is not suitable for an investor who is not liable to IT because the composite rate tax paid by the institution is not refundable to the investor, whatever his circumstances.

Thus tax-exempt investors must look elsewhere. For them investments in local authorities or in certain kinds of national savings (such as income bonds) will be more beneficial. Such income is taxable in principle but this fact is of course irrelevant to them. If IT at the basic rate is deducted at source by the paying institution it can be reclaimed by the investor. This contrasts with the situation described in the previous paragraph.

Some forms of investment produce interest that has been specified as tax-exempt. This applies to a first slice of annual interest on deposits in a British savings bank, ordinary account. It applies too to the return on National Savings Certificates (NSCs) whenever they are redeemed.[4] These investments may well appeal to the 'small investor' but as they pay low rates of interest which reflect their tax-exempt status they are likely to be very unattractive to tax-exempt investors. For them the effect is similar to the one we noted above when interest is received from banks and building societies. However, interest that is totally tax-exempt can be very attractive for the high income investor. It

Illustration 12.1

Investment	Fully taxable £	Bank £	NSC £
Investor (a)	12	9	8.50
Investor (b)	8.52[1]	9	8.50
Investor (c)	4.80[2]	5.07[3]	8.50

Notes:
(1) 12 less 29% thereof.
(2) 12 less 60% thereof.
(3) 9 is equivalent to 12.67 less basic rate tax at 29%: IT at 60% deducted from 12.67 leaves 5.07

is for this reason that a limit is imposed on the quantity of any such investment that can be held by any one individual.[5]

This discussion can now be illustrated with some figures. Three investments are assumed to be available, none of them producing capital gains. In one the interest is fully taxable and it produces a rate of return before tax of 12% per annum. The second is a bank deposit account paying 9% free of basic rate tax and the third is National Savings Certificates with an effective return of 8.5%. Illustration 12.1 shows the net of tax return on all these investments for (a) a tax exempt investor, (b) a basic rate taxpayer (assuming a rate of 29%), and (c) a top rate (60%) taxpayer.

Note how the order of preference differs, each investment being the best for one, but only one, of the investors. In practice the first two investments would not necessarily have a constant rate of interest over the five year period that has to be assumed for the purposes of comparison with the NSCs. They would show a lower rate of interest if redeemed within that period.[6] But this is not a taxation problem.

Let us now turn to investments which produce capital gains, with or without income as well. Equities, whether acquired direct or via unit trusts, are likely to produce gains, at any rate in the medium to long term. The potential investor will know that whereas dividends will be fully taxable as income (subject only to the tax credit adjustment which has been described in Chapter 7) any gains, after indexation, will be liable to tax when they are realized provided they and other gains together exceed the annual threshold. In fact for the private investor that threshold is quite substantial unless he finds himself selling a large piece of property all in one year. Shareholdings can be divided into smaller parcels and with a minimum of tax planning sold so as to take advantage of the threshold every year. Thus for many investors the effective liability to tax on gains can be zero.

This may lead investors to the potentially erroneous conclusion that they should always invest for gains. The market has different expectations about different companies and these are reflected in variations in the rates of return (on a current yield basis). Thus a low dividend yield reflects an expectation of future gains. However, tax-free capital gains are *relatively* more attractive to a high income, high tax rate investor than to an investor liable only at the basic rate. This being so, the share price may be expected to reflect the greater benefits to that higher rate investor and it may tend to rise above the price at which there is a net-of-tax advantage to the poorer man. This is a more subtle version of the principle stated at the beginning of this chapter that it is the net-of-tax rate of return that should be maximized.

Another reflection of this idea can be found in the prices and terms of issue of government securities. Most of these are redeemable at a stated time on terms that are known, usually at par value. Some of them will have been issued with an interest coupon at or near the market rate, and the latter may have changed since the time of issue. Others will have been issued, quite deliberately, at a discount to par value and with an interest coupon below the market rate so that part of the investor's reward will take the form of a capital gain of a known monetary amount if the stock is held to maturity. Furthermore all such capital gains are tax free by the terms of issue.[7] Thus the government issues some of its own securities on a basis which takes advantage of the investors' desire to reduce their tax burdens. That fact will itself affect the issue price and in the end the public revenue loss resulting from the CGT exemption and the low level of taxable income will be wholly or partly offset by the lower gross cost of servicing the National Debt. The tax capitalization effect on prices can be seen in the daily list of security prices published in *The Financial Times* and elsewhere. Where the price is below par value the running rate of interest will be greater than the nominal rate. More important is the yield to maturity. Low interest rate securities tend to have a lower yield to maturity because a higher component of that yield, the capital gain, is tax free. If the interest component is reduced by the basic rate of IT the yields to maturity tend to converge in those cases where the maturity dates are similar. Unless those dates are similar this convergence can be negatived by the term structure of interest rates.

A high proportion of personal investment takes place via financial institutions. We saw in Chapter 2 that considerable tax advantages are enjoyed by pension funds but lesser advantages can be enjoyed if funds are invested in institutions on terms whereby income and gains are taxed at institutional rates. A common example is life assurance with an endowment element. Premiums are paid on a regular basis and invested by the insurance company. The income and gains resulting are then taxed at special rates.[8] Eventually the endowment policy matures, either by the completion of the agreed term of years or on the death of the person whose life is assured, and its value is then paid out as a sum of money already fully taxed. The tax advantage to the investor lies in the difference between the rate of tax levied on the company and that which would have been levied on direct investment in shares and securities. In so far as the insurance company pays tax at a higher rate than the poorer investor there will be no tax advantage to him. This does not mean that such an investment is misguided as there are non-tax reasons, such as risk spreading and skilled portfolio management, for taking out an endowment policy.

Before concluding this section we will look briefly at three special schemes which are designed to provide tax advantages to the investor. All of them can be attacked as distorting fiscal neutrality but it has been argued that they aim to produce economic advantages for the country as a whole.

The first is the Business Expansion Scheme (BES) which was introduced in 1981.[9] The idea behind the scheme is that it would make available funds for the development of small businesses which were either too small or had too little past history to enable them to obtain funds in the conventional capital markets. The main tax incentive offered is considerable as it amounts to a reduction in taxable income for the year in which an approved investment is made. Thus an investment of £10000 can be made, in the case of a 60% rate taxpayer, at a net cost of only £4000. In addition gains on the investment were made free of capital gains tax from 1986. This sounds, and indeed is, remarkably favourable but against it must be set the risky nature of the investment, the requirement that it must be made for a period of not less than five years and the possibility that there may be difficulty in finding a willing buyer for the unquoted shares unless the company has prospered so far as being able to go, say, to the Unlisted Securities Market (USM). Thus it may be suggested that the BES is a good example of the potential dangers of being blinded by tax advantages. In fact various arrangements have been devised to mitigate the financial risks, and these have led to some tightening of the conditions under which BES relief can be given with the intention of reducing the degree of investment in assets such as property which are virtually risk free.

The second special scheme concerns employees acquiring shares in their employing company. It has been argued that such schemes improve employee motivation by giving them a financial interest in the success of their company. Under normal tax rules any such shares acquired on favourable conditions would give rise to additional income tax liability on the benefit received.[10] The legislation facilitating the special scheme has gone through various stages and remains complex.[11] It takes into account share options (where the employee is enabled to buy shares in the future at today's prices), share incentive schemes and approved profit-sharing schemes. The tax benefits are strictly limited and depend, of course, on the company offering the opportunities in the first place. The employee's investment decision may depend on whether the tax advantages are sufficient to outweigh the concentration of the risk of both the employment and the personal wealth in the same enterprise.

The third scheme, and the most recent, is the Personal Equity Plan (PEP) which started in January 1987.[12] An investor can invest up to £2400 each year in shares and is then able to reinvest dividends and gains free of tax so long as they remain within the 'plan'. The CGT benefit seems to be of little value for the small investor in view of the high threshold and there will be some administrative costs because of the formalities required in operating the 'plan' but the income reinvestment exemption offers a significant benefit along the lines of that available to pension funds.

RUNNING A FAMILY BUSINESS

Moving on from the private investor we will now look at the organization of smaller businesses. Large numbers of them exist, covering such enterprises as retail shops and market stalls, manufacturing and processing operations, service industries and professional practices. Often they will involve several members of a family but the points which follow do not depend necessarily on that fact.

The first decision must be whether to incorporate the business (i.e. form a company) or carry on as a sole trader or a partnership. The same business may progress through all of these stages and the timing of the changes may be important. Again it must be remembered that tax factors are only one element in the decision.

Consider first the case of a sole trader who employs other members of his family. Profits will belong to the trader and, if he prospers, he may be taxed on his income up to the top rate of IT. The position of other members of the family as employees can lead to two tax problems. The first is that the level of wages charged as a business expense may be challenged if it is thought to be inflated by family and income spreading motives so that it goes beyond a fair reward for the services rendered to the business.[13] The second is that there is a liability to pay national insurance contributions (NICS) and the level of these payments together with the scope of the benefits entitlement has to be compared with the position that would exist if these family employees became partners in the business.

Forming a partnership may have other advantages apart from those suggested by the problems stated above. The liability to capital gains tax on business assets would be spread between the partners and this would make available more than one slice of annual exemption and of retirement relief. Sharing ownership of the assets could have an effect on liability to IHT. However, all may not be plain sailing. The tax benefits depend on the existence of a genuine partnership. A sham, even with the benefit of a written agreement, just will not do.[14] This means that the existence of a true partnership affects relationships within the family. Trying to run a partnership when one of the partners is a dominant head of the household may cause more trouble than the expected tax savings can justify.

The next stage is the formation of a company. This is a radical change both commercially and in terms of the tax consequences. The main tax difference is that profits retained in the company are taxed at a fixed rate (probably the small companies rate in this situation) and the directors, who will be shareholders as well, can control their personal income tax liabilities and rates of IT by limiting the fees paid to them by the company. This contrasts with the sole trader or partnership where all profits are taxed at personal IT rates whether drawn out or not. The level of NICS will change as well.

The existence of a company produces a degree of flexibility in tax matters that is just not available to partnerships. To take one example, fees can be used to create a loss for the company, and this can be advantageous as the figures in Illustration 12.2 will show.

Using the IT rates for 1986/87 for all years the higher rates of personal IT start at incomes of £19535 for a single man. Suppose now that a company has profits, before paying fees to its two unmarried directors, of £30000 in Year 1 and £50000 in Year 2 and is expected to have £80000 in Year 3. One policy on fees may seem to be as shown under A.

Illustration 12.2

	Year 1 £	Year 2 £	Year 3 £	Total £
Policy A:				
Profit before fees	30000	50000	80000	160000
less: Fees	(30000)	(39070)*	(39070)*	(108140)
Taxable profit	Nil	£10930	£40930	£51860
CT at 29%	Nil	3169.70	11869.70	15039.40

* Limited to 2 × 19,535 to avoid paying IT at more than 29%, the rate of CT paid by the company on retained profits.

	Year 1 £	Year 2 £	Year 3 £	Total £
Policy B:				
Profit before fees	30000	50000	80000	160000
less: Fees	(39070)	(39070)	(39070)	(117210)
Loss relief		(9070)		
Taxable profit	£ Nil	£1860	£40930	£42790
CT at 29%	Nil	539.40	11869.70	12409.10

However, if the directors wish to enjoy their new prosperity and decide to draw out more than £19535 each in Year 3 the tax bill will increase as their rate of IT on the extra fees will be 40% or more whereas the company's lower profits will only reduce its tax bill at a rate of 29%.

Consider now the figures under B in the Illustration. The loss created in Year 1 reduces the taxable profit in Year 2. The extra fees in Year 1 may involve an earlier payment of IT on them. The extra fees in Year 1 can be left on loan to the company and then drawn out in Year 3 with no tax charge arising at that time. The effect overall is that the company has paid less CT (29% of £9070 = £2630.30 as shown in the Total column) and the directors have paid more IT (also 29% of £9070 on the extra fees in

Year 1) but the higher rate IT that would have been payable on extra fees in Year 3 has been avoided.

The balance of tax advantage need not lie always with the company. If a business is likely to produce capital gains on the sale of assets, and these gains cannot be rolled over,[15] company ownership of the assets can produce two disadvantages. The first is that a company does not enjoy an annual threshold, it is liable from the first £ of taxable gains. The second is that if and when gains are distributed to shareholders there may be a second charge to tax. A taxable gain on a company's assets, assuming it is reflected in the value of the shares, produces a potential taxable gain for the shareholders when they dispose of their shares.

Many other factors may arise in this context, not least the possible consequences of the death or retirement of the proprietors. We have covered only a few rather basic points but they should be sufficient to show that business organization decisions can be affected by taxation in complex ways and this is especially so as they must take into account possible further changes in the circumstances of the business and its owners. We will now move on from these proprietorship matters to look at some of the decisions which are taken in the course of commercial activity.

DECISIONS WITHIN THE BUSINESS

Many decisions within a business can be taken safely without regard to tax implications because these are either unimportant or non-existent. Nevertheless there are likely to be decisions about ongoing general policy matters in which tax is a relevant factor. We saw in Chapter 5 how attempts have been made to tax employee benefits. Even so employees may be provided with benefits which are either not taxable or which are taxable on the basis of a measure which falls short of the full benefit. It may be assumed that such benefits reduce the cost of labour if the employees compare the value of the untaxed benefits with the after-tax cash alternative and do not regard the tax advantages as merely offsetting the loss of freedom to spend equivalent cash sums as they wish. The tax consequences of capital gearing (leverage) were discussed in Chapter 8 on p. 134 but again the fact that there are apparent tax advantages does not preclude the possibility that the pre-tax cost of capital is increased and all or part of the benefit transferred, in effect, to the provider of capital.

It is in the more substantial individual transactions that careful planning may enable advantage to be taken of tax saving possibilities. Two examples will be given but almost any substantial transaction should be examined to see whether some variation in the commercial arrangements could lead to a tax saving for both parties, or for one of them. It is vital to remember that the facts of a transaction cannot be altered after the event (short of deliberate misrepresentation, which amounts to fraud). It should be borne in mind that a tax conscious party to a transaction may be able to save tax at the expense of another party who is unaware of the tax implications. There may be no reduction in the total tax revenues resulting but the payments may be shared in different proportions.

Let us start with a fairly simple example. A company is about to make a substantial sale of its products and the expected profit on it will be about £100 000. The sale is due to take place near the end of its AP but the purchaser is in the middle of its AP. Delaying the sale into the next AP, assuming there are no penalty clauses in the contract, will pass the profit into that AP. Of course this will reduce the reported profits for the current year but it may be possible to anticipate the delayed profit in the chairman's speech and so reduce any damage resulting from shareholder disappointment. The important thing is the tax effect. Liability to tax on the profit is delayed by a complete year. If we take the tax as £35 000 this may represent an interest saving of at least £3 500 or about 3½% of the profit itself. Of course the benefit of the timing delay may be lost if the rate of CT rises.

The second example is a little more complex and involves a more subtle approach. A company is interested in the acquisition of another company's business. The main alternatives are to acquire the shares, so that the other company becomes a wholly owned subsidiary, or to acquire the net assets (including goodwill) piecemeal. The taxation effects of these two approaches are quite different. Consider first the position of the vendors. If the shareholders sell their shares for cash they will be liable to CGT in the usual way. If they exchange their shares for shares in the bidding company no CGT will be due immediately because of the deferral provision on a share exchange (see Chapter 5, p. 78) but they will be left with shares they may not want or which they may find difficult to sell. Ideally they would wish to sell them year by year so as to take full advantage of the CGT thresholds.

From the viewpoint of the bidding company the new subsidiary is taken over as a whole and the trade continues as if the ownership had not changed because ownership of the assets remains with the same company. Should assets be transferred between the companies subsequently they will be covered by the group provisions and no capital gains tax will be chargeable. The buyer will take over any tax liabilities, actual or potential, which arise from the acquired company's earlier activities. This is a common form of acquisition and is comparatively straightforward.

Now consider the alternative method of acquisition, purchase of the assets direct. The tax system introduces a potential CGT liability when a company sells its assets and a further such liability if the company then distributes the net proceeds to its shareholders. If the selling company agrees to accept shares in the buying company, instead of cash, the CGT liability remains but the shares acquired may be less desirable than cash and may turn the vendor into an investment company.

Turning to the buying company, it will have acquired a bundle of assets. The trade represented by this bundle can no longer be treated as a continuing one as its ownership has changed from one company to another and so the assets have to be valued separately and calculations made of the capital allowances, capital gains, and other taxation consequences arising from the sale.

It is important to realize that these subsidiary valuations of the assets transferred may be crucial to the tax liabilities of both parties to the transaction. In Illustration 12.3 it is assumed that the assets sold consist of three items, goodwill, machinery and inventory. The first may produce a capital gain (30% tax rate assumed), the second an adjustment of capital allowances (35% tax rate) and the third will enter directly into the profit calculation (35% tax rate).

From the seller's point of view allocation of more of the total proceeds of £30 000 to goodwill would produce a lower tax liability in so far as gains are taxed at a lower rate than income. This would not be so if there is ACT available to reduce any tax on income and that ACT would otherwise remain unrelieved.[16]

From the buyer's point of view there can be no forseeable tax relief on the acquisition of goodwill, relief on the machinery will be spread over many years (on a 25% reducing balance basis) but relief on the inventory will be virtually immediate. Thus the purchaser may wish to maximize the value placed on inventory and minimize that placed on goodwill. This conflict between the interests of vendor and purchaser can be reconciled via an adjustment of the total price as shown under B (second negotiation).

Illustration 12.3

A. *First negotiation*:

	Goodwill £	Machinery £	Inventory £	Total £
Apportioned price	10 000	10 000	10 000	30 000
Tax on vendor	(3 000)	(3 500)	(3 500)	(10 000)
Net benefit to vendor	£7 000	£6 500	£6 500	£20 000
Tax relief to buyer	Nil	(3 500)*	(3 500)	(7 000)
Net cost to buyer	£10 000	£6 500	£6 500	£23 000

B. *Second negotiation*:

	Goodwill £	Machinery £	Inventory £	Total £
Apportioned price	5 000	10 000	16 000	31 000
Tax on vendor	(1 500)	(3 500)	(5 600)	(10 600)
Net benefit	£3 500	£6 500	£10 400	£20 400
Tax relief to buyer	Nil	(3 500)*	(5 600)	(9 810)
Net cost	£5 000	£6 500	£10 400	£21 900

* Spread over many years.

Under this new arrangement the total price is increased but its allocation to the assets is changed as well and, in particular, the value of goodwill is halved. A reduction in the value of machinery could also be envisaged as the relief to the buyer is spread over the years whereas the liability of the vendor is virtually immediate. Examination of the figures reveals that the buyer's tax relief is increased from £7 000 to £9 100 which more than covers the extra cost incurred. At the same time the vendor's tax bill rises from £10 000 to £10 600 but this still leaves the vendor with a net advantage of £600 compared with the figures in A. There are limits to this kind of apportionment in so far as it must be broadly reasonable, albeit subjective, and the illustration exaggerates a little in the interest of clarity. It does, however, show (a) which values should be taken at the upper end of the reasonable range, and (b) how this can be accommodated in negotiation by an adjustment of the total price. It is, of course, essential for the two parties to agree an apportionment before the figures are submitted to the tax authority.[17]

NOTES AND REFERENCES

1. He may, for instance, be entitled to the capital in a trust fund when he attains the specified age.
2. Under s.343, Taxes Act 1970, and ss. 26–27, Finance Act 1984.

3. For instance, 5% per half year is equal to 10.25% per year. The formula to derive an equivalent annual rate, r, is:

$$r = (1 + i)^n - 1$$

where i is the half yearly, quarterly or monthly rate and n is the number of periods in the year. Thus:

$$(1.05)^2 - 1 = 0.1025, \text{ or } 10.25\%$$

4. S.414, Taxes Act 1970, and s.34, Finance Act 1981.
5. Usually National Savings Certificates are limited to a maximum of £5 000 for each issue (but as the time of writing the figure for the current 31st issue has been raised to £10 000) – see the leaflets available at any post office.
6. For instance the 31st issues shows a return over 5 years of 7.85% but the year by year rates were 5.76%, 6.66% , 7.80%, 8.95% and 10.14%.
7. Under s.67, Capital Gains Tax Act 1979.
8. See Chapter II, Part XII, Taxes Act 1970.
9. Originally the Business Start-Up Scheme in Finance Act 1981, but renamed in 1983. It has been much amended since its introduction.
10. See, for instance, *Weight v. Salmon* 1935 19 TC 174, and s.186, Taxes Act 1970.
11. Most of the legislation can be found in Finance Acts 1973, 1980 and 1984.
12. S.39 and 8th Schedule Finance Act 1986.
13. Under S.130(a), Taxes Act 1970 – see *Copeman* v. *Wm Flood & Sons Ltd.* (1940) 24 TC 53 and similar cases.
14. There are several reported cases on this point – see, for example, *Dickenson* v. *Gross* (1927) 11 TC 614.
15. Under ss. 115–122, Capital Gains Tax Act 1979 (see Chapter 5, p.000).
16. In the case of the 'small company' ACT otherwise unrelieved would reduce the tax on the equivalent income to Nil.
17. See ss.77 and 81, Capital Allowances Act 1968.

EXERCISES AND DISCUSSION TOPICS

1. Henry Rudder owns a substantial portfolio of United Kingdom quoted equity investments worth £600 000 which he inherited from his father last year. The dividends are £40 000 p.a. (gross) and Henry's other income is over £50 000 p.a.

   He has called to see you because of his concern that a large part of the investment income will suffer income tax and wonders if there is any advantage in transferring the investments to a company in which he and his wife would hold the shares. The value of the investments has increased by £80 000 since his father's death. Moreover, he considers that his wife could be paid £2 000 p.a. as a director and that his five children, whose ages range from 9 years to 18 years, could be paid a similar sum for helping in the management of the investments. The profit remaining would, he believes, be retained in the company and suffer tax at a much lower rate.

   You are required to write a letter to Mr Rudder commenting on his proposals and indicating the extent to which they would be successful. Illustrate your letter with appropriate numerical examples.

   IoT, Associateship Intermediate Examination, Paper II, May 1986

R U Dunn
10 Through Street
Middlesborough
M15 5ED

J Brown Esq
Taxation Practitioner
1 High Street
Artfield AT1 1XX

31 October 1985

Dear James

Due to the present economic situation I am intending to commence in practice as an, insolvency practitioner with effect from 1 January 1986. As you are aware, I have been involved with this type of work for my present employers for a number of years, with the result that I am rather out of touch with taxation of the self-employed.

At this stage I can only guess at the level of fees to be earned in the future, but you may like to base your advice on fees of £20 000 in the first year rising to £40 000 over the following two years, with expenses accounting for approximately half the fee income. I shall be investing in office equipment costing approximately £12 000 during the course of the first few months.

I shall not be leaving my present employment until 31 December 1985 by which time I shall have earned about £14 000 in the current tax year. In view of my impending loss of job security my wife returned to teaching at Easter (paid from 1 April 1985) at a salary of £10 000 per annum.

Our only investment is approximately £40 000 in a building society on which we received £1400 on 30 June 1985 and expect about the same at the end of December.

I would like you to advise me of the points which I ought to be considering concerning my tax and national insurance position.

Your sincerely
Robert

You are required to reply to the above letter.
IoT Associateship Final Examination, Paper I, November 1985

3. You have been in business running a family company for many years and now wish to retire. You have received an offer for the business and this is likely to be acceptable to the minority shareholders. List the taxation aspects that need to be considered in agreeing the arrangements for and terms of the sale.

13 Tax avoidance

In Chapter 12 we saw that if business and personal affairs are to be arranged optimally taxation must be taken into account. In this chapter we shall go a stage further and examine how far such planning may go before it falls foul of legislative and other constraints. First of all we must look at avoidance in a more general way.

THE NATURE AND CAUSES OF AVOIDANCE

Tax 'avoidance' has to be distinguished from tax 'evasion', although in common parlance these words are often used interchangeably. In fact they tend to shade into each other at the margin but they can be clearly distinguished in principle. Evasion is an illegal act. It involves giving false or misleading information, or suppressing relevant information, so as to reduce or eliminate tax that is legally due. It can take many forms, some of them well known. A trader or farmer may sell goods for cash over and above his declared sales, especially where there is no itemized record of them, just a purported total of cash received. Services such as hairdressing and house decoration may be provided privately, the payer being unable to claim tax relief on the outlay and the recipient asking for payment in cash (quite possibly a reduced amount) so that there is no record of the transaction. An employee may acquire a second, part-time, or casual job which by itself is below the tax threshold and keep his main job secret from the second employer.

Tax evasion may take the form of claims for reliefs that are not due. These may be expenses claims where the money was not actually spent (receipted bills being acquired by other means) or, perhaps, a claim by a single man on the basis that he is married.

Tax evasion of this nature is believed to be widespread and elimination of it is virtually impossible in a free society (and probably so even in a controlled society). Rather like trying to eliminate burglary, the cost of the manpower required to check and supervise people's activities would far outweigh the value of any benefits that might result, quite apart from their effect on the quality of life of innocent and guilty alike. Various estimates have been made of the extent of tax evasion in the UK, and these suggest that income suppressed is equal to 5% or more of the known GNP.[1]

Tax avoidance may shade into tax evasion in the context of avoidance schemes which involve a sequence of legal formalities that must be taken at the right times and in the right order.[2] There may be a temptation to ante-date crucial documents or to prepare records of formal meetings which should have taken place and did not. This temptation is particularly strong if the avoidance possibility was not foreseen but becomes obvious with hindsight, and an attempt is then made to produce evidence of 'facts' which did not actually happen at the alleged time.

Let us consider, therefore, the kinds of activities that amount to tax avoidance and which are legal (i.e. are not evasion). Many of them amount to doing no more than taking advantage of opportunities presented by the tax laws themselves. We saw in the previous chapter that a business may be run as a partnership or as a company. In so far as the taxation consequences influence the decision this is a form of tax avoidance, but not one which most people would regard as being morally wrong. Similarly, we have seen how the private investor will take tax 'efficiency' into account in choosing from the range of investment opportunities. In both cases the tax factor is influencing the decision, but it will be observed that these decisions have legal and financial consequences quite apart from their effect on taxation liability or relief.

Another area of tax avoidance consists of making sure that the reliefs available under the tax laws are not lost inadvertently. Thus an individual may spread his realizations for capital gains tax purposes over two or more years so as to use up a multiple of the annual threshold before paying any tax. This is not easily done unless the assets can be sold piecemeal and this fact may influence the choice of investment. Thus a single property may carry a potential CGT liability, whereas a holding of a quoted share or security may not. Similarly a transfer of assets may be arranged to take advantage of the reliefs provided by IHT, especially those pertaining to transfers between spouses.

There are many such examples and from them it is apparent that the opportunity to avoid tax will vary according to the particular circumstances of the taxpayer. It has been pointed out that such opportunities detract from the equity of the tax system; in particular horizontal equity may be lost, and vertical equity may lose the degree of progressivity that was intended. This leads us to the question whether this loss of equity is inherent in all tax systems. Some have argued that it is not.[3]

Most tax avoidance opportunities arise from two factors.

1. The restricted definition of the scope of the tax base, and
2. Differing rates of tax (including zero rates) being applied.

The first of these can be seen if we look again at the definition of 'income'. In Chapter 5 we considered the arguments for a comprehensive income tax (CIT) and we saw that a tax on capital gains was an attempt to widen the scope of the tax on flows to cover those receipts which, like income, may add to personal spending power. We have also seen that not only are these two sources taxed at different rates, but that there are various thresholds and exemptions designed to give relief in special circumstances. Furthermore we note that there is no CGT on death.

Kay and others have argued that the only way to overcome these avoidance possibilities is to introduce a tax on expenditure which would be imposed irrespective of the source of the money used.[4] Even then there would be some tax avoidance opportunity if other countries retained their present tax systems as those disadvantaged by the expenditure tax would no doubt seek to move their affairs to a country which was more advantageous to them. Thus people might live and invest in an expenditure tax country while saving, and then move to an income tax country when dis-saving.[5]

Any discussion of tax system design in this context would become extensive and it would be more realistic therefore if we looked at the tax avoidance position as it exists now in the UK.

LEGISLATION TO COUNTER TAX AVOIDANCE

Let us consider first the legislative approach to tax avoidance. The position taken in the UK until recently was that where unacceptable tax avoidance was taking place it should be countered by specific legislation designed to deal with the particular avoidance device.[6] An early example was a device known as 'bond washing'. This consists of selling a security *cum div* and buying it back *ex div* at a lower price. The regular holder would gain by the difference between the two prices, on which no tax might be due. The short-term holder would receive the income payment to offset the fall in the price between buying and selling. The point was that the short-term holder would be chosen as someone with a low tax rate whereas the regular holder had a high tax rate on his income. This device was first countered in its more elementary forms about half a century ago.[7]

A more complex arrangement known as dividend stripping was used widely in the 1950s. This would involve a company with accumulated profits which, if paid out as dividends, would attract high rates of IT. The shares in the company were sold to a share dealing company (i.e. a company trading in shares and liable to tax on its 'income' from such transactions) which arranged for the first company to declare a dividend out of the accumulated profits. Once that company had been denuded of its profits its shares could be sold back to the original shareholders at a much lower price. The effect was to leave the original shareholders with a cash surplus because they received more than they paid (and no CGT liability at that time) while the dealing company had a large dividend (taxable) and an equally large trading loss on its share transactions. Being a dealing company it could set off the loss against dividend income.[8]

This device was countered by legislation in 1955 but it was found all too soon that variants of it were being invented (such as removing the profits before they existed!) and that these escaped the legislation.[9] Eventually in 1960 a more general form of legislation was devised and this still exists.[10] This legislation is concerned with so-called 'transactions in securities'. It specifies certain types of transaction and decrees that if they are undertaken with the sole or main object of securing a tax advantage that advantage shall be counteracted. The legislation is complex and not always clearly expressed but its effect can be illustrated from two of the decided cases.

In the Clearly case there were two companies, each of which was owned jointly by two ladies. One of the companies had cash to spare and the ladies did not wish to pay IT on any dividend declared to distribute that cash. They therefore arranged to sell their shares in one of the companies to the other company for cash. By this means one company became a wholly owned subsidiary of the other and the ladies received their cash as the proceeds of sale of the shares, not as income. However, the court decided that this was a 'transaction in securities' and the money was therefore to be taxed as if it was a dividend.[11]

In the second case a Scottish company with accumulated profits and cash resources was threatened by a takeover bid. In order to foil it the major shareholders borrowed money on loan in order to buy shares from the minority at a price above the bid price. Subsequently, under a scheme of capital reconstruction sanctioned by the Court of

Session, reserves were capitalized and then shares were redeemed in cash and the loans repaid by the borrowers. The court held in this case that there was a 'transaction in securities' but it had taken place for non-tax reasons. It recognized that in devising its defence strategy the shareholders had taken the taxation consequences into account.[12]

Before we leave the subject of anti-avoidance legislation it is worth glancing briefly at an alternative approach. This consists of a general section which empowers the tax authority to challenge tax reduction schemes. An example can be taken from New Zealand which has the following law.

'Every arrangement made or entered into, whether before or after the commencement of this Act, shall be absolutely void as against the Commissioner for income tax purposes if and to the extent that, directly or indirectly, —

(a) Its purpose or effect is tax avoidance; or

(b) Where it has two or more purposes or effects, one of its purposes or effects (not being a merely incidental purpose or effect) is tax avoidance, whether or not any other or others of its purposes and effects relate to, or are referable to, ordinary business or family dealings, —

whether or not any person affected by that arrangement is a party thereto'.[13]

It is apparent that this is a very wide ranging section although it should be borne in mind that its scope may be narrowed by judicial interpretation. A similar section in the Australian legislation has been so construed narrowly. Part of the trouble is, of course, that it would be unreasonable to apply the section in circumstances where the tax system itself gives the taxpayer a choice in the arrangement of his financial or business affairs. The UK has no such general section beyond the 'transactions in securities' legislation described above, but as we shall now see the courts have been inclined in recent years to take a more restrictive view of what may be allowed in the way of tax avoidance.

THE JUDICIAL APPROACH TO TAX AVOIDANCE

The traditional approach of the UK judiciary has been to look at the letter of the law rather than trying to make equitable or moral judgements about taxation. If the drafting of tax legislation is deficient in relation to Parliament's intention the courts will not seek to provide a remedy. Only Parliament itself can do so by passing new legislation.

This does not mean that the courts are blind to reality. They will not, for instance, be bound by a document which purports to govern a legal relationship if it is clear that the reality is different. This point has arisen in cases such as those of a business partnership between a father and his children evidenced by a deed but where the course of events makes it clear that no true partnership exists.[14]

However, if it is clear that a legal formality exists and that it has created rights and obligations for the parties concerned the courts will be unwilling to ignore its tax consequences. The leading case on this point concerned the Duke of Westminister.[15]

The facts were quite simple. The Duke employed people on his estate but their wages were not deductible in taxing his considerable income. He decided therefore to make payments to seven of them under deed of covenant, the payments then becoming deductible from his income because they qualified as annual payments.[16] The covenanted payments were for seven years or more and were not conditional on the recipient remaining in the Duke's employ. It was admitted that the employees were expected to be content with lower wages to the extent that they received these payments.

The tax authority challenged the arrangement as far as the House of Lords and this led to the celebrated judgement of Lord Tomlin, part of which reads as follows:

'Every man is entitled if he can to arrange his affairs so that the tax attaching under the appropriate acts is less than it otherwise would be. If he succeeds in ordering them so as to secure this result, then, however unappreciative the Commissioners of Inland Revenue or his fellow taxpayers may be of his ingenuity, he cannot be compelled to pay an increased tax. . .'[17]

Of course, the Duke's employees were entitled in law to payment of their wages in full as well as to the covenanted amounts. There had been a change in the Duke's formal obligations and this remained true even if they were not enforced. Although the possibility was suggested, there was no evidence of a collateral contract whereby the employees agreed to take a lower wage and not to pursue their rights under the deed if their employment ceased. Had there been such a contract the court's decision may well have been different.

As the decades passed and tax avoidance schemes became more common and more sophisticated some members of the judiciary began to express their concern about the apparent effect of the Duke of Westminister doctrine. Eventually in 1981 the House of Lords found itself able to take a fresh approach in a case which involved a series of pre-ordained transactions.[18] The facts of the case will be set out here both to show the nature of tax avoidance schemes and to explain the background to the court's decision.

A farming company, W.T. Ramsay Ltd., had realized a substantial capital gain from the sale of land and was faced with a correspondingly large tax bill. The scheme it adopted was devised to create a capital loss which could be subtracted from the gain. The scheme proceeded in steps as follows.

1.   Ramsay (R) invested in the shares of a company (CM) created especially for the scheme.
2.   R then lent money to CM in the form of two loans, each at 11% per annum, the first for 30 years, the second for 31 years.
3.   Under the terms of issue of the loans the interest rate on the first could be and was reduced to zero, and that on the second was doubled.
4.   The second loan was then assigned at its increased market value. It was argued on technical grounds that the 'gain' on this loan was not a taxable gain (just as losses on most loans are not allowable losses).
5.   CM then repaid both loans, the first at par value, as specified in the terms of issue, the second at the enhanced market value.
6.   As a result of repaying the loans there were no assets left in CM and the shares owned by R became worthless. This created an allowable loss of £175 000 to set against the gain on the land already referred to above.

It should be borne in mind that all of the events described above took place in 1973 between 23 February and 9 March and that, apart form the costs of professional advice and other small outlays, R was no worse off at the end of the series of transactions that it had been at the beginning – except for the hoped for tax relief.

The approach adopted by the House of Lords was to look at the series of transactions as a whole and by doing so it came to the conclusion that they had no business purpose (other than tax avoidance) and that the company suffered no actual loss. The particular transaction that produced the 'loss' could not be isolated from the corresponding gain that arose from the assignment of the second loan with its enhanced interest rate.

This decision was seen as spelling the end of a tax avoidance industry which had developed off-the-peg schemes designed to deal with many common situations. What seemed more important was how it would affect more mundane examples of tax planning which had not previously been attacked. The next case on the subject, involving the Burmah Oil Company, did not take the discussion much further,[19] so we will move immediately to a new watershed in the case of *Furniss* v. *Dawson*.[20]

The Furniss arrangement did not involve the kind of artificial self-cancelling arrangement used by Ramsay. It arose out of an intention by the shareholders in a family company to sell their shares to an independent purchaser. Instead of doing this directly for cash they were advised to set up another company, Greenjacket, in the Isle of Man, and exchange their shares for shares in Greenjacket. In turn and without delay Greenjacket then sold the shares to the independent purchaser.

The apparent effect of this scheme was that the original shareholders escaped capital gains tax because they had exchanged shares for shares, not cash[21] and Greenjacket was not liable because it had made no gain, having acquired the shares at market value. Note, however, that the original shareholders were not in the same position as they would have been without the scheme as the cash was tied up in Greenjacket.

The High Court and the Court of Appeal both found that they could distinguish Furniss from Ramsay and decided that the arrangements were effective as a tax avoidance scheme. However, the House of Lords took the opposite view. It decided that because there was a prearranged series of transactions and because the insertion of Greenjacket had no commercial or business purpose tax must be paid as if there had been a direct sale of the shares for cash. The fact that the insertion of Greenjacket had a continuing effect on the outcome of the transaction as it concerned the sellers of the original shares was held to be of no consequence.

The House of Lords also made clear its view that the definition of what is unacceptable tax avoidance would have to develop case by case as it was not amenable to statutory definition. This aspect of the decision creates considerable problems for those who have to make decisions on the basis of what is and is not acceptable. Not least of these problems is the time the courts may take to reach a final decision on a new set of facts. The shareholders in the Furniss case were particularly hard hit as their transactions actually took place in 1971 (i.e. nearly ten years before the Ramsay decision) and were not thought to be invalid, even by the Court of Appeal, after the final Ramsay decision was available.[22]

As the matter stands at the time of writing there is an urgent need for more guidance, a need which has led to discussions between professional bodies and Inland Revenue officials. These have made it clear that a number of tax planning devices will not be challenged but they still leave a large grey area.[23] The alternative of pursuing a scheme all the way to the House of Lords for their authoritative judgement can be a very expensive undertaking.

Where then does all this leave us? In an increasingly complex world the battle between the tax avoider and the tax authority will no doubt continue. It consumes a large amount of highly skilled labour on both sides and may be one of the more significant costs of operating a tax system. It is, therefore, an important factor to be borne in mind in designing a tax system. It can be discouraged in the longer term only by devising a logically consistent system with marginal tax rates as low as possible so as to reduce the potential benefit of any scheme.

NOTES AND REFERENCES

1. See O'Higgins, M., 'Aggregate Measures of Tax Evasion: An Assessment', in *British Tax Review*, Sweet & Maxwell, London, (1981), at pages 286–302 and 367–378, and Dilnot, A. and Morris, C.N.', What Do We Know About the Black Economy?', in *Fiscal Studies*, Vol. 2, No. 1, Basil Blackwell, Oxford (March 1981), at pages 58–73. See also Smith, S., *The Shadow Economy*, Oxford University Press, Oxford (1986).
2. For an interesting description of the procedures involved in more complex schemes see Tutt, N., *The Tax Raiders, The Rossminster Affair*, Financial Training Publications, London (1985).
3. A full discussion of this point and the points which follow is contained in Kay, J.A., 'The Economics of Tax Avoidance', in *British Tax Review*, Sweet & Maxwell, London (1979), at pages 354–365.
4. At page 364 of the article referenced in note 3.
5. This possibility was recognized by the Meade Committee, Institute for Fiscal Studies, *The Structure and Reform of Direct Taxation*, George Allen & Unwin, London (1978). See page 17.
6. This approach was approved by the *Final Report of the Royal Commission on Taxation*, Cmd. 9474, HMSO, London (1955), at pp. 309–310, and has often been referred to subsequently in discussion of the topic.
7. The present legislation is contained in s. 469, Taxes Act 1970.
8. See, for example, *J.P. Harrison (Watford) Ltd. v Griffiths* (1962) 40 TC 281, (1963) AC 1.
9. An example can be found in a case which failed on timing grounds, *Greenberg v. CIR* (1971) 47 TC 240, (1972) AC 109.
10. Now ss. 460–468, Taxes Act 1970.
11. *CIR v. Cleary* (1967) 44 TC 399, (1968) AC 766.
12. *CIR v. Brebner* (1967) 43 TC 705, 2AC 18.
13. S.99, Income Tax Act 1976 (New Zealand).
14. For example, *Dickinson v. Gross* (1927) 11 TC 614.
15. *Duke of Westminster v. CIR* (1935) 19 TC 490, (1936) AC 1.
16. See now s. 52, Taxes Act 1970, but note the restrictions to and limitations of relief in ss. 434–459.
17. At page 520 of 19 TC (note 15 above)
18. *W.T. Ramsay Ltd. v. CIR* (1981) 54 TC 101, 1 All ER 865.
19. *CIR v. Burmah Oil Co. Ltd.* (1981) 54 TC 200.
20. *Furniss v. Dawson* (1984) 55 TC 324, 1 All ER 530.
21. Relief under s. 85, CGT Act 1979 (company reconstructions and amalgamations).
22. The actual dates are as follows:
   Furniss transactions completed 20 December 1971.
   Ramsay decision in the House of Lords 12 March 1981.
   There was an exceptionally long delay between the original tribunal decision in Furniss (21 January 1976) and the final decision in the House of Lords (9 February 1984).
23. For a summary of a more up-to-date position see, for example, the most recent edition of

Tolley's Tax Planning, Tolley Publishing, London. In the 1986 edition the relevant article is headed '*Furniss* v. *Dawson* – The Future of Tax Planning' by R.M. Ballard.

EXERCISES AND DISCUSSION TOPICS

1. The decision to operate a business as a company may be made, at least partly, on the basis of tax advantages. Would you describe this as tax planning (i.e. acceptable by most standards) or tax avoidance (possibly unacceptable)? If the former how do you distinguish it from the Ramsay case?
2. Explain why the House of Lords in making its decision in the Ramsay case did not regard itself as overturning the decision in the Duke of Westminster's case.
3. The owner of a business pays wages to his wife and family although they give him only negligible assistance. Discuss whether this amounts to tax evasion or avoidance. Would it make any difference if he recorded the wages in his books but did not actually pay them to the purported recipients?

14 Enforcement

So far we have looked at many of the criteria that should be observed in the design of a tax system, considering the UK in particular. We are now going to look at some factors which can ruin an otherwise sensible and acceptable design. A tax system is designed to tax people in certain ways, but no one with practical experience will ignore the likelihood that it will fail to work as designed. Even to work approximately as intended means that the natural desire of the designated taxpayers to pay less, or no, tax must be overcome and administrators must have the resources to apply the tax laws correctly, efficiently and effectively.

GENERAL ISSUES

In the sections which follow we shall look at the legal provisions needed for effective implementation of tax policy. Before doing that we shall put them into context by looking at the possible consequences of inefficient implementation of tax law and at the problems that must be solved to secure an effective administration.

When a tax system is being designed or amended the proponents tend to assume that their purposes will be achieved. If people are to be taxed on their income (as defined) it is assumed that this will happen, likewise if taxes are to be imposed on assets passing at death, or on sales of goods and services. We have seen already that such taxes may not be borne in the way envisaged because people change their financial arrangements legally in order to avoid the intended burden. Thus a man may be able to arrange to enjoy the fruits of his investments in the form of capital gains or exempt income.

Beyond this, however, is the man who suppresses the existence or size of his income, assets or sales. To put it bluntly, he evades the tax legally due by fradulent means. This may amount to no more than a deliberate decision to neglect his legal duty to report his full income etc. Such cases are common in all countries and are sometimes referred to as the black or underground economy. Often the suppressed income and sales will have to go hand in hand and will lead to a consequential need to suppress the existence of assets acquired out of the proceeds of the undisclosed transactions.

Now it is inevitable that taxes are unpopular (even among those who receive a net benefit through social security subsidies) so it may be wondered why tax evasion should be regarded as undesirable. One answer is the way it can distort the intention of Parliament in the design of the tax system. Some people are better placed to evade taxes and thereby bear a less than equitable burden. It is not just a question of everyone having the same opportunity to evade and differing only by their respective tendencies to be law abiding.

Tax evasion is not confined to one class of people. Opportunities can arise in many ways. The rich man with multinational interests may be able to hide earnings and assets outside the country to which he owes his main allegiance by reason of his nationality, domicile or residence. The company director may benefit privately from work done by employees of his company. The poorer craftsman may ply his trade openly as an employee but work for cash in the evenings and at weekends. Where this so-called moonlighting is done for householders they will seldom have any incentive to disclose to the tax authority the fact that payments have been made.

Thus it is essential in designing an effective tax system to try to minimize the opportunities for, and rewards of, evasion. This means that some potential subjects of taxation are excluded from serious consideration. Thus if drugs such as cannabis were legalized and then taxed (on the same arguments as those used for tobacco and alcohol) there could be problems of evasion as the informal channels now used to evade illegality might remain in being to evade taxation.

Even if the design minimizes the risk of evasion by basing the taxes on clearly defined and ascertainable bases it is still necessary to ensure that the law can be enforced. There must be an administrative structure to ensure that people are brought face to face with their legal responsibilities. A vital part of any such structure is the people who operate it. It is likely that the officials concerned will be dealing collectively with millions of taxpayers. If they fail to fulfil their specified duties evasion may become the accepted way of life and even the stability of the national political system may be undermined.

One problem that seems to arise in many countries is bribery of the tax officials. A poorly paid official may be wide open to bribery because of the relatively large amounts of tax he is due to collect. This is not just a question of low standards of public morality, although the national ethos may stem from beliefs (justified or not) about the standards observed by those in high office. The system itself may fail to provide adequate cross-checks to protect the official against temptation. Furthermore, a low level of reward may fail to attract recruits of sufficient ability to detect the more sophisticated opportunities for evasion, or may attract only the more unscrupulous who enter the service in anticipation of the rewards to be obtained from bribery.[1]

A related problem can arise even in a highly developed society such as the UK. Tax planning requires the use of well trained, high quality minds. If the pay of tax officials is allowed to decline the best of them may be attracted by the rewards obtainable from advising taxpayers.[2] The result is a lower standard of administration and a reduced ability to counter attempted avoidance and evasion. Either of these distorts the intended design and may bring the system into disrepute if things go too far.

All these points notwithstanding, even the best officials can only enforce the system as intended if they have effective powers to do so. These powers must be consistent with the political and social *mores* of the country concerned. Thus in some countries officials may have considerable power to make discretionary decisions and to exact penalties for non-compliance. In others, such as the UK, officials must act within the law and are subject to challenge in the courts if they go beyond their powers or apply the law incorrectly.

The position in the UK has been the subject of a full review in recent years and in the next section we will look at the report of the Keith Committee before going on to consider the main enforcement provisions.

THE KEITH COMMITTEE

The Committee on the Enforcement Powers of the Revenue Departments (Chairman, Lord Keith of Kinkel) was set up by the government in 1980 because of concern that had been expressed about the balance existing between the need to ensure and enforce compliance with tax law and the need to avoid excessive burdens and pressures on taxpayers and others. It reported in four volumes over the period 1983/85.[3]

The committee collected and published a great deal of information about the activities of the tax authorities and about the rationale and results of those activities under a variety of headings. It considered too the evidence and arguments put forward by taxpayers and their representative organizations. The result is a very detailed account, presented in a way which reveals some consistent principles and regular themes. Many of these themes are summarized in the remainder of this section because of the light they throw on problems inherent in the operation of a tax system.

The committee laid down six principles to be kept in mind in guiding their work. They were as follows (slightly abbreviated).

(1) Enforcement powers should be precise, and logically formulated, and should so far as practicable be harmonized over the whole direct and indirect tax field.
(2) The scope for administrative discretion should be reduced to a minimum... In this way, everyone knows where they stand, and compliance is likely to be improved. If everyone is treated alike, grounds for complaint are minimized, provided always that the sanction is regarded as broadly fair.
(3) Routine regulatory mechanisms should not, in the tax field, be fenced with criminal sanctions. Automatic civil surcharges and penalties are more appropriate and more reliable in their application.
(4) All enforcement procedures should be subject to ultimate judicial control both broadly and in matters of detail, and such control should be capable of being applied in a summary and expeditious way.
(5) Opportunities for successful concealment of facts relevant to tax liability should be reduced.
(6) Effective criminal sanctions should be available to check the incidence of deliberate and serious frauds.[4]

The committee recognized that enforcement powers can cause friction between individuals and that the law by itself is not enough to secure the smooth operation of the tax system. As they put it:

'... a great deal depends on the standard of training given by both Departments to their officers. The human element is of paramount importance, and no pains should be spared so that the outlook and conduct of individual tax officers is up to the proper standard in their dealings with the public. That is not a matter that can be legislated for.'[5]

One of the committee's persistent themes is that the tax authority depends primarily on the taxpayer for the information needed to assess tax liability of most kinds. Liability to IT, CT and VAT depend largely on documentary evidence which only the taxpayer or his agents possess. Thus, unlike a commercial dispute about the circumstances of a transaction between two parties, the tax authority's problem may lie in finding out that the taxable transaction occurred at all. The essential enforcement procedures involve collecting relevant information, checking that information, assessing and collecting the tax due and imposing penalties on defaulting or fraudulent taxpayers as an encouragement to greater standards of honest compliance. Each of these factors will now be considered in the light of the report.

Relevant information starts with the taxpayer, and in his case it starts with the proposition that he should notify the tax authority of his liability whether imposed on his own income, whether as an employer responsible for collecting PAYE tax or as a trader liable to charge and account for VAT. It may be appropriate also for him to notify changes in circumstances which involve new or different liabilities. The evidence in the UK is that most people starting to trade approach the tax offices voluntarily for guidance, but without a statutory obligation, and penalties, the less scrupulous could escape the tax net with every hope of getting away with it. Even where such people receive payments from others these may be ascribed to fictitious recipients such as Mickey Mouse of Sunset Boulevard[6] or to the current occupant of 10 Downing Street, London SW1!

Once it is known that a person (which word includes a company) has a potential or actual liability to tax of any kind the provision of information can be put on a regular footing. In the case of income and capital gains the normal arrangement in the UK is for an annual return to be issued at the beginning of each tax year.[7] PAYE tax withheld by an employer is the subject of a monthly return and tax payment, plus an end of year report listing the details for each employee. VAT is reported and collected every three months.

Three issues arise in any case where tax liability depends on the provision of information by the taxpayer. The first is that if the information is supplied late tax legitimately due may be paid late, and this represents a clear financial advantage to the taxpayer. Not only is this unfair to those who pay at the proper time, it reduces the tax yield for that year and may increase the incidence of bad debts as the tax liability accumulates. Businesses which are in financial difficulty succumb all too easily to the temptation to use the tax collected from employees and customers as a source of finance.[8]

The second issue is the bunching of the work load for both the tax administration and the taxpayer. This is most noticeable in the case of annual returns of income. The committee noted that in the UK the problem had been overcome by failure to enforce the 30 day time limit, but felt that this was very unsatisfactory and proposed an alternative system which allowed for the need to provide reasonable time for the preparation of business accounts whatever accounting date may have been chosen.[9] The many businesses which had accounting years ending on 31 March could not be expected to produce their accounts by 5 May. For one thing the burden on the accounting profession would be intolerable.

Thirdly there is the question of what is to be done if the information is not provided at all. The answer adopted here is to give the tax authority the power to assess tax due on an estimated basis using their best judgement. A trader who fails to report his business income one year may be judged on the basis of past profits and of trends in his trade generally. If he accepts the estimate and pays the tax that may be evidence, usable in the following year, that his actual profit was greater than the estimate. A similar procedure is used in the case of VAT. Of course, most traders' response to such estimates is to produce the requred information, and this means that other, more formal, penalties for failure to supply information may not be needed very often.

It should not be assumed from the preceding discussion that the tax authority depends solely on the taxpayer for its information. Information about one taxpayer may be found in that provided by another, advertisements and news items in the media may reveal facts not otherwise known, and there are specific powers to obtain information from third parties. The latter will be listed later but it can be noted here that they cover many sources of income or gains where the payer or agent can be required, under threat of penalty, to give details. This may involve the provider of the information is a considerable administrative burden and cost but his legal duty is clear. However, the provision of all details about payments large or small would not be cost effective for the tax administrators and a minimum amount is usually specified in the notice, even if not in the underlying legislative power.

Two particular problems arise on the provision of information by third parties. The first is the extent to which government departments could or should co-operate in exchanging information which may have been supplied in confidence for quite different purposes. For instance, the contents of census forms might be very useful to the tax authority, but if it were believed that they were being so used people's willingness to complete the forms accurately would be sharply reduced. So far such exchanges have been confined to those between the two tax authorities. It is clear, for instance that the interests of the CCE (VAT) and the BIR (IT) in a particular trader will overlap.[10] The other problem is that of confidentiality in the relationship between a taxpayer and his professional advisers. The Keith Committee recognized that there were difficulties at the borderline but identified a clear distinction between, say, professional advice on tax planning which could not fairly be disclosed to 'the other side' and professional knowledge of the facts of transactions such as property sales derived from conveyancing work.[11]

Having obtained its information the tax authority needs to check it for accuracy, looking for inadvertent or deliberate error. It does this in two ways. Firstly it can cross check it in the tax office and this may include raising points of doubt with the taxpayer either by correspondence or by interview. Secondly an official may check information by visiting the trader's premises. The former is the more common practice of the Inland Revenue in dealing with IT, CT, etc., the latter is widely used in checking PAYE tax and VAT.

Cross checking in the tax office includes reconciling third party information and comparing the pattern and trends in business accounts with those of similar businesses. A rate of gross profits lower than that usually found in a particular trade may itself be a cause for enquiry. Attention is usually concentrated on those cases which give the greatest grounds for suspicion and an enquiry may end up as an attempted full reconciliation of income, savings and living costs.[12]

In the case of VAT, on the other hand, there has to be more emphasis on the detailed transaction records and checking of these is done by regular audit visits to the business premises. The visits have the backing of statutory powers but they are usually made at a time and place agreed with the business concerned. The CCE say that the primary aim of these visits is to ensure that records are being properly kept and decisions about liability at the borderline correctly made, and to give advice. Nevertheless, a significant proportion of such visits produce additional liability.[13] A similar approach is taken in the visits made to check PAYE records.[14]

What then is the tax authority's remedy if it decides that the information being provided by the taxpayer is deficient in some respect? Reference was made above to the use of estimated assessments where no information has been received at the appropriate time. This weapon is also used if the authority is unwilling to accept the accuracy of the information actually supplied. It is a very powerful weapon as it places the onus on the taxpayer to show that the assessment is excessive and if his records are deficient he may find it very difficult to do this. It means too that, quite apart from any formal procedures to obtain access to private records such as bank accounts, there will be little sympathy in any appeal tribunal for a taxpayer who denies that he understated his liability and yet refuses to allow access to those records which would throw light on the matter.[15]

However, the taxpayer is not without some rights in the matter. The most important is that of appeal to an independent tribunal.[16] If he feels that the tax authority is taking an unreasonable line he can argue his case before that tribunal (or get someone to do it for him) and if he then feels that its decision is wrong in law he can appeal to the courts. Note that he cannot appeal to the courts on a finding of fact unless he disputes a secondary fact on the grounds that it is not supported by the primary facts as found.[17]

Once a tax liability has been settled, with or without the taxpayer's agreement, there remains the collection of the tax due. Again the less scrupulous taxpayer might accept the liability but ignore the normal requests for payment, thereby gaining a relative advantage over fellow taxpayers who do pay. There are three main powers available to coerce him to pay, and they are not mutually exclusive.

The first power enables the tax authority to claim interest at a commercial rate on the debt. This power removes the financial incentive to delay payment except in so far as the delay leads to the debt becoming that of an insolvent company which cannot pay. It has been suggested that in some cases this is done deliberately, the moving spirits behind the business then moving on to operate it through another company. This has been referred to as the 'phoenix syndrome'.[18] There may also be collection problems if the taxpayer has transferred his assets and himself to a foreign country with no intention of returning to the UK.

The second power lies in the ability to recover the amount due by distraint. This means that the authority can enter premises with a bailiff and lay claim to goods with a view to selling them in satisfaction of the debt. This power is widely used but in the overwhelming majority of cases produces a very rapid cash settlement.[19] The third power is the normal remedy of recovery through the civil courts on the same basis as that available to any other creditor. It is not used very often and the delays inherent in the process may increase the risk that the creditor and his assets will disappear.[20]

Finally, what means are available to discourage the taxpayer from an incomplete disclosure of information, perhaps in the hope that he will escape his full liability? There are two kinds of remedy, civil and criminal, and they will be covered in that order.

The main civil remedies are provided in the tax legislation itself. The idea lying behind them is that the taxpayer who provides full and complete information and pays promptly shall not be disadvantaged compared with one who is, at best, careless of his statutory responsibilities or, at worst, sets out deliberately to deceive. The tax authority can look to three remedies, all of which may be used together in any one case.

(1) To raise further tax assessments for the years concerned, including the past years

which would be time barred in normal circumstances.[21]

(2)   To collect interest at a commercial rate on the additional tax which would have been due in past years if correct information had been supplied on time.

(3)   To levy monetary penalties, usually related to the tax liability understated but also varying in size according to the nature of the offence and to the degree of co-operation given in the investigation of the omissions and understatements.

All of these remedies are subject to formal procedures, usually involving the appeal tribunal, but in practice most cases are settled by a legally enforceable agreement whereby the taxpayer agrees in writing to pay a stated sum in respect of his liability to tax, interest and penalties for the years specified. Even so the tribunal route is always open to the taxpayer and a decision to use it is not treated as 'lack of cooperation' in negotiating penalties due. The main inhibiting factor seems to be the additional cost of mounting a formal case for the purpose of a quasi-judicial hearing before the tribunal.[22]

Going beyond civil proceedings, but not necessarily producing more revenue for the tax authority there may be criminal proceedings leading to the possibility of imprisonment as well as or instead of financial penalties. In addition the first two civil remedies listed above would still be enforced. Criminal proceedings are confined to those cases where fraudulent behaviour can be shown up to the higher standard of proof required for such purposes. Partly because of the nature of the tax such proceedings are more common in VAT offences than for IT. The statistics suggest that cases are only pursued to the criminal courts where the tax lost is substantial and the chances of a successful prosecution are high. Very few prosecutions fail. It has been suggested that such prosecutions are not really necessary in view of the civil penalties available. The counter argument is that it is only by criminal prosecution and conviction, publicly reported, that honest taxpayers will be reassured and potentially dishonest ones discouraged. It should be borne in mind that the civil route produces no publicity in the UK, although the idea of publishing the names of defaulters has been tried elsewhere and has been suggested for use in the UK.[23]

A special kind of problem arises in the case where there has been a deliberate and premeditated fraud. The main evidence of the facts is likely to be held by the taxpayer or his agents. Where serious fraud is suspected a notice requiring production of that evidence, the exact nature and extent of which will not be known, will result in its destruction or removal elsewhere. To overcome this problem tax administrators have been given powers, under judicial safeguard, to enter premises without warning and not necessarily during normal business hours. Such 'raids' may involve the police and may include personal searches. Although the statistics of the results of such searches are reassuring there can be no doubt that they consist of an erosion of civil liberty and personal privacy. Unfortunately the evidence of the participation of the general criminal fraternity in VAT fraud, at least, suggests that they are inevitable.[24]

Our general review of the requirements of effective tax enforcement is now complete. In the remainder of this chapter we will add some flesh to part of the skeleton by looking at the current UK statutes as they concern, first, the provision of information and, then, the penalties for false or incomplete disclosure.

INFORMATION POWERS IN THE UK

So far as IT is concerned the main information requirements are brought together in the Taxes Management Act 1970. S.7 requires people to give notice if they are chargeable to IT and have not delivered a statutory return. The penalty for failure to comply may be up to £100. S.8 follows this up by setting out in some detail the requirement to complete a return of income source by source. S.93 prescribes a penalty of £50 plus £10 per day (limited by reference to the tax actually due) for failure to submit the information required. Similar provisions apply to CT and CGT.

The Act goes on in ss.13–19 to deal with the information that is to be supplied by third parties. This includes taxable income received by but not belonging to the recipient, lists of lodgers, details of employees' emoluments, fees and commissions paid to people other than employees, and details of leases of land and buildings. Again the requirements are backed up in s.98 by penalties, the effect of which is similar to that described for s.93 except that there can be no limit by reference to the tax due.

The collection of information may be active as well as passive. Ss.110–111 give a right to enter and inspect land in order to establish its annual value and a right to inspect other assets for the purposes of CGT. In s.20 (as amended by Finance Act 1976) there is a more general right to inspect and copy documents relevant to tax liability either at the tax office or elsewhere. In extreme cases s.20C enables a warrant to be obtained to enter premises, by force if necessary, in order to seize and remove documents believed to be required as evidence of fraud. On a more regular basis there is a right to inspect wages records for the purposes of PAYE audit[25] and, in the context of the special problems of casual work in the building industry, to inspect records and documents relating to sub-contractors.[26]

The main VAT information powers were consolidated in the VAT Act 1983 but have since been amended in the Finance Act 1985 following consideration of the Keith Committee's recommendations. Much of the detail is dealt with through statutory instruments.

The CCE are given the power to make regulations requiring people who make or receive a supply of goods or taxable services to notify them of the fact and of any changes in circumstances. Furthermore CCE may demand to see relevant documents, to take copies or extracts, or to remove them for a reasonable time.[27] They can take samples in order to establish the category of the goods although they must pay for them at cost price if they are not returned to the trader.[28]

The VAT legislation is more specific about the business records that must be maintained and the period for which they must be retained.[29] It also deals specificially with the issues that arise when records are kept on computer and hard copy may not be available.[30]

We have seen already that the administration of VAT is much more concerned with the primary records of a business than is IT. Thus, for VAT there is general power for an 'authorized person' to enter business premises at a reasonable time, as well as a more draconian power to enter forcibly.[31] The latter includes a power to search people but at least it lays down that a woman or girl can only be searched by a woman. Can a man be searched by a woman? The law does not seem to prohibit it!

As would be expected these information powers are backed by penalties for failure to comply. Failure to notify liability may result in a penalty equal to 30% of the relevant tax or £50 if greater. If information is not supplied or records not kept the penalty is either a fixed sum or a percentage of the tax due and can be repeated on a day-to-day basis as long as the failure continues. The penalty is greater if there has been a previous failure. If records, although adequate, have not been preserved for the stated time, now six years, there is a penalty of £500.[32]

So far we have looked at the penalties for failure to supply information or keep records. Where there is some element of deliberate understatement of tax due or other concealment other penalties can be levied, as we shall see in the next section.

PENALTY PROVISIONS IN THE UK

We have seen already (on pp. 198–202) that the deterrent used most widely in the UK consists of financial penalties rather than criminal proceedings. Such a system can only operate effectively if the scale of penalties for 'wrong-doing' (to use a deliberately vague word) is clearly set out. This is the legislation that we shall now consider.

For IT purposes the main penalty section is to be found in s.95, Taxes Management Act 1970. It relates to the delivery of an incorrect return, making an incorrect statement for the purposes of claiming an allowance, deduction or relief or submitting incorrect accounts. For the penalty to be incurred the error must be made fraudulently or negligently. The penalty prescribed is £50 plus the amount of the tax that would have been lost because of the error. In the case of fraud the tax lost part of the penalty may be doubled. In addition to the penalty interest is chargeable on the additional tax due, calculated from the date when it should have been paid.[33]

The result of these penalties and charges may be considerable. A taxpayer who *negligently* reduces his tax bill by £1 000 per year for six years (and such a reduction could hardly be less than negligence) might face the following bill:

	£
Recovery of tax lost	6 000
Interest thereon, say[34]	2 500
Penalty	£6 000
	£14 500

It should be borne in mind that if the error took place over a longer period there is a power to make out of-time assessments[35] and interest and penalties will be chargeable on those amounts as well. The interest will then be proportionately larger as it relates to a longer period.

This is not quite the end of the story. The BIR has power to mitigate penalties, but not interest.[36] It is clear from the Keith Committee's report that it will usually do so in proportion to the gravity of the offence and the degree of co-operation received in the investigation.[37] Only tax lost and interest thereon are recoverable if the case is the subject of criminal prosecution, which takes place under the general criminal law, not under the tax statutes.

So far as VAT is concerned the penalty provisions were completely revised by Finance Act 1985 following consideration of the Keith Committee's recommendations. Before that the VAT penalties concentrated on criminal prosecution and the main change has been to introduce civil penalties for which the required standard of proof is lower.

The first of the civil penalties in Finance Act 1985 is to be found in s. 13. This concerns dishonesty as a result of which tax due is underpaid or a tax refund is overpaid. The penalty prescribed is the amount of the tax that would have been evaded (in addition to the tax itself) and it can be reduced by up to one half in so far as the person concerned is co-operative in the investigation. In addition s. 18 charges interest on the tax underpaid in past years.

Even though the required standard of proof is lower in civil proceedings it may still be the case that the understatement results from neglect or carelessness rather than dishonesty. This is covered by s. 14 which also covers those businesses which accept an assessment (such as an estimated assessment) which understates the true liability. Following an idea put forward by the Keith Committee[38] the test of neglect is an objective one based on the proportion of the true tax that would have been lost if the error had not been discovered. Initially the test is 30% of the true tax, but as amounts rise this becomes £10000 (in the true tax range £33333 – £200000) and then 5% of the true tax. The power to levy penalties is also available where there is error on a lesser scale (15% of the true tax) but it continues over several years. In all such cases the fixed penalty is 30% of the tax that would have been lost.

As with IT there is now provision in ss. 21–22 to ensure that in the more serious cases (dishonesty but not neglect) an assessment or additional assessment can be made to recover tax due beyond the normal six year time limit. Such penal and tax recovery machinery is not, however, appropriate to those small businesses which tend to be late in meeting their statutory responsibility to submit a quarterly return and pay the VAT due. These cases are now covered by the 'default surcharge' prescribed by s. 19.

A business only comes within this section if there are two defaults within a period of 12 months. If this happens the business is notified that a surcharge period exists ending on the first anniversary of the second quarter which was in default. A further (third) default within this period will then produce liability to the penalty (surcharge) and will further extend the surcharge period. The latter is important because the size of the penalty increases in stages with each default in the same surcharge period. Thus a surcharge period which starts off as one year may become virtually continuous if there are regular defaults year by year. The surcharge is calculated as £30 or 5% of the outstanding tax if greater on a first default, rising to £30 or 30% of the outstanding tax. The effect of the default surcharge is to make it unprofitable for the trader to play the system by delaying payment of VAT collected from customers. It is no longer necessary for the CCE to start formal proceedings for recovery, nor is there any need to become involved in complicated interest charge calculations for tax delayed for short periods.

In addition to these civil remedies there are specified criminal sanctions for VAT. The main provisions are now to be found in 6th Schedule, Finance Act 1985, which also sets out the offences to which they apply. Broadly the penalties which may be imposed are three times the amount of tax which would have been lost (sbject to any overriding statutory maximum fine for such offences), imprisonment of up to six months on summary conviction, or imprisonment of up to seven years on indictment. The court may impose the financial penalty in addition to or instead of imprisonment. It will be noticed that the potential financial penalty is three times that which can be levied under civil proceedings for dishonesty. The civil and criminal penalties cannot both be imposed but the tax lost and interest thereon is always recoverable.

In this section we have looked at the main deterrent penalties used in the administration of IT and VAT, and in the previous section we looked at the information powers. There are many other such provisions in the legislation, although some are of little practical significance. Nevertheless it is important to bear in mind that the imposition of penalties is not an everyday occurrence. Most of the work done in settling tax liabilities, both by the officials and by the taxpayer and his representatives, is carried on in a normal commercial manner and as often as not without personal antipathy. The importance of penalties lies in their existence as an encouragement to the honest to remain so and in the power they give to counter deliberate dishonesty. They are used only in a small minority of cases but even so the delicate balance between tax enforcement and personal liberty must be monitored constantly.

NOTES AND REFERENCES

1. See Muten, L., 'Leading issues of tax policy in developing countries', in Peacock A. and Forte F. (eds.), *The Political Economy of Taxation*, Basil Blackwell, London (1981).
2. See correspondence between the President of the Institute of Taxation and the Board of Inland Revenue reproduced in *Taxation Practitioner*, August 1986, and the House of Commons reply by the Financial Secretary to the Treasury (Mr Norman Lamont) to a question set down by Mr Tim Smith, MP. Also paras. 125–128 of the *Report of the Board of Inland Revenue for the Year Ended 31 December 1985*, Cmnd. 9381, HMSO, London (1986).
3. Volumes 1 & 2, Cmnd. 8822 (1983), Volume 3, Cmnd. 9120 (1984) and Volume 4, Cmnd. 9440 (1985), HMSO, London. Hereafter referred to as the Keith Committee.
4. Keith Committee, para. 1.5.1.
5. *Ibid.*, para. 1.9.1.
6. This example is taken from the Keith Committee, para. 2.3.1.
7. In fact many taxpayers in the UK do not receive an annual return, and some receive a non-statutory form – see Keith Committee, Chapter 6.
8. The financial problems of loss-making professional football clubs are often brought to a head by non-payment of PAYE tax deducted from players' wages and VAT due on gate receipts.
9. Keith Committee, paras. 3.1.20 and 3.1.25.
10. *Ibid.*, Chapter 23.
11. *Ibid.*, Chapter 26.
12. *Ibid.*, Chapters 10, 11 and 13.
13. *Ibid.*, Chapter 4.
14. *Ibid.*, Chapter 12.
15. *Ibid.*, sections 10.5 and 11.5 cover these procedures.
16. In the case of the Inland Revenue there are General and Special Commissioners. VAT has its own tribunal.
17. The leading case is *Edwards* v. *Bairstow and Harrison* (1955) 36 TC 207 and 3 All ER 48. The question at issue was whether the purchase and sale of five cotton mills (primary facts) amounted to an adventure in the nature of trade (a secondary fact).
18. Keith Committee, paras. 24.4.1 to 24.4.6.
19. *Ibid.*, section 24.2.
20. *Ibid.*, para. 24.1.1.
21. The normal time limit is 6 years from the end of the year of assessment concerned, but if the taxpayer has died assessments cannot be made after the end of the third year following the year of death – see Taxes Management Act 1980, ss. 34 and 40.
22. Keith Committee, Chapters 16–21.
23. *Ibid.*, Chapter 22.
24. *Ibid.*, sections 9.16 to 9.23.

25. Regulation 32 of the Income Tax (Employments) Regulations 1973.
26. Regulation 11 of the Income Tax (Sub-contractors in the Building Industry) Regulations 1975.
27. Para. 8, 7th Schedule, Value Added Tax Act 1983, and para. 3, 7th Schedule, Finance Act 1985.
28. Para. 9, 7th Schedule, Value Added Tax Act 1983.
29. Para. 7, 7th Schedule, Value Added Tax Act 1983, and para. 1, 7th Schedule, Finance Act 1985.
30. S. 10, Finance Act 1985.
31. Para. 10, 7th Schedule, Value Added Tax Act 1983, and para. 5, 7th Schedule, Finance Act 1985.
32. S. 17, Finance Act 1985.
33. S. 88, Taxes Management Act 1970.
34. The interest rate is varied from time to time by Treasury Order. The calculations in the example assume a rate of about 10% per annum for an average period of about four years, which is probably conservative. Note that the interest is simple, not compound, but is not deductible in any income calculation for tax purposes.
35. Ss. 36–37, Taxes Management Act 1970.
36. S. 102, Taxes Management Act 1970.
37. See Keith Committee, Chapters 17 and 20.
38. Discussed by the Keith Committee in Chapter 18.

EXERCISES AND DISCUSSION TOPICS

1. Discuss ways in which a tax system, although well designed with equity in mind, may become inequitable because of the opportunities it offers to a few citizens to evade their proper liability. Can you think of possible subjects for taxation which could not be used because of the evasion possibilities which would arise?
2. It is well recognized that civil penalties for tax evasion increase the public revenue, whereas criminal penalties, particularly imprisonment, increase public expenditure. Discuss reasons why the latter are still regarded as a necesary feature of tax enforcement procedures and why nevertheless they are little used.
3. The main source of information for tax assessment and collection is the taxpayer.

   (a) What other types of information are available to check the information received from that source?
   (b) Can you think of taxable activities for which this kind of check is unlikely to be adequate?

15   Future trends and developments

In the course of this book we have looked at a number (but not all) of the taxes levied in the UK[1] and at the principles which enable us to look critically at the way they are levied. In this final chapter we shall try to bring together some of the threads from earlier discussion in an attempt to answer the question 'Where do we go from here?'

This is not an idle question. Business men and private individuals are making investment decisions which depend on expected outcomes over long periods and those outcomes may be affected critically by changes in tax law and policy. Of course they are affected to a greater extent by other unforeseen events – wars, changes in energy prices and so on – but that is no reason to ignore the potential effect of tax changes.

In order to limit the discussion consideration will be confined to the UK, but even then international factors may produce constraints (for instance, because of EC harmonization rules). Before looking at the policies some attention must be paid to the spending framework.

THE FRAMEWORK OF GOVERNMENT FINANCIAL POLICY

We saw in Chapter 1 (Table 1.3) the broad spectrum of government spending.[2] In so far as trends in taxation and spending must be linked, albeit not exactly, it is clear that the spending commitments will bear on the taxes that need to be collected in total, even if not on the distribution of revenue between the individual sources. The direction of the trend may be very important as it is easier to reform the tax system when the revenue requirement is falling as no one need be made obviously worse off.

What then are the long-term prospects under the main expenditure headings? This may depend partly on political value judgements and the complexion of future governments, but it depends, too, on hard facts. For instance, an important element in the social security budget is the scheme for giving relief to the unemployed. The number unemployed is a fact,[3] whatever it may owe to past policies. The question of who is to be entitled to relief and at what level is a political decision. The prospects for reducing the level of unemployment (recorded at well over 3 million at the time of writing) depend also on political decisions but these are constrained by the economic realities. Economic forecasters suggest that the prospects for reducing the level significantly over the next few years are very limited within the existing constraints. Thus it appears that the prospects for reducing this element of the social security budget are poor unless harsh

TAXATION POLICY 209

decisions are made about the level of support. Such decisions may be made by failing to apply full inflation indexation to the existing payments.

Another large item in the social security budget is the support given to the elderly and here again facts exist which seem likely to have a vital impact on future government spending. The demographic pattern in the UK is such that the ratio between those of working age and those over retirement age is changing adversely, partly because of birth rate patterns and partly because more people are living to the age of 75 and beyond.[4] This change can be forecast very accurately for 20 years or more because it concerns people already living.

The crux of the matter is that there will be relatively fewer producers, who also consume, and more consumers who do not produce. Given that state pensions have to be paid out of current taxes and given the increased need of the very elderly for social and medical care the implication for government spending is all too clear.

Again political decisions may be made to counter these trends. Appropriate medical and social care may be increased at a slower rate than the increase in the elderly population, perhaps forcing the younger members of the families concerned to take on more responsibility. State pension policies may be varied so as to reduce the automatic payments to the better off elderly (those with company or public service pensions and/or significant investment income) while maintaining or improving support for those who depend solely on the state pension. These would be hard political decisions which might be able to do no more than hold back the level of spending in real terms or as a proportion of GNP.

The proportionate increase in the elderly population may be accompanied by a compensating decrease in the population of school age, another group of consumers who do not produce. However, this does not follow automatically as the birth rates which determine these changes are at least two generations apart.[5] Even if there are fewer children, recent experience in the UK does not suggest that it is easy to reduce spending on education. The required reduction in the number of teachers may be too rapid to be dealt with by 'natural wastage' (i.e. retirements and resignations). At the same time if all recruitment ceased all training establishments would have to be closed and there would be serious distortion in the age distribution of the teaching profession to the point where it was predominantely elderly. Neither would be sensible measures if the birth rate then stabilized or rose again. Then there is the question of school buildings. Closing schools, whether they are seen as physical or social entities (and they are both) is widely disliked, but so is the alternative of allowing them to operate well below capacity if financially inefficient. It is always easier to expand than to contract.

These examples of the unemployed, the elderly and education show some of the issues facing future governments in seeking to keep significant items of public spending under control over the next few decades. Many other problems exist, defence not least, all of which may make it very difficult to reduce taxes or even to hold them at their present level. Of course views will differ about the desirable size of the PSBR, about the necessary level of defence spending and so on, but there will be no easy solutions. The history of a government first elected in 1979 with a commitment to cutting public expenditure is, perhaps, an awful warning to its successors.[6]

TAXATION POLICY

In the light of the discussion about public spending it is most important that the taxes levied to finance it should do as little harm to the economy as is possible. Any taxes which discourage the creation of new employment or drive profitable industry out of the country are inconsistent with the country's needs. In a recent discussion document the Confederation of British Industry commented:

'Our present tax system is lacking in basic rationale or logic, is the subject of wide dis-satisfaction and is frequently changed. It cannot therefore be conducive to competitiveness and growth.'[7]

Similar comments have been made by many other observers.

What then are the main defects that are perceived by these commentators? They differ to some extent according to their political stance and to self-interest, but some general themes can be identified. Thus it is now widely accepted that there must be a closer relationship between the tax and social security systems. On the whole, recent discussion has shown an improving tendency to look at the relative costs and to consider the indirect effects, often the most important, of any 'bright ideas'.

First come the more revolutionary proposals of which the most important is the idea of an expenditure tax (discussed in Chapter 3). Great claims are made for this tax in terms of its effect on the economy and on simplicity of administration. The greatest difficulties seem to lie in the transition from the present system and in reconciling it with the tax systems of other countries given that business and investment crosses frontiers on a massive scale. The present writer's belief is that the most that can be expected in the foreseeable future is that some of the tax's ideas, in particular relief for saving, may be imported into the present system. Thus there may be some development of the idea that lies behind PEP.[8] Unfortunately this will do nothing to improve simplicity.

There may be stronger moves towards mitigating the adverse effect of present taxes by reducing the rates of tax in return for the withdrawal of many special exemptions and reliefs. The underlying argument is that special reliefs are bound to distort the economic balance while a high rate of tax tends to increase disincentive effects at the margin.[9] Thus employees may be discouraged by high marginal rates at the same time that they are seeking non-cash benefits if those benefits are not fully taxed at their cash equivalent.

Taxes imposed on industrial and commercial activity can have particularly undesirable effects on the economy. Special reliefs on certain kinds of capital expenditure may discriminate between capital intensive and labour intensive activity, when what is wanted for long-term success is an undistorted decision between the two. Taxes which are imposed on industrial costs are uncertain in their effects and in so far as they fall on the firm may make it impossible to compete adequately against foreign firms who are not so burdened.

At the time of writing the trend towards lower tax rates and the withdrawal of special reliefs does seem to be gathering momentum. The US tax proposals reveal a sharp reduction in tax rates, but both company taxable profits and personal taxable incomes will rise so that it does not follow that tax liabilities will be less.[10] Something similar happened in the UK in 1984 when the rate of CT was reduced in stages but many reliefs allowable in calculting taxable profits were withdrawn.[11]

In considering the possibility of further developments along these lines the political climate has to be considered. The UK government elected in 1979 was committed to free movement of capital across frontiers and in that climate was constrained to operate a tax system which was compatible with those of its main trading partners, especially in the OECD. For instance, differences in company tax systems can distort international investment unless any differences can be resolved through bilateral agreements dealing with double taxation.[12]

At the same time the 1979 government was committed to lowering the rate of tax and eliminating distortion. Unfortunately, it may be argued that it has added new distortions and has failed to eliminate some of the most damaging.

A change to a left-wing government might produce sharp change of course and thereby invalidate many of the investment decisions made in recent years. The precise policy of the Labour party is not yet clear but it does seem to be thinking in terms of higher rates of tax on high earners together with an increased commitment to certain forms of government spending, such as state pensions. Its policies may also mean that the UK will cease to be an open economy for transfers of capital across frontiers.[13] Whether such policies will improve or harm the level of economic prosperity is a matter for the reader's individual judgement.

The Alliance parties may attain a position of greater influence and do seem to be open to ideas of serious tax reform along the lines discussed above.[14] They too seem to envisage heavier taxation of the reasonably well-to-do and greater benefits for selected categories of the needy. It seems to be less 'doctrinaire' in such matters than the Labour party, but whether its more open stance will survive the constraints of practical politics remains to be seen.

All political parties owe a debt to their supporting interest groups and this must affect their attitude to particular aspects of any tax reform programme. The reforms in the USA were achieved by a concerted effort to produce an agreed package which, on the surface, hit most of the special pleaders but which could be presented as being advantageous to all of them through its effect on general economic prosperity. The UK reform has tended to be piecemeal so that every individual proposal has to battle through against the opposition of the particular groups who perceive themselves as being directly disadvantaged. Of course those who may benefit say very little.

In the next section we will look at the particular taxes in the UK. Strictly we need to produce a fully costed general overview of any changes envisaged, but to do so in this context would be little more than idle speculation. To set out the desirable and possible direction of change for each tax, bearing in mind the needs of the country generally, must suffice.

THE INDIRECT TAXES

It will be convenient to look first at the indirect taxes. The excise taxes on tobacco products and alcohol are likely to affect the prosperity of only those industries directly concerned. It seems unlikely that any case can or will be made for substantial revision. There may be growing social concern about excessive consumption of alcohol but given the ease of private manufacture (from elderberry wine onwards – or upwards) a substantial increase in tax is another matter. The tax rate on diesel oil (derv) is high relative to the tax on petrol as compared with that relationship in many other countries, and it has been suggested that this was the result of an attempt to protect the indigenous motor industry which was ill prepared to produce and sell diesel engined cars. There may be some change here over the next few years but the general level of oil taxes will depend on trends in world oil prices. The desire to use the tax system to encourage energy conservation seems to be less noticeable than it was a few years ago. The main industrial objection to the excise tax is that has to be borne as a cost, unlike VAT which can be set off. Thus the excise tax burden on fuel should be kept low enough to avoid any rise in the costs of UK-based industry above those of its competitiors abroad.

VAT is almost entirely a tax on the consumer except where it falls on exempt activities, especially financial services. Thus it has little impact on industrial costs, but a different question that does arise is whether food and other necessities should continue to be zero rated in contrast with the policies adopted by the other members of the EC.[15] The argument against widening the present scope of the tax is that to do so would increase the cost of living (which might result in higher wage settlements) and would remove the present slightly progressive structure of the tax. The counter arguments are that the increased revenue could be used to reduce taxes which are more damaging to the economy and which also increase the cost of living, albeit less obviously. It can be argued as well that VAT is not a suitable tax for introducing progressivity into the tax system and that the relief of poverty should be directed more precisely at the poor. It is unlikely that politicians, of whatever hue, will be able to overcome a natural reluctance to be seen apparently imposing higher taxes on the poor, although the consequential reduction in costs of administration may yet carry some weight.[16]

A tax which may well increase the cost of living, although few outside business management are aware of it, is the employers' contribution to National Insurance. It seems highly unlikely that this tax is borne by the employee, in which case it is a cost to the employer and all or most of it will be passed on to the consumer if the employer is to remain profitable. This means that it enters into the costs of industry located in the UK and may thereby reduce international competitiveness (in which import substitution should not be forgotten) as well as increasing UK prices. However, the yield is considerable and not easily replaced. Nevertheless, there is steady pressure from the CBI and elsewhere to reduce this tax and this pressure has had some success in recent years.[17] It is just possible that there could be a trade-off between widening the scope of VAT and reducing the burden of employers' contributions given that the effect on the cost of living would be in opposite directions and the improvement in industrial competitiveness could produce more employment.

Finally in this group of indirect taxes are the local, municipal rates. They have been subjected to much dislike and even more study. The most recent proposal is that they should be replaced, in whole or in part, by a flat rate tax per capita.[18] This seems to be a mainly political question but rates imposed on industrial premises are also an economic one as they are a cost, albeit not a large one in most cases, and they may cause locational distortion because of their varying levels from one municipality to another. On the other side of the coin is the total relief from rates of all agricultural property. Given the steps that have been taken already to hold down municipal spending by government controls and the declining profitability of agriculture it seems unlikely that there will be significant changes in industrial and agricultural rating.

DIRECT TAXES

Turning now to direct taxes, and especially to income taxes, several lively issues arise some of which are known to be in the process of serious reconsideration or reform.

It has been noted already that the Conservative government first elected in 1979 is committed to a programme of reducing the rate of tax and in this it had succeeded to some extent at the time of writing.[19] Whether this process can continue may depend on the progress of the economy over the next few years but some further reduction in the basic rate of IT seems likely, if only for presentational reasons. In so far as the case for a reduction in the rate of tax is based on the disincentive argument it may be that the higher rates, rising to 60%, are also open to some further reduction. However, suggestions of inordinately high rises in higher earnings (multiples of the rate of increase in the RPI) may suggest that this is politically inappropriate.

If a government of left-wing tendencies is elected any such reduction is most unlikely and some increases may be expected. There is in fact some evidence that people are prepared to pay more of these visible taxes if they feel that the extra money is being used for worthy causes, such as improved support for those who really need it.[20]

The scope for substantial changes in the threshold of IT (outside the normal indexation rule) may be tied up with two factors, the link with NICS and the restructuring of the taxation of married couples. We have seen that the thresholds for IT and NICS are not the same and that employees' NICS cease before IT reaches the upper limit of its basic rate band. Both contributions represent taxation and there seem to be strong reasons for aggregating them, especially as both will shortly be collected under the same computerized deduction scheme. There would be some logic too if IT was put on the same periodic basis as NICS, PAYE ceasing to be cumulative. This would be a big reform. The main objection appears to be the mistaken belief, still widely held, that NICS represent a form of insurance premium. Politicians feel inevitably that this makes NICS more acceptable than IT.

Computerization may also make it feasible to integrate the IT system with social security. The revenue cost of removing the poverty trap by raising the IT threshold would be impossibly high because all taxpayers benefit whether rich or poor. However, some rationalization of social security provisions could reduce the problem and ensure that effective tax rates in excess of 100% did not occur. It is inevitable that such reforms can only be envisaged if the net revenue cost (tax lost plus additional grants) is small.[21]

Turning next to the taxation of married couples, it is very widely held that it must be reformed. The Green Paper published in 1986[22] favours separate (independent) taxation with transferable allowances so that a husband with a non-working wife receives a double allowance. Unfortunately transferability undermines the principle of independence and it has been opposed both on that and on incentive grounds.[23] It does seem that the route to be adopted will depend on the flavour of the government in power after the next general election, which must take place not later than 1988. Whichever plan is adopted some people must be worse off relatively, although this fact may be obscured by phasing in the new allowance structure over several years and by failing to index those allowances which are not to be 'reduced'.

The IT changes that have been discussed are unlikely to take place without some loss of tax revenue and/or increased spending on social security (in real terms). The question of how these losses can be met cannot be ignored, convenient though it may be to do so. Increasing the basic and other rates of IT is one solution, although its effects may be harmful to economic growth and avoidance and evasion may be further encouraged. One possible candidate for reform is CGT. Unlike the inflation element in interest receiveable gains are now indexed[24] so that as time passes chargeable gains will reflect real gains. Gains then become an accretion in spending power and as such, apart from some roll-over situations, would seem to be capable of being taxed at the same rate as income. At the same time the present threshold is high and encourages CGT planning aimed at making full use of it each year. For most people the threshold eliminates CGT altogether unless they have the misfortune to sell a large asset owned for many years (e.g. freehold premises) in circumstances whereby they are unable to spread the chargeable gain over several tax years.

It has indeed been suggested that these indexed gains should be taxed as income in the normal way with no special threshold.[25] This would broaden the base of IT and would either produce higher revenues or would enable the rate of tax to be reduced (or the normal threshold to be increased). The equity case for doing this seems to be a strong one. However, so long as a progressive rate structure remained it would be necessary to allow 'spreading' of a unusually large gain (large by the criterion of the individual's normal level of gains) by some form of top-slicing relief. It would also be desirable to reconsider taxation of capital gains on death, the tax being imposed on lifetime gifts already.[26] This would mean that elderly investors would not be locked into their existing assets by the prospect of tax-free gains for their estate. This too would raise extra revenues but would cause some loss of IHT as the CGT payable would reduce the estate of the deceased.

Every opportunity should be taken to widen the IT base and it seems likely that the trend towards the assessment of non-monetary benefits will continue. In the case of company cars and other employment benefits the legal position is reasonably clear although questions of apportionment between business and private use give rise to practical problems. Two other benefits are likely to provoke continuing argument, share option schemes and housing. The former is linked with the general encouragement of direct savings, and in so far as option benefits are liable to CGT would be affected by any change in CGT along the lines suggested.[27] The latter is part of a wider problem.

The housing market in the UK has been distorted by many tax and non-tax factors over recent decades and there can be no doubt that house prices are higher and investment in owner-occupied housing greater than if the tax reliefs did not exist. Pressure is mounting for the elimination of the mortgage interest relief,[28] especially as it is believed that parts of many house purchase loans are obtained not to buy the house but to buy other assets such as motor cars. The main issue in the end may be how to phase out this relief without disrupting the level of house prices to the serious detriment of existing owners. As a first step withdrawal of relief on any excess over the basic rate of IT seems to be favoured. Keeping the loan limit fixed is, of course, a form of gradual withdrawal and it affects the first time buyer last of all.[29]

Of the other reliefs on housing the roll-over relief for CGT seems to be unavoidable but will lose significance anyway as the gain derives from the indexed years after 1982. The question of taxing the notional benefit from house occupation is much more difficult politically and no such development is at all likely unless it could be linked to a sharp reduction in the rate of tax. There would be serious practical problems in the need to agree a notional value for each house so occupied. It was this problem more than anything which led to the previous tax on occupation being phased out in 1963 at a time when the number of owner-occupied houses in the UK was much smaller than it is now.[30]

Turning now to savings, the proponents of an expenditures tax can rightly claim that there would be few problems under their scheme as all savings into registered assets would be made tax free. If IT is retained as the principal direct tax the question remains whether savings should be encouraged by tax relief and, if so, how should the approved categories be decided and defined. As we have seen in earlier chapters the existing reliefs are concentrated on pension funds and retirement annuities, share option schemes, the BES and the PEP. In addition, special tax arrangements apply to the income and gains derived from certain National Savings schemes and from certain institutional savings schemes such as endowment policies. Most of these reliefs and arrangements limit the qualifying amounts and are subject to various restrictions and conditions. Altogether it looks and is a hotchpotch and adds significantly to the complexity of the system. It would be a very brave man who could argue that this collection of bits and pieces benefits the economy of the UK.

Future development in this area may depend considerably on the political complexion of future governments. The Labour Party tends to favour investment via the public sector. The Conservative Party has a strong ideological commitment to the investment of personal savings directly via the financial markets. The topic is so varied that it is difficult not to become bogged down in the detail but an attempt to cover the main possibilities is made in the paragraphs which follow.

The main reliefs aimed at pension provision for retirement are deeply entrenched in both the tax and financial systems of the UK and are unlikely to be changed, with the possible exception of removing for future years the tax exemption of the lump sum element of the benefits.[31] The reliefs in respect of National Savings reflect the needs of the government to borrow from many sources and the Treasury is unlikely to give up the present variety of incentives at its disposal. The other reliefs for savings all seem to be open to challenge on policy grounds as well as on grounds of their contribution to the complexity of the system.

Share option schemes encourage directors and employees to invest in their employing company (or its holding company). This may seem to be a good idea from an incentive point of view but it ties the employee even more to his employer so that he may lose both his job and his savings if the company fails. Those who have the means to do so will spread their investment risk, especially as commercial and industrial conditions can change very rapidly. Surely, what is required is the ability to respond rapidly in a changing world, not a heavier commitment to a particular *status quo*.

The BES has been fraught with difficulties of definition since its inception and it is not clear whether most of the enterprises which have benefitted would have been unable to attract necessary finance without it.[32] Furthermore, it is possible that the tax relief may often have been 'capitalized' in the sense that the benefit may have gone only partly to the investor, the remainder being absorbed in sustaining a low rate of return and/or in enhanced rewards to the operators of the business.

Similar issues may arise with the PEP. The annual savings allowed for inclusion in the scheme are small in relation to the minimum economic size for an investment in equities. Again the main beneficiaries may be the plan operators rather than the investors. It is likely that many of the richer investors would have made the investments anyway, while for the small investor the plan seems to limit investment to too narrow a front for risk to be spread adequately.

The more fundamental objection to such schemes in that they narrow the tax base while providing no clearly identifiable economic benefits to the country. The alternative of a wider tax base with a lower nominal rate of tax may be more beneficial to the economy. It may also be the case that some of the problems that these schemes are intended to solve are not tax problems at all but institutional finance problems. It must be accepted nevertheless that we are dealing here with wide questions of political philosophy which may go beyond the shorter-term economics of the argument.

Before leaving personal taxes we will look at possible developments in IHT (formerly CTT). The impact of and yield from this tax has been eroded steadily since the change of government in 1979[33] so the main question is whether this erosion will continue even to the extent of complete abolition, or will it be reversed? The answer depends almost entirely on the political complexion of future governments. A Conservative government might take the view that the tax was no longer worth collecting, but it might find some opposition even within its own ranks to the idea of complete abolition. It could perhaps, link the abolition of IHT to the incorporation of CGT into the IT system on the lines described above, especially if CGT was collected on death at IT rates and, periodically, on trust assets. A left-wing government, on the other hand, would certainly wish to have a direct tax on wealth and might seek to make the present IHT much more effective. Even so, it might have problems about doing this if its main targets had taken the precaution of transferring their wealth, or a substantial part of it, abroad. Presumably most such transfers would take place before that government came to power, anticipating the general election result. For some people, opinion poll forecasts can have a monetary value.

If IHT is to stay in its present form there are two areas of development which have growing support. These are the gradual withdrawal of the reliefs for agriculture and for forestry. There is some strong evidence for the view that these reliefs are now capitalized in the price of the assets concerned and that such assets are now owned by wealthy men who wish to minimize tax liability.[34] The result, especially in agriculture, is that the small scale entrepreneur, the working farmer, is being priced out of the market. The same arguments do not apply to the relief for other business assets as the market for them is not dominated by wealthy investors seeking tax advantages.

Turning finally to companies, we have seen that considerable changes have been made in the taxation of companies since 1984.[35] It has been suggested that, consistent with an expenditure tax, they should only be taxed on distributions, but this seems unlikely to happen in the forseeable future. The main question is whether the new system will survive intact. The CBI has objected already to the withdrawal of the accelerated capital allowance,[36] but it seems unlikely that the government which made the change will accede quickly to pressure to reverse it. Nevertheless, the complete absence of any inflation adjustment in the new system, either for depreciation or for working capital, may well lead to changes if (when?) the inflation rate rises and industry falls on hard times.[37] Such changes need not be dependant on the political complexion of the government in power at the crucial time.

Many of these thoughts on the possibilites for change do depend on the nature of the governments that take office in future decades. If this analysis is correct it reflects one of the continuing problems of British politics, the desire of governments to change the policies of their predecessor, often on ideological grounds. A result of this is that the tax system lacks stability, and frequent enforced changes mean greater complexity (if only because of the transitional arrangements), greater costs and more uncertainty about their direct and indirect effects. In an ideal world the system would be stable, changing only in response to long-term changes in the economy and in international circumstances. Perhaps after all a change to an expenditure tax base would enable the UK tax system to get rid of the mountain of dead wood created by past changes and give it a new start – but the practical and political obstacles are still formidable.

NOTES AND REFERENCES

1. Not, for instance, petroleum revenue tax (PRT) which can have a vital effect on oil exploration and production but is rather specialized.
2. The government also produces an annual White Paper, *The Government's Expenditure Plans*. The one published in January 1986, Cmnd 9702, covered the period up to 1988/89.
3. The measure of unemployment depends on the definitions used, but whether within the definition or not the actual number is a fact. This does not imply that the number is ascertainable precisely by normal statistical processes.
4. See *Social Trends*, HMSO, London (1985), in Chapter 1, in which the forecasts go up to the year 2001. Longer projections have been made which reveal a continuing trend in the direction indicated.
5. *Ibid.*, Chapter 3. The number of school pupils in the UK was expected to fall from 11.3 million in 1976 to 8.9 million in 1991 (Table 3.2). The rate of change in particular age groups was greater than the overall figures indicate.
6. See the White Paper, *The Government's Expenditure Plans, 1986–87 to 1988–89*, Cmnd. 9702. Chart 1.2 shows that public expenditure as a percentage of GDP rose sharply after 1979 and that the 1978/79 level was only due to be regained in 1986/87. Chart 1.11 shows very clearly that social security and health are taking a rising proportion of the total and that the overall reduction has been achieved by cuts elsewhere, especially in support for industry and trade.
7. *Tax – Time for Change: A CBI discussion document*, Confederation of British Industry, London (December 1985), at page 11.
8. Personal equity plans, introduced in the Finance Act 1986 – see s. 39 and 8th Schedule. See also Chapter 14.
9. See, for instance, the First and Second Reports of the (Irish) Commission on Taxation, published in July 1982 and March 1984, The Stationery Office Dublin. The Irish experience is particularly interesting as they have a history of using specific incentives with apparent success.
10. For brief accounts of the changes see *The Economist* for 23 and 30 August, 1986.
11. As a result of ss. 18, 48 and 58, Finance Act 1984.
12. The special complexities of the UK/USA bilateral treaty for the relief of double taxation is attributable largely to the differences between the company tax systems in the two countries.
13. See reports in *The Times* for 19 September 1986 (statement by the Shadow Chancellor) and 3 October 1986 (party conference report).
14. See, for instance, *Fairness and Enterprise: Tax Reform Proposals*, SDP Green Paper No. 21, SDP, London (July 1985).
15. The EC is relevant here because considerable progress has been made in harmonizing VAT in the member states and the UK is bound by the Community's directives.
16. See Chapter 10 and Sandford, C. T., Godwin, M. R., Hardwick, P. J. W. and Butterworth, M. I., *Costs and Benefits of VAT*, Heinmann Educational Books, London (1981) for a discussion of the cost savings which may result from having a single rate.
17. See Chapter 7 of *Tax – Time for Change: A CBI discussion document*, Confederation of British Industry, London (1985). The contribution rate was reduced from 13.7% in 1980 to 10.45% in 1986, but the latter is now imposed on all earnings, the upper limit having been abolished.
18. Green Paper, *Paying for Local Government*, Cmnd. 9714, HMSO, London (1986), especially Chapter 3.
19. The basic rate and higher rates of IT have been reduced significantly but this has been paid for, in part, by increases in the rate of VAT and in some excise duties.
20. For instance, see *Social Trends*, HMSO, London (1986), at pages 17–18. For a wider discussion see Lewis, A., *The Psychology of Taxation*, Martin Robertson, Oxford (1982).

21. An extended discussion of these issues can be found in Dilnot, A. W., Kay, J. A., and Morris, C. N., *The Reform of Social Security*, Institute for Fiscal Studies, London (1985).
22. Green Paper, *The Reform of Personal Taxation*, Cmnd. 9756, HMSO, London (1986).
23. See, for instance, Morris, N. and Stark, G. *The Reform of Personal Taxation, IFS Commentary*, IFS, London (May 1986).
24. But only gains accruing from April 1982.
25. Chapter 3 of the CBI Report (see note 17 above).
26. CGT on transfers by way of gift is subject to an option to pass the accrued gain to the donee rather than pay the tax due at the time of transfer – see s. 79, Finance Act 1980.
27. CGT, not IT, is chargeable where the scheme falls within s. 38 and 10th Schedule, Finance Act 1984.
28. For instance, by bodies such as the CBI in their Report referred to in note 7 above, and by the National Federation of Housing Associations in their *Inquiry into British Housing* (The Duke of Edinburgh's Committee) London (1985).
29. The qualifying maximum loan of £25 000 was first fixed in April 1974 and was increased to £30 000 in April 1983. Meanwhile the RPI has increased to more than three times its 1974 value.
30. See Chart 8.1 in *Social Trends*, HMSO, London (1985). Owner occupied houses in the UK exceeded 13 million in 1983 and represented about 60% of the total housing stock.
31. The tax-free lump sum paid as part of the retirement provision is a common feature of public sector schemes and because of its tax-free nature is widely adopted elsewhere. There seems to be no logical reason why it should be tax free when relief has already been given both for the contributions to the fund and on the income and gains accruing to the fund.
32. The scheme started in 1981 as the Business Start-Up Scheme. Changes in scope and definition, many of them substantial were made every year up to and including 1986.
33. See Sutherland, A., 'Capital Transfer Tax: Adieu', in *Fiscal Studies*, Vol. 5, No. 3 (1984). The *Financial Statement and Budget Report, 1986–87* (HM Treasury, March 1986) shows a small increase in the expected revenue for 1986/87 but as Sutherland explains in his article there is some buoyancy in the revenues because of the transitional provisions dating from the change from estate duty in 1974. It will take some years for the lifetime gifts exclusion to affect revenues because of the fact that they are still taxable if death occurs within seven years.
34. See Chapter 6.
35. In Chapters 7 and 9.
36. See note 7. The discussion is in Chapter 5 of that report.
37. For a discussion of the potential effects as inflation rates rise see Devereux, M. P. and Mayer, C. P., *Corporation Tax: The Impact of the 1984 Budget*, IFS, London (1984).

Appendix: Rates of Tax and Reliefs, Finance Act 1987

This Appendix has two sections as follows.

1. The tables in the first section list rates of tax and reliefs up to and including those for 1987/88 which were introduced in the 1987 Finance Act. These tables concentrate on matters referred to in the text and do not pretend to be complete for all purposes. For additional information see the annual publications such as *Tolley's Tax Data* and the *Allied Hambro Tax Guide*.

2. The second section is a commentary on the effect on the main text of the changes made in the spring and early summer of 1987. Because of the general election in June 1987 many of the proposals in the original Finance Bill (published immediately after the budget) were deleted from the pre-election Finance Act, but these deleted proposals were re-introduced in a new Finance Bill which was published on 3 July and which will become the Finance (No. 2) Act 1987. The bracketed number at the beginning of each paragraph is the page number in the main text.

1. TABLES OF RATES OF TAX AND RELIEFS

a. Income tax

	1984/85	1985/86	1986/87	1987/88
Basic rate (%)	30	30	29	27
Basic rate band (£)	15,400	16,200	17,200	17,900
Higher rate bands (£) –				
40%	2,800	3,000	3,000	2,500
45%	4,900	5,200	5,200	5,000
50%	7,500	7,900	7,900	7,900
55%	7,500	7,900	7,900	7,900
60%		remainder		
Personal reliefs (£) –				
Single man or woman	2,005	2,205	2,335	2,425
Married man	3,155	3,455	3,655	3,795
Wife's earnings (maximum)	2,005	2,205	2,335	2,425

	1984/85	1985/86	1986/87	1987/88
Age allowance – single	2,490	2,690	2,850	2,960
– 80 years or more – single				3,070
Age allowance – married	3,955	4,255	4,505	4,675
– 80 years or more – married				4,845
Income limit for age allowance	8,100	8,800	9,400	9,800
Reduction for excess income	2/3	2/3	2/3	2/3
Additional allowance for children				
(single parent)	1,150	1,250	1,320	1,370
Blind person	360	360	360	540
Dependent relatives –				
Women claimants (unmarried)	145	145	145	145
Others	100	100	100	100
Housekeeper	100	100	100	100
Services of son or daughter	55	55	55	55
Widow's bereavement	1,150	1,250	1,320	1,370
Benefits in kind – motor cars (£) –				
Under four years old and original				
market value up to	16,000	17,500	19,250	19,250
Up to 1,300 cc	375	410	450	
Up to 1,400 cc				525
1,301 to 1,800 cc	480	525	575	
1,401 to 2,000 cc				700
1,801 cc or more	750	825	900	
2,001 cc or more				1,100

Lower amounts are provided for cars more than four years old, and larger amounts for more expensive cars. The scale is halved if business mileage exceeds 17,999 and increased by 50% if it is 2,500 or less.

There are also scale charges related to engine capacity if petrol is provided by the employer for private journeys.

For 1988/89 the scale rates for cars are to be increased by about 10% but the rates for the use of petrol will not be changed. Thus the figures in the last column above will become £580, £770 and £1,210 respectively.

b. National Insurance

	6.10.85–5.4.86	1986/87	1987/88
Class I contributions – employees (not contracted out)			
Lower weekly limit (£)	35.50	38.00	39.00
Upper limit of 5% rate	54.99	59.99	64.99
Upper limit of 7% rate	89.99	94.99	99.99
Upper limit of 9% rate	264.99	284.99	295.00
Class I contributions – employers (not contracted out)			
As for employees except –			
Upper limit of 9% rate	129.99	139.99	149.99
Thereafter 10.45% (no upper limit)			

	1985/86	1986/87	1987/88
Class 4 contributions –			
Lower annual limit	4,150	4,450	4,590
Upper annual limit	13,780	14,820	15,350
Percentage rate	6.3	6.3	6.3
(50% thereof deductible for income tax)			
Retirement pensions (basic) –			
Married	3,056	3,187	3,289
Single	1,909	1,991	2,054
Widow's pension	1,909	1,991	2,054
Unemployment benefit and sick pay vary with particular circumstances.			

c. Capital gains tax

	1984/85	1985/86	1986/87	1987/88
Rate of tax (%)	30	30	30	30
Threshold (£)	5,600	5,900	6,300	6,600
Retirement relief qualifying age	60	60	60	60
Relief per qualifying year	*	10,000	10,000	12,500
Maximum relief	100,000	100,000	100,000	125,00
* Different basis				

Price index numbers for CGT

	1982	1983	1984	1985	1986	1987
January	—	325.9	342.6	359.8	379.7	394.5*
February	—	327.3	344.0	362.7	381.1	100.4*
March	313.4	327.9	345.1	366.1	381.6	100.6*
April	319.7	332.5	349.7	373.9	385.3	101.8*
May	322.0	333.9	351.0	375.6	386.0	101.9*
June	322.9	334.7	351.9	376.4	385.8	101.9*
July	323.0	336.5	351.5	375.7	384.7	
August	323.1	338.0	354.8	376.7	385.9	
September	322.9	339.5	355.5	376.5	387.8	
October	324.5	340.7	357.7	377.1	388.4	
November	326.1	341.9	358.8	378.4	391.7	
December	325.5	342.8	358.5	378.9	393.0	

* The RPI was re-based to 100 in January 1987. Thus, for sales of assets from February 1987 where the purchase was before January 1987 the closing index number must be multiplied by 3.945. Tables have been published by the Inland Revenue to show the adjustment factor for all months by reference to all possible purchase dates but, as will be apparent, these are rather unwieldy and have not been reproduced here.

d. Inheritance tax

Rates of tax (%) – 17.3.86 to 16.3.87	On death	Lifetime
First £71,000	0	0
£71,001–£95,000	30	15
£95,001–£129,000	35	17½
£129,001–£164,000	40	20
£164,001–£206,000	45	22½
£206,001–£257,000	50	25
£257,001–£317,000	55	27½
£317,001 upwards	60	30

Tapering of tax due if transfer more than 3 years before death	
3–4 years	80% payable
4–5 years	60% payable
5–6 years	40% payable
6–7 years	20% payable

Rates of tax (%) from 17.3.87	On death	Lifetime
First £90,000	0	0
£90,001–£140,000	30	15
£140,001–£220,000	40	20
£220,001–£330,000	50	25
£330,001+	60	30

Tapering percentages as before

e. Corporation tax

Years from 1 April	1984/85	1985/86	1986/87	1987/88
Full rate of CT (%)	45	40	35	35
Small company rate (%)	30	30	29	27
Small company limit (£)	100,000	100,000	100,000	100,000
Small company fraction	3/80	1/40	3/200	1/50
Capital gains reduction	1/3	1/4	1/7	Nil*

* Assuming the post-election Finance Bill becomes law as it stands. See note re page 112 below.

ACT fraction (years to 5 April)	3/7	3/7	29/71	27/73

2. BUDGET 1987 COMMENTARY

Chapter 2

(4) The up-dated version of Table 1.1 may be found in Table 6B3 of the Financial Statement and Budget Report, 1987–88, H. M. Treasury, March 1987.

(6) The up-dated version of Table 1.2 may be found in Table 6.7 of the publication referred to in the previous note.

(9) The up-dated version of Table 1.3 may be found in Table 5.1 of the publication referred to in the previous two notes.

(11) A more recent version of Table 1.5 appears in Economic trends for May 1986.

(22) From 1987/88 the special threshold for the elderly was further increased for those aged 80 or more (S.26, Finance Act 1987). Both sets of figures are shown in Table 1a above.

(23) For 1987/88 the basic rate of IT was reduced to 27% but the higher rates were not changed (S.20, Finance Act 1987). Combined with the increased threshold this reduced the average rate of tax on £100,000 from 50.7% to 50.2%. However the indexed equivalent income would be about £103,900 on which the average tax rate would be 50.6%. At this income level the reduction in the basic rate is almost cancelled out by the Chancellor's failure to index the higher rate bands.

(23) The post-election Finance Bill proposes a partial exemption for profit-related pay (PRP) (Clauses 1–17 and 1st Schedule) Provided the scheme is approved either for a company or for an employment unit thereof, the employee is to be exempt from tax on one half of the profit-related element up to a maximum of £3,000 or 20% of total pay if less. Thus, an employee with an income of £15,000, of which £3,000 is profit-related, would find his tax bill reduced by 27% of £1,500 = £405. National Insurance is not to be affected. The rationale of the exemption is that by encouraging PRP schemes it should improve flexibility in the labour market, especially when profits decline.

(24) Tax free lump sums are to be limited to £150,000 on pension schemes approved after 16 March 1987. This restriction was not implemented in the pre-election Finance Act but has been re-introduced in the 3rd Schedule of the post-election Finance Bill.

(25) The portability of pensions should be improved under a new scheme which is due to start on 4 January 1988. These personal pension schemes may replace employers' schemes and the schemes for the self-employed. Tax relief will be given for contributions up to 17½% of income (27½% if aged over 50 years). The new proposed legislation is in Clauses 18–57 and the 2nd Schedule of the post-election Finance Bill.

(26) With a basic rate of 27% the net cost to the father is £730. Note how the lower tax rate reduces the benefit of covenanting.

(30) Example 2.1. In 1987/88 the net interest received would be £146 (i.e. £200 less 27%).

(31) Example 2.2. In 1987/88 there would be no abatement on an income of £9,700 because the income limit has been raised to £9,800 (see Table 1a). Re-work the example on an income of £10,200 using the 1987/88 tax rates and reliefs. Maximum abatement now applies at an income of £10,602 and the effective marginal rate between £9,800 and £10,602 is 45.01%.

(31) Example 2.3. The effect of the 1987/88 rates is discussed above in the context of page (23).

(33) Example 2.5. See above (note re page 26) for the effect of the lower basic rate for 1987/88.

Chapter 4

(57) Note that the aggregation of a wife's income with her husband's does not take place for the tax year in which the marriage occurs (S.36, Finance Act 1976).

(57) For 1987/88 a further increase in the threshold for the elderly was given to those aged 80 years or more. The figures are shown in Table 1a.

(66) Example 4.1. For 1987/88 the tax saving would be £369,90, the increased difference between the two tax thresholds being more than offset by the reduction in the basic rate.

(66) Example 4.2. For 1987/88 the tax saving on an income of £5,000 is £463.05 (or £479.25 if aged 80 years or more). On an income of £10,000 the new income limit reduces the age reliefs to £2,827 and £4,542 respectively but the saving is unchanged, viz.

$$(4,542 - 2,827) \text{ at } 27\% = £463.05 \qquad (£479.25 \text{ if over 80 years})$$

(67) Example 4.3. For 1987/88 the tax on a combined income of £11,000 is £1,675.35 in (a) and £1,290 in (b).

(67) Example 4.4. For 1987/88 the tax on the normal basis is £8,773 and on the optional basis is £7,957.

(68) Example 4.5. For 1987/88 the husband's tax to the date of death is £2,100.60 and the widow's tax is £595.35.

(69) Example 4.6. For 1987/88 the husband's tax is £3,450.60 and the wife's £965.25.

Chapter 5

(82) The BES investment limit is £40,000 in any one tax year. Because this led to a bunching of investments at the end of a tax year it is now provided (S.42, Finance Act 1987) that up to £5,000 invested in the first half of one year may be relieved against income of the previous year (but not so as to exceed the normal £40,000 limit).

(184) The Chancellor repeated his assertion (note 44) when increasing the benefit scale for 1988/89 by 10%. See Table 1a and the note at the end thereof for the detailed figures.

Chapter 6

(100) From 17.3.87 the tax threshold was increased substantially (probably to reflect the sharp rise in the price of houses) and the number of rate bands reduced from 7 to 4, see Table 1d above (S.57, Finance Act 1987).

(102) Before 17.3.87 transfers to an interest in possession trust were taxable immediately. The post-election Finance Bill proposes that from that date they will be treated as a PET. Transfers to a discretionary trust would still have been taxable and steps have been taken to prevent discretionary trusts being disguised as short-term interest in possession trusts.

(103) From 17.3.87 minority shareholdings in an unquoted company are to attract the 50% reduction provided the holding exceeds 25% of the shares in the company (S.58 and 8th Schedule, Finance Act 1987).

(105) The yields of IHT show increases in 1986/87 and 1987/88 (forecast). This will be due in part to significant increases in stock market and real estate prices over the last few years. In addition, yields of the previous tax, CTT, were affected by the change in

1975 from second deceased spouse exemption to first spouse exemption as at present and this effect has now worked its way through the system as spouses entitled to the pre-1975 exemption have died.

(106) Example 6.1. If Mr Neer had died on 17.3.87 then the tax due on the same asset values but at the new rates would have fallen to £3,150.

(107) Example 6.2 From 17.3.87 the assets shown in this example fall below the taxable threshold.

Chapter 7

(110) For the twelve months ending on 31.3.88 the total tax would be the same but the grossed-up dividend is £389,041 (i.e. 284,000 × 100/73) as the basic rate tax imputed to it at the new rate of 27% is £105,041.

(110–11) The charity's refund is reduced to £1,050.41 for 1987/88 and the total cash benefit falls to £3,890.41.

Shareholder B would pay additional tax as follows for that year –

	£	
Cash dividend received	2,840	
Tax credit 27/73	1,050	(nearest £)
Gross income	3,890	
Tax thereon at 50%	1,945	
less: Tax credit	1,050	
Tax still due	895	

(112) The post-election Finance Bill proposes that from 17.3.87 capital gains are to be taxed at the same rate as income and so the fractional deduction is to be abolished (Clause 74).

(113) The benefit of the delayed payment of MCT by pre-1965 companies is being withdrawn in stages over three years starting with the first AP commencing after 17.3.87. Thus by 1991 all companies will be required to pay their MCT 9 months after the end of each AP (S.36 and 6th Schedule, Finance Act 1987).

(114) As a corollary of the proposal to revise the treatment of capital gains (see note re page 112 above) ACT is to be set-off against the CT on gains as well as that on income. The maximum rate of set-off for 1987–88 would have been 27% of the underlying income and gains, leaving the company (if it is not a small company) to pay MCT of not less than 8% thereof (i.e. the difference between 35% and 27%).

(115) The small companies rate has been reduced to 27% from 1.4.87 in line with the reduction in the basic rate of IT. The abatement fraction becomes 1/50 and so the abatement in the illustration becomes £5,000 and the effective marginal rate in the abatement band rises to 37% (S.22, Finance Act 1987).

(119) The post-election Finance Bill proposes legislation to eliminate from 17.3.87 a device whereby interest was 'paid' in one AP but not received by a recipient in the same group until the following AP, thereby separating tax relief and tax liability by 12 months (Clause 60).

(120–1) Example 7.1. If all of these transactions had taken place one year later the ACT fraction would have been 27/73 and the total ACT due £33,287.67. The total tax due (ACT plus MCT) would still be £260,000.

(121–2) Example 7.2. One year later the actual net payment would be altered to reflect the 27% basic rate of IT. Thus the first item of interest received would be £1460 (i.e. 73% of £2,000).

(122–3) Example 7.3. Under the proposals contained in the post-election Finance Bill the capital gain would have been taxed in full, the ACT would be calculated as 27/73 of the dividends and the ACT set-off would only be restricted if it exceeded 27% of the aggregate of taxable income plus gains.

(124) Example 7.5. Assuming the same profits etc., but one year later, the effect of the 1987 Finance Act and the post-election Finance Bill would have been as follows –

£

	£
Income	250,000
Gains (full amount)	50,000
F.I.I. (grossed-up) 25,000 × 100/73	34,246
Total	334,246
Corporation tax due –	
35% of profits excluding F.I.I. (300,000)	105,000
less: Abatement	
$(500,000 - 334,246) \times \dfrac{300,000}{334,246} \times \dfrac{1}{50}$	2,975
	102,025

Note how the inclusion of the full gains would have increased the tax liability for this company over that for the previous year (see the main text).

(125) Example 7.6. The principle of this calculation is not affected by the 1987 changes but the numerical result will be affected by the reduction in the rate of tax to 27%. The gain will still be excluded in calculating the distributable income.

(125–6) Example 7.7. This example is not affected by the 1987 changes except for the change in the rate of ACT to 27/73.

(127) Note 11. From 1.4.87 the tax on £100,000 becomes £27,000 and the marginal rate in the abatement band is

$$\frac{148,000}{400,000} \times 100 = 37\%$$

Chapter 8

(133) Under the Tax Reform Act of 1986 the main tax rate for US companies is reduced to 34%, but the general scheme of the calculation shown in the main text remains the same.

Chapter 9

(144) It may be observed here that costs incurred by employers to provide retraining for redundant employees who are about to leave or have left them were not generally deductible and so specific legislation was introduced to deal with the problem (S.35 and 5th Schedule, Finance Act 1987).

Chapter 10

(161) At the time of writing there has been active discussion about the possibility of

reducing the scope of the zero-rated categories to achieve greater conformity with other members of the European Community. Presumably some proportion of the increased yield of VAT resulting would be needed to increase welfare benefits paid to those people on very low incomes whose cost of living would have been increased significantly.

(162) The 1987 budget proposed changes in those regulations which deal with the matching of taxable inputs and exempt outputs. Broadly, the intention is to attempt specific matching rather than pro-rata methods as the latter can be manipulated to gain a tax advantage. The new regulations are made under the authority of S12, Finance Act 1987.

(164) Small businesses (defined as those with turnover below £250,000 per annum) may now account for VAT on an annual basis. Furthermore they may use a cash basis of accounting rather than the more normal accrual basis. This means that sales are chargeable only when the cash is received and relief for bad debts follows automatically in so far as cash is not received. These revised regulations are made on the authority of S.11, Finance Act 1987.

(165) The excise taxes were not changed in the 1987 budget except for a reduction in the duty on unleaded petrol which had the effect of reducing its price to the same level as the leaded variety (S.1, Finance Act 1987). The failure to change most of these taxes is, of course, equivalent to a reduction in real terms.

(166) On-course betting duty has been abolished (S.2, Finance Act 1987).

(166) Vehicle excise duties were not changed in the 1987 budget apart from some minor reliefs affecting farm and recovery vehicles.

(166) Rates on residential property in Scotland have been replaced by a lump-sum tax called the Community Charge which will be levied on all resident adults. This new tax is to be extended to England and Wales under proposals which have been tabled by the re-elected government.

(167) Note 6. The registration limit for 1987/88 is £21,300 per year (or £7,250 in any quarter) (S.14, Finance Act 1987).

(167) Note 14. At the time of writing (July 1987) the pump price has risen to about 175p per gallon. This means that the VAT has increased proportionately but the excise duty is unaltered, and so the relative tax burden has fallen slightly.

Chapter 11

(170) Under S.1, Finance Act 1987 the excise duty on unleaded petrol was reduced with the intention of removing a possible disincentive as its price exclusive of tax tends to be higher than that of the more common leaded petrol. However, as is the case with derv, not everyone has a free choice: older cars cannot be adapted to use unleaded petrol.

(175) Table 11.2. As rates of excise duty were not altered in the 1987 budget the effect was to reduce yields for 1987/88 as follows when comparison is made with the indexed equivalent for 1986/87.

	£ million
Petrol and derv	−245
Vehicle excise duty	−95
Tobacco	−105
Alcoholic beverages	−105

(Figures from Table 4.1, Financial Statement and Budget Report 1987-88, H. M. Treasury, March 1987.)

The lower figures shown above for the vehicle excise and alcoholic beverage duty reductions when compared with the figures shown in Table 11.2 reflect a lower rate of general price inflation.

Chapter 12

(180) From 6 April 1987 half of an investment made in the first six months of a tax year can be set against income of the previous tax year but the carry back is limited to £5,000 in total, and cannot be used to increase the relief for the year beyond £40,000 (S.42, Finance Act 1987).

(181) Various amendments were proposed in the 1987 budget and are included in the post-election Finance Bill (Clause 59). These included the case where employee share options in one company are exchanged for options in a take-over bidder. Although the other amendments proposed were minor any one of them may have been crucial to a particular case and they would have added further complexity to this legislation. This complexity is typical of any relief in which equity of treatment is being sought between 'equivalent' situations in the complex financial world in which we live.

Chapter 13

(193) On 24 March 1987 the Court of Appeal decided in the case of Craven v. White, and in two others which it heard simultaneously, that the Ramsay principle could not be applied where the final step in a series of transactions had not been determined when the series started. The Court was of the opinion that to apply Ramsay in such circumstances would make its effect too wide-ranging. It is expected that these cases will be further considered by the House of Lords, which, it may be noted, overturned the decision of the Court of Appeal in favour of the taxpayer in the Ramsay case itself. Perhaps history will not repeat itself on this occasion.

Chapter 14

(200) This argument about the behavioural consequences of the use of census data was applied in a BBC Television programme, *The Secret Society*, (22 April 1987) to the use of the electoral register for other (including commercial) purposes. However the two cases may be differentiated in so far as the electoral roll is a public document whereas the individual census forms are intended to be kept confidential because of the very personal nature of some of the information that is being sought.

(204) The post-election Finance Bill (Clauses 85–90) attempts to strengthen the interest provision by applying it to all tax due when it is paid late even if the actual liability had been in dispute at the due date. In return interest is to be added to tax that is overpaid when it is refunded after the due date for payment.

(204) The post-election Finance Bill (Clauses 82–4) proposes increases in the penalties imposed on companies which fail to complete their annual returns in due time, the amount of the fixed penalty being increased for repeated failures. After the initial fixed penalty further amounts are to be charged as a percentage of the tax due.

Chapter 15

(210) The proposals for tax exemption of a part of profit-related pay (PRP) may be useful in this context – see Appendix item related to page (23) above.

(211) The 1987 budget change in the taxation of unleaded petrol is relevant in the context of using the tax systems to achieve, or to not frustrate, public policy aims, in this case the reduction of lead pollution in the atmosphere.

(213) The reduction in the basic rate to 27% has been noted already. The government's stated aim is to reduce it to 25%. It may be observed however that the top rate of 60% was not reduced in the 1987 budget.

(213) The decision in 1987 to reduce the IT burden in real terms by reducing the basic rate rather than by increasing the thresholds beyond indexation may reflect in part a desire not to increase the married man's allowance at a time when its effective abolition is envisaged. The form of abolition proposed in the Green paper involves increasing the single person's allowance by half the difference between it and the married allowance.

(213–4) It is relevant to observe here that the 1987 budget proposed to tax company gains as income (i.e. at 35% except for small companies) and that where gains received by individuals are taxed at all the tax rate is now 3 points *above* the basic rate of IT (i.e. 30% rather than 27%). Of course individuals whose incomes are taxed at the top marginal rate of 60% will still prefer gains to income, as will those whose gains are covered by the annual threshold (provided the pre-tax rates of return are the same).

(214) Capital gains on houses would still produce a chargeable gain in many parts of the country even if fully indexed. House prices in London and the South East have outpaced the RPI quite significantly over recent years.

(215) The tax exemption of lump sums will be restricted, for new contracts, to a maximum of £150,000 under the post-election Finance Bill. Schemes had been devised which 'exploited' the exemption generally available.

(215) It must be remembered that share option schemes have been popular with senior executives because they provide an opportunity to receive a reward which is untaxed or taxed at a low rate. They may also be necessary to enable UK companies to keep talented managers in competition against American and other foreign companies which regard such schemes as a normal element in the remuneration package. The potential benefits on the rapidly rising stock markets of recent years have been considerable.

(216) The yield of IHT is beginning to rise, partly because of rapidly rising property and share prices, but also because of a technical factor which relates back to the change from ED to CTT in 1975 when the tax liability of the surviving spouse was altered. Before 1975 tax was collected on the first death, since then it has been collected, in effect, on the second death.

Statutory references

Table of decided cases

Bibliography

BOOKS

Accounting Standards Committee, SSAP 16, *Current Cost Accounting*, , London (1980).

Accounting Standards Committee, SSAP 3, *Accounting for Value Added Tax*, ASC, London (1973).

Askari, H., Cummings, J.T. and Glover, M., *Taxation and Tax Policies in the Middle East*, Butterworths, London (1982).

Board of Inland Revenue, *Report for the Year Ended 31st December 1985*, 128th Report, Cmnd. 9831, HMSO, London (1986).

Brown, C.V., *Taxation and the Incentive to Work*, Oxford University Press, Oxford (1983).

Brown, C.V. and Jackson, P.M., *Public Sector Economics*, Martin Robinson, Oxford (1982).

Central Statistical Office, *Social Trends*, HMSO, London (1985 and 1986).

Commission on Taxation, *First and Second Reports*, The Stationery Office, Dublin (1982 and 1984).

HM Commissioners of Customs and Excise, *General Guide, VAT Notices*, HMSO, London.

HM Commissioners of Customs and Excise, *76th Report, for the Year Ended 31st March 1985*, Cmnd. 9655, HMSO, London (1985).

The Committee on the Enforcement Powers of the Revenue Departments (Chairman, Lord Keith of Kinkel), Cmnd. 8822, 9120 and 9440, HMSO, London (1983, 1984 and 1985).

Confederation of British Industry, Tax – Time for Change, CBI, London (1985).

Devereux, M.P. and Mayer, C.P., *Corporation Tax: The Impact of the 1984 Budget*, Institute for Fiscal Studies, London (1984).

Dilnot, A.W., Kay, J.J. and Morris, C.N., *The Reform of Social Security*, Clarendon Press, Oxford (1984).

Duke of Edinburgh's Committee – see National Federation of Housing Associations.

Equal Opportunities Commission, *Income Tax and Sex Discrimination*, EOC, Manchester (1978).

Field, F. *The Wealth Report*, Routledge and Kegan Paul, London (1979).

Gatney, D.J., Skadden, D.H. and Wheeler, J.E., *Principles of Federal Income Taxation*,

Mcgraw-Hill, New York (1982).

Gower, L.C.B., *Principles of Modern Company Law*, Stevens, London (1979).

Green Paper, *Corporation Tax*, Cmnd. 8456 HMSO, London (1982).

Green Paper, *Paying for Local Government*, Cmnd. 9714, HMSO, London (1986).

Green Paper, *Proposals for a Tax Credit System*, Cmnd. 5116, HMSO London (1972).

Green Paper, *The Reform of Personal Taxation*, Cmnd. 9756. HMSO, London (1986).

Green Paper, *The Taxation of Husband and Wife*, Cmnd. 8093, HMSO, London (1980).

Green Paper, *Wealth Tax*, Cmnd. 5704 HMSO, London (1974).

Grout, V., *Tolley's Tax Cases*, Tolley Publishing Co., Croydon (1986 and annually).

Halpern, L., *Taxes in France*, Butterworths, London (1980).

Hicks, J.R., *Value and Capital: An Enquiry into Some Fundamental Principles of Economic Theory*, Oxford University Press, Oxford (1946).

Hills, J., *Savings and Fiscal Privilege*, IFS Report Series No. 9, Institute for Fiscal Studies, London (1984).

Inflation Accounting Committee (Chairman F.E.P. Sandilands), *Inflation Accounting: Report of the Inflation Accounting Committee*, Cmnd. 6225, HMSO, London (1975).

Institute of Chartered Accountants in England and Wales, *Tax Digests*: see under Mead, D.F. and under Parker, M.

Inland Revenue Statistics, 1984, HMSO, London (1985).

Inland Revenue explanatory pamphlet, *Residents and Non-Residents – Liability to Tax in the UK*, IR 20, Board of Inland Revenue, London (1983).

Institute for Fiscal Studies, *The Structure and Reform of Direct Taxation*, Report of a Committee Chaired by Professor J.E. Meade, George Allen & Unwin, London (1978).

Kaldor, N., *An Expenditure Tax*, Allen & Unwin, London (1955).

Kay, J.A. and King, M.A., *The British Tax System*, Oxford University Press, Oxford (1983).

Keith Committee – see Committee on the Enforcement Powers of the Revenue Departments.

Lewis, A. *The Psychology of Taxation*, Martin Robertson, Oxford (1982).

Maslow, A.H., *Motivation and Personality*, Harper and Row, New York (1954).

Mead, D.F., 'Residence and Domicile', *Tax Digest No. 11*, Institute of Chartered Accountants in England and Wales, London (1982).

Meade Committee – see under Institute for Fiscal Studies.

Morris, C.N. and Stark, G., *The Reform of Personal Taxation*, IFS Commentary, Institute for Fiscal Studies, London (1986).

National Economic Development Office (NEDO), *Value Added Tax*, HMSO, London (1971).

National Federation of Housing Associations, *Enquiry into British Housing* (The Duke of Edinburgh's Committee), NFHA, London (1985).

Organisation for Economic Co-operation and Development, *Revenue Statistics of OECD Member Countries, 1965–82*, OECD, Paris (1983).

Parker, M. (ed.), 'Corporate Taxes Around the World', *Tax Digests Nos. 39 and 40*, Institute of Chartered Accountants in England and Wales, London (1985).

Peacock, A. and Forte, F., *The Political Economy of Taxation*, Basil Blackwell, Oxford (1981).

Pechman, J.A. (ed.), *Comprehensive Income Taxation*, Brookings, Washington DC (1977).

Pen, J., *Income Distribution*, Pelican, London (1974).

Reddaway, W.B., *The Effects of Selective Employment Tax, First Report: The Distributive Trades*, HMSO, London (1970).

Robinson, A. and Sandford, C., *Tax Policy-Making in the United Kingdom*, Heinemann Educational Books, London (1983).

Report of the Royal Commission on Taxation, Queen's Printer, Ottowa (1966).

Royal Commission on the Distribution of Income and Wealth, *Report No. 1*, Cmnd. 6171, HMSO, London (1975).

Royal Commission on the Taxation of Profits and Income, *Second Report*, Cmd. 9105, HMSO, London (1954).

Royal Commission on the Taxation of Profits and Income, *Final Report*, Cmd. 9474, HMSO, London (1955).

Sandilands Committee – see under Inflation Accounting Committee.

Sandford, C.T., *Hidden Costs of Taxation*, Institute for Fiscal Studies, London (1973).

Sandford, C.T., Godwin, M.R., Hardwick, P.J.W. and Butterworth, M.I., *Costs and Benefits of VAT*, Heinemann Educational Books, London (1981).

Slevin, K.S., *Retirement Relief*, CCH Editions, Bicester (1986).

Smith, Adam, *An Enquiry into the Nature and Causes of the Wealth of Nations*, Clarendon Press, Oxford (1776 reprinted 1976).

Smith, S., *The Shadow Economy*, Oxford University Press, Oxford (1986).

Social Democratic Party, *Fairness and Enterprise: Tax Reform Proposals*, SDP Green Paper No. 21, SDP, London (1985)

Social Trends – see under Central Statistical Office.

Tolley's Tax Planning, Tolley Publishing, Croydon (1986).

HM Treasury, *Financial Statement and Budget Report, 1986–87*, HMSO, London (1986).

Tutt, N., *The Tax Raiders, The Rossminster Affair*, Financial Training Publications, London (1985).

University of Wisconsin Institute for Research on Poverty, *Final Report of the New Jersey Graduated Work Incentive Experiment in New Jersey and Pennsylvania*, University of Wisconsin, Wisconsin (1973).

'Which?' *Tax Saving Guide*, Consumer's Association, London (March 1986 and annually).

White Paper, *The Government's Expenditure Plans*, Cmnd. 9702, HMSO, London (1986).

ARTICLES

Ballard, R.M., '*Furniss* v. *Dawson* – The Future of Tax Planning', in *Tolley's Tax Planning* (1986).

Chown, J.F., 'The Harmonization of Corporation Tax in the EEC', in *British Tax Review* (1976), page 39.

Dilnot, A. and Morris, C.N., 'What Do We Know About the Black Economy?', in *Fiscal Studies*, Volume 2, Number 1 (1981), at pages 58–73.

Goude, R., 'The Economic Definition of Income', in Pechmann, J.J. (ed.),

Comprehensive Income Taxation (1977).

Harrison, A., 'Recent Changes in the Distribution of Personal Wealth in Britain', in Field, F. (ed.), *The Wealth Report*, (1979).

Jeffrey-Cook, J., 'A Year Beginning on April 6', in *British Tax Review* (1977), pages 68–69

Kay, J.A., 'The Economics of Tax Avoidance', in *British Tax Review*, (1979), at pages 354–365.

Muten, L., 'Leading Issues of Tax Policy in Developing Countries', in Peacock, A. and Forte, F., *The Political Economy of Taxation* (1981).

O'Higgins, M., 'Aggregate Measures of Tax Evasion: An Assessment', in *British Tax Review* (1981), at pages 286–302 and 367–378.

Sutherland, A., 'Capital Transfer Tax: Adieu', in *Fiscal Studies*, Volume 5, Number 3 (1984), at pages 63–83.

Index